D0218078

Study Guide 1

Name		
Identifying Accounting Terms	22 Pts.	
Identifying Accounting Concepts and Practices	18 Pts.	
Analyzing How Transactions Change an Accounting Equation	10 Pts.	
Analyzing How Transactions Change Owner's Equity in an Accounting Equation	12 Pts.	
Total	62 Pts.	

Part One—Identifying Accounting Terms

Directions: Select the one term in Column I that best fits each definition in Column II. Print the letter identifying your choice in the Answers column.

Column I	Column II	Answers
A. account	1. Planning, recording, analyzing, and interpreting financial information. (p. 6) *Accounting*	1. **D**
B. account balance	2. A planned process for providing financial information that will be useful to management. (p. 6) *Accounting System*	2. **G**
C. account title	3. Organized summaries of a business's financial activities. (p. 6) *Accounting Records*	3. **F**
D. accounting	4. Financial reports that summarize the financial condition and operations of a business. (p. 6) *Financial Statements*	4. **N**
E. accounting equation	5. A business that performs an activity for a fee. (p. 6) *Service Business*	5. **T**
F. accounting records	6. A business owned by one person. (p. 6) *Proprietorship*	6. **Q**
G. accounting system	7. Anything of value that is owned. (p. 8) *Asset*	7. **H**
H. asset	8. Financial rights to the assets of a business. (p. 8) *Equities*	8. **K**
I. business ethics	9. An amount owed by a business. (p. 8) *liability*	9. **O**
J. capital	10. The amount remaining after the value of all liabilities is subtracted from the value of all assets. (p. 8) *Owner's Equity*	10. **P**
K. equities	11. An equation showing the relationship among assets, liabilities, and owner's equity. (p. 8) *Accounting Equation*	11. **E**
L. ethics	12. The principles of right and wrong that guide an individual in making decisions. (p. 8) *Ethics*	12. **L**
M. expense	13. The use of ethics in making business decisions. (p. 8) *Business Ethics*	13. **I**
N. financial statements	14. A business activity that changes assets, liabilities, or owner's equity. (p. 10) *Transaction*	14. **U**
O. liability	15. A record summarizing all the information pertaining to a single item in the accounting equation. (p. 10) *Account*	15. **A**
P. owner's equity	16. The name given to an account. (p. 10) *Account tittle*	16. **C**
Q. proprietorship	17. The amount in an account. (p. 10) *Account Balance*	17. **B**
R. revenue	18. The account used to summarize the owner's equity in a business. (p. 10) *Capital*	18. **J**
S. sale on account	19. An increase in owner's equity resulting from the operation of a business. (p. 14) *Revenue*	19. **R**
T. service business	20. A sale for which cash will be received at a later date. (p. 14) *Sale on Account*	20. **S**
U. transaction	21. A decrease in owner's equity resulting from the operation of a business. (p. 15) *Expense*	21. **M**
V. withdrawals	22. Assets taken out of a business for the owner's personal use. (p. 16) *Withdrawals*	22. **V**

Part Two—Identifying Accounting Concepts and Practices

Directions: Place a *T* for True or an *F* for False in the Answers column to show whether each of the following statements is true or false.

Answers

1. Accounting is the language of business. (p. 6)

1. _T_

2. Keeping personal and business records separate is an application of the business entity concept. (p. 6)

2. _T_

3. Assets such as cash and supplies have value because they can be used to acquire other assets or be used to operate a business. (p. 8)

3. _T_

4. The relationship among assets, liabilities, and owner's equity can be written as an equation. (p. 8)

4. _F_

5. The accounting equation does not have to be in balance to be correct. (p. 8)
   It needs to be in balance.

5. _F_

6. The sum of the assets and liabilities of a business always equals the investment of the business owner. (p. 10)

6. _F_

7. Recording business costs in terms of hours required to complete projects is an application of the unit of measurement concept. (p. 10)

7. _F_

8. The capital account is an owner's equity account. (p. 10)

8. _T_

9. If two amounts are recorded on the same side of the accounting equation, the equation will no longer be in balance. (p. 11)

9. _F_

10. When a company pays insurance premiums in advance to an insurer, it records the payment as a liability because the insurer owes future coverage. (p. 11)

10. _F_

11. When items are bought and paid for later this is referred to as buying on account. (p. 12)

11. _T_

12. When cash is paid on account, a liability is increased. (p. 12)

12. _F_

13. When cash is received from a sale, the total amount of both assets and owner's equity is increased. (p. 14)

13. _T_

14. A sale for which cash will be received at a later date is called a charge sale. (p. 14)

14. _T_

15. The accounting concept Realization of Revenue is applied when revenue is recorded at the time goods or services are sold. (p. 14)

15. _T_

16. When cash is paid for expenses, the business has more equity. (p. 15)

16. _F_

17. When a company receives cash from a customer for a prior sale, the transaction increases the cash account balance and increases the accounts receivable balance. (p. 16)

17. _F_

18. A withdrawal decreases owner's equity. (p. 16)

18. _T_

Name _____Mayra Flores_____ Date __1/28/13__ Class __1A__

Part Three—Analyzing How Transactions Change an Accounting Equation

Directions: For each of the following transactions, select the two accounts in the accounting equation that are changed. Decide if each account is increased or decreased. Place a "+" in the column if the account is increased. Place a "−" in the column if the account is decreased.

Transactions

1–2. Received cash from owner J. Nichols as an investment. (p. 10)
3–4. Paid cash for supplies. (p. 11)
5–6. Paid cash for insurance. (p. 11)
7–8. Bought supplies on account from Suburban Office Supplies. (p. 12)
9–10. Paid cash on account to Suburban Office Supplies. (p. 12)

Trans. No.	Assets			=	Liabilities	+	Owner's Equity
	Cash +	Supplies +	Prepaid Insurance	=	Accts. Pay.—Suburban Office Supplies	+	J. Nichols, Capital
1–2.	+						+
3–4.	−	+					
5–6.	−		+				
7–8.	−	+			+		
9–10.	−				−		

Part Four—Analyzing How Transactions Change Owner's Equity in an Accounting Equation

Directions: For each of the following transactions, select the two accounts in the accounting equation that are changed. Decide if each account is increased or decreased. Place a "+" in the column if the account is increased. Place a "−" in the column if the account is decreased.

Transactions

1–2.	Received cash from sales. (p. 14)
3–4.	Sold services on account to Imagination Station. (p. 14)
5–6.	Paid cash for rent. (p. 15)
7–8.	Paid cash for telephone bill. (p. 15)
9–10.	Received cash on account from Imagination Station. (p. 16)
11–12.	Paid cash to owner J. Nichols for personal use. (p. 16)

Trans. No.	Assets				= Liabilities	+ Owner's Equity
	Cash +	Accts. Rec.—Imagination Station +	Supplies +	Prepaid Insurance =	Accts. Pay.—Ling Music Supplies +	J. Nichols, Capital
1–2.	+					+
3–4.		+				+
5–6.	−					− (exp.)
7–8.	−					− (exp.)
9–10.	+	−				
11–12.	−					− (withdrawal)

1-1 WORK TOGETHER, p. 9

Completing the accounting equation

Assets	=	Liabilities	+	Owner's Equity
11,000		3,000		8,000
10,000		4,000		6,000
63,000		35,000		28,000

Completing the accounting equation

Assets	=	Liabilities	+	Owner's Equity
30,000		17,000		13,000
80,000		60,000		20,000
51,000		25,000		26,000

1-2 WORK TOGETHER, p. 13

Determining how transactions change an accounting equation

Trans. No.	Assets	=	Liabilities	+	Owner's Equity
1.	supplies +		A/P +		
2.	110 (cash) + increase				+ (310) owner's equity + increase (capital)
3.	pr insurance " 110 100 + / —				
4.	110 (cash —		210 — A/P.		

capital drawing. is

Determining how transactions change an accounting equation

Trans. No.	Assets	=	Liabilities	+	Owner's Equity
1.	Cash. +				Capital +
2.	— Supplies +		A/P +		
3.	sup + cash , —				
4.	prins +, —				
5.	cash + — 110		—		

1-3 WORK TOGETHER, p. 17

Determining how transactions change an accounting equation

Trans. No.	Assets				=	Liabilities	+	Owner's Equity
	Cash	+	Accts. Rec.— Bowman Co.	+ Supplies +	Prepaid Insurance	=	Accts. Pay.— Maxwell Co.	+	Susan Sanders, Capital
1.	+	+						+
2.		+						+
3.	−							−
4.	+	−						
5.	−							−

1 − 1
1 − 2

1

Determining how transactions change an accounting equation

Trans. No.	Assets				= Liabilities +	Owner's Equity
	Cash	Accts. Rec.— + Navarro Co. +	Supplies +	Prepaid Insurance =	Accts. Pay.— Barrett Co. +	Vincent Orr, Capital
1.	+	+				+
2.	+	+				+
3.	+	—				+
4.	—					— withdrawal
5.	—					— expense

1-1 APPLICATION PROBLEM, p. 19

Completing the accounting equation

Assets	=	Liabilities	+	Owner's Equity
95,000		51,000		44,000
64,000		44,000		20,000
4,000		3,500		2,500
138,000		70,000		68,000
19,000		8,000		11,000
16,000		4,000		12,000
35,000		13,000		22,000
169,000		120,000		49,000
8,000		4,800		3,200
86,000		48,000		38,000
12,000		5,000		7,000
30,000		8,000		22,000
47,000		24,000		23,000
22,000		29,000		13,000
57,000		21,000		36,000
125,000		69,000		56,000
11,000		5,000		6,000
5,300		2,000		3,300

Determining how transactions change an accounting equation

Trans. No.	Assets			=	Liabilities		+	Owner's Equity
	Cash	+ Supplies	+ Prepaid Insurance	=	Accts. Pay.— Five Star Supply	+ Accts. Pay.— Riverland Co.	+	Calvin Parrish, Capital
Beg. Bal. 1.	0 +3,000	0	0		0	0		0 +3,000
New Bal.	3,000	0	0		0	0		3,000
2.	−1,600		−1,600	−1,600				−1,600
New Bal.	1,400							1,400
3.		+700						+700
New Bal.	1,400	+700		+700				2,100
4.		+300		+300	+300			
New Bal.	1,400	1,000	1,600	+700	300			3,000
5.	−700			−700				
New Bal.	700	1,000	1,600	0	300			3,000
6.	−200				−200			
New Bal.	500	1,000	1,600		100			3,000
7.	−100	+100						
New Bal.	400	1,100	1,600		100			3,000
8.	+1,500							+1,500
New Bal.	1,900	1,100	1,600	0	100			4,500

6,000

Name _Mayra Flores_   Date _1/28/13_ Class _____

1-3 APPLICATION PROBLEM, p. 20

Determining how revenue, expense, and withdrawal transactions change an accounting equation

Trans. No.	Cash	+ Accts. Rec.—Lisa Lee	+ Supplies	+ Prepaid Insurance	= Accts. Pay.—Kline Co.	+ Peter Smith, Capital
Beg. Bal. 1.	625 −300	0	375	300	200	1,100 −300 (expense)
New Bal. 2.	325 −150.	0	375	300	200	800 −150.
New Bal. 3.	+175 +800		375	300	200	+650 800 (revenue)
New Bal. 4.	975 −100.	20.00	375	300	200	1,450 −100 (expense)
New Bal. 5.	875	+400.00	375	300	200	1,350 +400. (revenue)
New Bal. 6.	875 +650	+400.00	375	300	200	1,750 +650
New Bal. 7.	1,525.− −35	400	375	300	200	2,400. −35 (expense)
New Bal. 8.	1,490.− +300	400 −300	375	300	200	2,365 +300
New Bal.	1,790.−	100	375	300	200	2,365

Determining how transactions change an accounting equation

Trans. No.	Cash	Accts. Rec.— + Ana Santiago	Supplies +	Prepaid Insurance =	Accts. Pay.— Delta Co. +	Marion Cassidy, Capital
				Assets	= Liabilities +	Owner's Equity
Beg. Bal.	2,300	0	200	100	1,800	800
1.	−400					−400 (expense)
New Bal.	1,900	0	200	100	1,800	400 *3200*
2.	+ 500					+500 (Invest)
New Bal.	2,400	0	200	100	1,800	900
3.	−50					−50 (expense)
New Bal.	2,350	0	200	100	1,800	850
4.	1,025	0				+1,025
New Bal.	3,375	0	200	100	1,800	1,875
5.			+ 450		+450	
New Bal.	3,375	0	650	100	2,250	1,875
6.		+730				
New Bal.	3,375	+730	650	100	2,250	2,605
7.	−660					−660
New Bal.	2,715	730	650	100	2,250	1,945
8.	−150		150			
New Bal.	2,565	730	800	100	2,250	1,945
9.	+400	−400				
New Bal.	2,965	330	800	100	2,250	1,945
10.	−1,500	330	800		−1500	
New Bal.	1,465	330	800	100	750	1,945
11.	−100	330	800	+100		
New Bal.	1,365	330	800	900	750	1,945 =
12.	+1,230	300	800			1,230 =
New Bal.	2,595	300	800	200	750	3,175 =
13.	−1,200	300	800	200	750	−1,200 =
New Bal.	1,395	300	800	200	750	≠ 1975
14.						

Left margin handwritten totals: 2000, 27000, 2650, 3675, 4,25, 4,55, 4,195, 1,195, 4,195, 2,695, 2,695, 3925, 2560

1-5 CHALLENGE PROBLEM, p. 22

Determining how transactions change an accounting equation

1.

Trans. No.	Assets				= Liabilities +	Owner's Equity
	Cash	Accts. Rec.— + Mary Lou Pier +	Supplies +	Prepaid Insurance	Accts. Pay.— = Kollasch Co. +	Zachary Martin, Capital
Beg. Bal. 1.	8,552	1,748	1,485 − 400	615	3,145	9,255 − 400
New Bal. 2.	8,552	1,748	1,085	615	3,145 + 250	7,855 12,000 − 250 (expense)
New Bal. 3.	8,552	1,748	1,085	615	3,395	8,605
	THIS TRANS. DOEB NOT AFFECT Zacharias Repair shop.					
New Bal. 4.	8,552 − 120	1,748	1,085	615	3,395 − 120	8,605
New Bal.	8,432	1,748	1,085	615	3,275	8,605

(margin notes: 2,000, 12000, 11,880)

2.

a) Because he owns his property

b) You want to keep your cash ready for expenses.

Study Guide 2

Name	Perfect Score	Your Score
Identifying Accounting Terms	5 Pts.	
Analyzing Transactions into Debit and Credit Parts	20 Pts.	
Identifying Changes in Accounts	15 Pts.	
Total	40 Pts.	

Part One—Identifying Accounting Terms

Directions: Select the one term in Column I that best fits each definition in Column II. Print the letter identifying your choice in the Answers column.

Column I	Column II	Answers
A. chart of accounts	1. An accounting device used to analyze transactions. (p. 29)	1. _E_
B. credit	2. An amount recorded on the left side of a T account. (p. 29)	2. _C_
C. debit	3. An amount recorded on the right side of a T account. (p. 29)	3. _B_
D. normal balance	4. The side of the account that is increased. (p. 29)	4. _D_
E. T account	5. A list of accounts used by a business. (p. 32)	5. _A_

Part Two—Analyzing Transactions into Debit and Credit Parts

Directions: Analyze each of the following transactions into debit and credit parts. Print the letter identifying your choice in the proper Answers columns.

Account Titles

A. Cash
B. Accounts Receivable—
    Imagination Station
C. Supplies
D. Prepaid Insurance
E. Accounts Payable—
    Suburban Office Supplies
F. J. Nichols, Capital
G. J. Nichols, Drawing
H. Sales
I. Rent Expense

Answers

	Debit		Credit
1–2. Received cash from owner as an investment. (p. 32)	1. A	2.	F
3–4. Paid cash for supplies. (p. 33)	3. C	4.	A
5–6. Paid cash for insurance. (p. 34)	5. D	6.	A
7–8. Bought supplies on account from Suburban Office Supplies. (p. 35)	7. C	8.	E
9–10. Paid cash on account to Suburban Office Supplies. (p. 36)	9. E	10.	A
11–12. Received cash from sales. (p. 38)	11. A	12.	H
13–14. Sold services on account to Imagination Station. (p. 39)	13. B	14.	H
15–16. Paid cash for rent. (p. 40)	15. I	16.	A
17–18. Received cash on account from Imagination Station. (p. 41)	17. A	18.	B
19–20. Paid cash to owner for personal use. (p. 42)	19. G	20.	A

Part Three—Identifying Changes in Accounts

Directions: For each of the following items, select the choice that best completes the statement. Print the letter identifying your choice in the Answers column.

Answers

1. The values of all things owned (assets) are on the account equation's (A) left side (B) right side (C) credit side (D) none of these. (p. 28)

1. _A_

2. The values of all equities or claims against the assets (liabilities and owner's equity) are on the accounting equation's (A) left side (B) right side (C) debit side (D) none of these. (p. 28)

2. _B_

3. An amount recorded on the left side of a T account is a (A) debit (B) credit (C) normal balance (D) none of these. (p. 29)

3. _A_

4. An amount recorded on the right side of a T account is a (A) debit (B) credit (C) normal balance (D) none of these. (p. 29)

4. _B_

5. The normal balance side of any asset account is the (A) debit side (B) credit side (C) right side (D) none of these. (p. 29)

5. _A_

6. The normal balance side of any liability account is the (A) debit side (B) credit side (C) left side (D) none of these. (p. 29)

6. _B_

7. The normal balance side of an owner's capital account is the (A) debit side (B) credit side (C) left side (D) none of these. (p. 29)

7. _B_

8. Debits must equal credits (A) in a T account (B) on the equation's left side (C) on the equation's right side (D) for each transaction. (p. 32)

8. _D_

9. Decreases in an asset account are shown on a T account's (A) debit side (B) credit side (C) balance side (D) none of these. (p. 30)

9. _B_

10. Increases in an asset account are shown on a T account's (A) debit side (B) credit side (C) right side (D) none of these. (p. 30)

10. _A_

11. Decreases in any liability account are shown on a T account's (A) debit side (B) credit side (C) right side (D) none of these. (p. 30)

11. _A_

12. Increases in a revenue account are shown on a T account's (A) debit side (B) credit side (C) left side (D) none of these. (p. 38)

12. _B_

13. The normal balance side of any revenue account is the (A) debit side (B) credit side (C) left side (D) none of these. (p. 38)

13. _B_

14. The normal balance side of any expense account is the (A) debit side (B) credit side (C) right side (D) none of these. (p. 40)

14. _A_

15. The normal balance side of an owner's drawing account is the (A) debit side (B) credit side (C) left side (D) none of these. (p. 42)

15. _A_

2-1 WORK TOGETHER, p. 31

Determining the normal balance, increase, and decrease sides for accounts

Cash

Debit	Credit
↑ Increase	Decrease ↓
N. Balance	

A/R

Debit	Credit
↑ Normal Balance	decrease ↓
Increase	

Supplies

Debit	Credit
↑ N. Balance	↓

Prepaid Insurance

Debit	Credit
↑ Increase	Decreased ↓

A/P Miller Supplies

Debit	Credit
↓ Decrease	Increase ↑

A/P office Supplies

Debit	Credit
↓ Decrease	Normal Balance ↑ (liability)

Jeff Dixon

Debit	Credit
↓ Decreased	Normal ↑ Balance
	Increase

Determining the normal balance, increase, and decrease sides for accounts

Cash.

Debit	Credit.
Normal B.	
Increase	Decreased

A/R Lee McCann.

Debit	Credit
Normal B.	

A/R Sonya Lopez

Debit.	Credit.
Normal B.	

Supplies.

Debit	Credit
Normal B.	

Prepaid Ins.

Debit	Credit.
Normal B.	

A/P topline Supplies

Debit	Credit
Increase	Decreased

Vickie Monson Capital

Debit	Credit
Decreased.	Inscreased (Normal Balance)

COPYRIGHT © SOUTH-WESTERN CENGAGE LEARNING

2-2 WORK TOGETHER, p. 37

Analyzing transactions into debit and credit parts

Apr. 1.

Cash	
Debit	Credit
↑ 5,000.=	Decreased ↓
Increased	
N. Balance	

Kim Park, Capital	
Debit	Credit
↑	$5,000.= ↑ N. Balance
	Increase

Apr. 2.

Supplies	
Normal B. Debit	Credit
↑ 50.=	↓
Increase	Decreased

Cash	
Debit	Credit
↑ ↑ Increase	50.= ↓
N. Balance	Decrease

Apr. 5.

Prepaid Ins.	
Debit	Credit
↑ 75.=	↓
N. Balance	

Cash	
Debit	Credit
↓ Normal Balance	75.= ↑

Apr. 6.

Supplies	
Debit	Credit
↑ 100.=	↓
N. Balance	

A.P / Bales Supplies	
Debit	Credit
↓	100.= ↑
Decrease	N. Balance Increase

Apr. 9.

Cash	
Debit	Credit
↓ N. Balance	(50) ↑

A/P Bales Supplies	
Debit	Credit
(50) ↓ Decrease	Increase ↑ N. Balance

Analyzing transactions into debit and credit parts

Sept. 1.

Cash

Debit	Credit
↑ 2,000.= N. Balance	↓

Derrick Hoffman, Capital

Debit	Credit
↓ decrease	2,000.= N. Balance Increase ↑

Sept. 4.

Prepaid Insurance

Debit	Credit
300 ↑ N. Balance Increase	300.= ↓ decrease

Cash

Debit	Credit
↑ N. Balance. 300.=	↓

Sept. 5.

Supplies

Debit	Credit
↑ N. Balance	100.= ↓

Cash

Credit	Debit
↑ N. Balance Increase. 100.=	Decreased ↓

Sept. 6.

Supplies

Debit	Credit
↑ 230.= N. Balance	↓

A/P - Nash Supply

Debit	Credit
↓ Decrease	230. N. Balance Increase ↑

Sept. 11.

Cash

Debit	Credit
↑	115.— ↓

A/P Nash Supply

Debit	Credit
115.— ↓ Decrease	N. Balance Increase ↑

2-3 WORK TOGETHER, p. 44

Analyzing revenue, expense, and withdrawal transactions into debit and credit parts

Apr. 10.

Cash
600.—

Sales
600.—

Apr. 18.

Cash
425

A/Rec Sam Ericksen.
425

Apr. 11.

A/R Sam Erickson
850

Sales
850

Apr. 20.

Cash
300.—

Kathy Bergan, Drawing
300.—

Apr. 14.

Cash
250

Rent Exp.
250.

Analyzing revenue, expense, and withdrawal transactions into debit and credit parts

Sept. 13.

Cash

1,500 = ✓

Sales

1,500 ✓

Sept. 15.

A/R – Jan Roe

500 ✓

Sales ✓

500. =

Sept. 16.

Cash

450

✓

utilities Exp.

450 ✓

Sept. 18.

Cash

250 ✓

A/R don. Rr

250

Sept. 21.

Cash

700 ✓

Derrick H Drawing

700 ✓

2-1 APPLICATION PROBLEM, p. 46

Debit First

Determining the normal balance, increase, and decrease sides for accounts

1	2	3	4	5	6	7	8
Account	Account Classification	Account's Normal Balance		Increase Side		Decrease Side	
		Debit	Credit	Debit	Credit	Debit	Credit
Cash	Asset	✔		✔			✔
Act/Recv-Jens Ol.	Asset	✓		✓			✓
A/R -Tori N	Asset	✓		✓			✓
Supplies	Asset	✓		✓			✓
Prepaid Ins .	Asset	✓		✓			✓
A/P - Unit Co.	Liability	✓	✓	✓	✓	✓	✓
Juan Reo, Capital	Owner's Equity		✓	✓	✓	✓	✓

Analyzing transactions into debit and credit parts

March 1.

Cash	
1,000.00	

Hal Rosen, Capital	
	1,000.00

March 1.

Prepaid Ins.	
Debit 400.00	Credit

Cash	
Debit	Credit 400.00

March 3.

Supplies	
Debit 600.00	Credit

Ac/P All star Co.	
	Credit 600.00

March 5.

Supplies	
Debit 100	Credit

Cash	
Debit	Credit 100

March 8.

All star Co.	
Debit 400.—	Credit

Cash	
Debit	Credit 400

2-3 APPLICATION PROBLEM, p. 47

Analyzing revenue, expense, and withdrawal transactions into debit and credit parts

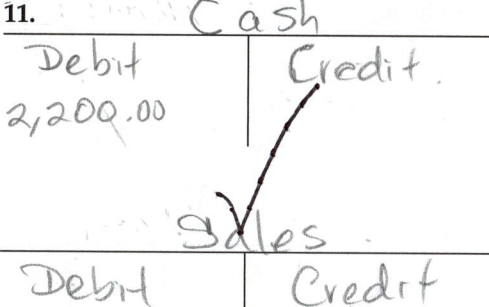

March 11.

Cash

Debit	Credit
2,200.00	

Sales

Debit	Credit
	2,200.=

March 12.

Cash

Debit	Credit
	150.00

Advertizing.

Debit	Credit
150.=	

March 14.

A/R Dominic

Debit	Credit
1,700	

Dominik Field.

	Credit
	1,700

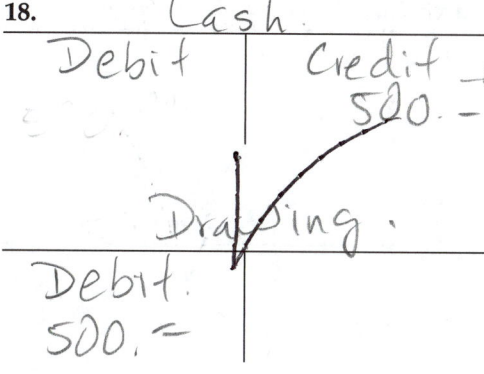

March 18.

Cash

Debit	Credit
	500.-

Drawing.

Debit	
500.=	

March 19.

Cash

1,000.=	

Dominik Field.

	1,000.-

Analyzing revenue, expense, and withdrawal transactions into debit and credit parts

March 25.

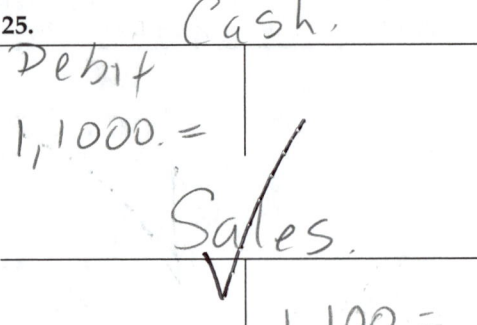

Cash.

Debit
1,1000.=

Sales.
1,100.=

March 28.

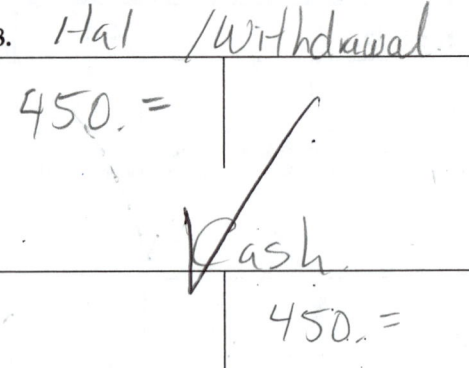

Hal /Withdrawal
450.=

Cash.
450.=

March 26.

A/Recv Dominick Field
500.=

Sales
500.=

March 29.

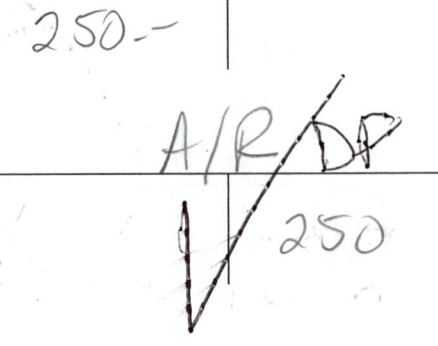

Cash
250.−

A/R DP
250

March 27.

Advertizing Expense.
125.=

Cash
125.=

2-5 MASTERY PROBLEM, p. 47

Analyzing transactions into debit and credit parts

Cash	
(1) 2,700.00	(2) 500.00
(4) 850.00	(4) 300.00
(11) 1,900.00	(5) 275.00
(11) 900.00	(10) 75.00
(13) 500.00	(15) 25.00
(30) 200.00	(16) 50.00
	(22) 55.00
	(23) 95.00
	(26) 400.00

Vicki Land, Capital	
	(1) 2,700
	(11) 1,900.=

Vickie Lands, Drawing
(26) 400

A/R - Alston Goff	
(8) 700.00	(13) 500.00

Sales	
	(4) 850.00
	(8) 700.00
	(11) 900.00
	(25) 450.00

A/R - Josie Leveson	
(25) 450.00	(30) 200.00

Advertising Expense
(23) 95.00

Supplies
(4) 300.00
(9) 200.=
(12) 130.=

Miscellaneous Exp.
(2) 500

Prepaid Ins.
(5) 275.-

Rent Exp.
(2) 800.00

A/P - North End Supply
(12) 130

Prepaid Exp.
(10) 75.00

A/P - Bethany Supplies	
(16) 50	(9) 200.-

Utilities
(22) 55.00

Analyzing transactions recorded in T accounts

1	2	3	4	5	6
Trans. No.	Accounts Affected	Account Classification	Entered in Account as a		Description of Transaction
			Debit	Credit	
1.	Cash	Asset	✔		Received cash from owner as investment
	Adriana Janek, Capital	Owner's Equity		✔	
2.	Utilitie Exp.	Owner's Equity (Expense)	✓		Paid Cash for utilities
	Cash	Asset		✓	
3.	Miscellaneous Exp.	owner's equity. Exp.	✓		Paid $cash for miscell.
	Cash	Asset		✓	
4.	Supplies	Asset	✓		Bough supplies on Account
	Act/P - Tri City Supplies	Liability		✓	
5.	Cash	Asset	✓		Receiv cash from sales
	Sales	owner's equity.		✓	
6.	Advertisin Exp	owner's equity	✓		Paid cash for advert
	Cash	Asset		✓	
7.	Rent Exp	owner's equity Expense	✓		Paid cash for rent
	Cash	Asset		✓	
8.	Cash	Asset	✓		Received cash from sales
	Sales	Owner's Equity Revenue		✓	
9.	Cash	Asset	✓		Received Cash from sales
	Sales	Owner's Equi Revenue		✓	
10.	Supplies	Asset	✓		Paid cash for supplies
	Cash	Asset		✓	
11.	A/P - Tri City Supplies	liability	✗		Paid cash on account.
	Cash	Asset		✓	
12.	Adriana Janek Drawing	owner's equity	✗		Paid cash to owner for personal.
	Cash	Asset		✓	
13.	A/R - Ralph	Asset	✓		Sold Service on Account to Ralph Dahl.
	Sales	Owner's Equity		✓	

Study Guide 3

Name	Mayra Flores	Perfect Score	Your Score
	Identifying Accounting Terms	13 Pts.	
	Identifying Accounting Concepts and Practices	17 Pts.	
	Analyzing a Five-Column Journal	10 Pts.	
	Recording Transactions in a Five-Column Journal	20 Pts.	
	Total	60 Pts.	

Part One—Identifying Accounting Terms

Directions: Select the one term in Column I that best fits each definition in Column II. Print the letter identifying your choice in the Answers column.

Column I	Column II	Answers
A. check	1. A form for recording transactions in chronological order. (p. 56) *Journal.*	1. _F_
B. double-entry accounting	2. Recording transactions in a journal. (p. 56) *Journalizing*	2. _G._
C. entry *Sales/Credit*	3. A journal amount column headed with an account title. (p. 57) *Special amount column.*	3. _M_
D. general amount column	4. A journal amount column that is not headed with an account title. (p. 57) *General Amount Column.*	4. _D_
E. invoice	5. Information for each transaction recorded in a journal. (p. 57) *Entry*	5. _C_
F. journal	6. The recording of debit and credit parts of a transaction. (p. 57) *double-entry accounting*	6. _B_
G. journalizing *Sales Invoice Check.*	7. A business paper from which information is obtained for a journal entry. (p. 57) *Source document*	7. _L_
H. memorandum	8. A business form ordering a bank to pay cash from a bank account. (p. 58) *Check*	8. _A_
I. proving cash	9. A form describing the goods or services sold, the quantity, and the price. (p. 58) *Invoice*	9. _E_
J. receipt	10. An invoice used as a source document for recording a sale on account. (p. 58) *Sales Invoice*	10. _K_
K. sales invoice	11. A business form giving written acknowledgment for cash received. (p. 58) *Receipt.*	11. _J_
L. source document	12. A form on which a brief message is written describing a transaction. (p. 58) *Memorandum*	12. _H_
M. special amount column	13. Determining that the amount of cash agrees with the accounting records. (p. 76) *Proving Cash.*	13. _I_

Part Two—Identifying Accounting Concepts and Practices

Directions: Place a *T* for True or an *F* for False in the Answers column to show whether each of the following statements is true or false.

1. Information in a journal includes the debit and credit parts of each transaction recorded in one place. (p. 56)

1. _T_

2. The Objective Evidence accounting concept requires that there be proof that a transaction did occur. (p. 57)

2. _T_

3. Examples of source documents include checks, sales invoices, memorandums, and letters. (p. 57)

3. _F_

4. A check is the source document used when items are paid in cash. (p. 58)

4. _T_

5. The source document for all cash payments is a sales invoice. (p. 58)

5. _F_

6. A receipt is the source document for cash received from transactions other than sales. (p. 59)

6. _T_

7. A calculator tape is the source document for daily sales. (p. 59)

7. _T_

8. The source document used when supplies are bought on account is a memorandum. (p. 64)

8. _T_

9. The source document used when supplies bought on account are paid for is a check. (p. 65)

9. _T_

10. The journal columns used to record receiving cash from sales are cash debit and sales credit. (p. 67)

10. _T_

11. The source document *sales invoice* is abbreviated as SI in a journal entry. (p. 68)

11. _F_

12. The journal columns used to record paying cash for rent are general debit and cash credit. (p. 69)

12. _T_

13. The journal columns used to record paying cash to the owner for personal use are general debit and cash credit. (p. 71)

13. _T_

14. To prove a journal page, the total debit amounts are compared with the total credit amounts to be sure they are equal. (p. 73)

14. _T_

15. Double lines across column totals mean that the totals have been verified as correct. (p. 74)

15. _T_

16. To correct an error in a journal, simply erase the incorrect item and write the correct item in the same place. (p. 77)

16. _F_

17. Dollars and cents signs and decimal points should be used when writing amounts on ruled accounting pages. (p. 77)

17. _F_

Name _____Mayra Flores_____ Date _____ Class _____

Part Three—Analyzing a Five-Column Journal

Directions: The columns of the journal below are identified with capital letters. For each of the following items, decide which column is being described. Print the letter identifying your choice in the Answers column.

JOURNAL   PAGE

	DATE		ACCOUNT TITLE	DOC. NO.	POST. REF.	GENERAL DEBIT	GENERAL CREDIT	SALES CREDIT	CASH DEBIT	CASH CREDIT	
1	A	✓	B	C	D	E	F	G	H	I	1
2											2
3											3

Answers

1. Write the year for the first entry on a journal page. (p. 60)

    1. __A__

2. Write the name of the month for the first entry. (p. 60)

    2. __A__

3. Write the account title for an amount in the General Credit column. (p. 60)

    3. __B__

4. Write the credit amount when cash is received from the owner as an investment. (p. 60)

    4. __F__

5. Write the source document number for an entry. (p. 60)

    5. __C__

6. Write the account title for an amount in the General Debit column. (p. 60)

    6. __B__

7. Write the amount credited to Sales. (p. 67)

    7. __G__

8. Indicate with a check mark that no account title needs to be written for an entry. (p. 67) ✓

    8. __B__

9. Write the amount debited to Rent Expense. (p. 69)

    9. __E__

10. Write the debit amount when cash is received from sales. (p. 70)

    10. __H__

Part Four—Recording Transactions in a Five-Column Journal

Directions: The columns of the journal below are identified with capital letters. For each of the following transactions, decide which debit and credit amount columns will be used. Print the letters identifying your choice in the proper Answers columns.

JOURNAL   PAGE

DATE	ACCOUNT TITLE	DOC. NO.	POST. REF.	GENERAL DEBIT	GENERAL CREDIT	SALES CREDIT	CASH DEBIT	CASH CREDIT
A	B	C	D	E	F	G	H	I

Answers

		Debit	Credit
1–2.	Received cash from owner as an investment. (p. 60)	1. H	2. F
3–4.	Paid cash for supplies. (p. 61)	3. E	4. I
5–6.	Paid cash for insurance. (p. 63)	5. E	6. I
7–8.	Bought supplies on account. (p. 64)	7. E	8. F
9–10.	Paid cash on account. (p. 65)	9. E	10. I
11–12.	Received cash from sales. (p. 67)	11. H	12. G
13–14.	Sold services on account. (p. 68)	13. E	14. G
15–16.	Paid cash for an expense. (p. 69)	15. E	16. I
17–18.	Received cash on account. (p. 70)	17. H	18. F
19–20.	Paid cash to owner for personal use. (p. 71)	19. E	20. I

3-1, 3-2, 3-3, and 3-4   WORK TOGETHER, pp. 62, 66, 72, 78

3-1 Journalizing entries in a five-column journal
3-2 Journalizing entries in a five-column journal
3-3 Journalizing transactions that affect owner's equity in a five-column journal
3-4 Proving and ruling a journal

JOURNAL

PAGE 1

	DATE	ACCOUNT TITLE	DOC. NO.	POST. REF.	GENERAL DEBIT	GENERAL CREDIT	SALES CREDIT	CASH DEBIT	CASH CREDIT	
1	Apr 1	Norm Derrey Capital	R1			150000		150000		1
2	2	Supplies	C1		37500				37500	2
3			R1		✱50000	30000		30000		3
4	3	Supplies	C1		95000				95000	4
5	4	Prepaid Insurance	C2		120000				120000	5
6										6
7	Apr 1	Supplies	M1		50000					7
8		Acct. Pay- Palm Supply				50000				8
9	7	Prepaid Ins	C2		30000				30000	9
10	9	Acct. Payable- Palm Supply	C3		25000				25000	10
11	Jan 5	Prepaid Insurance	C2		40000				40000	11
12	9	Supplies	M1		30000				30000	12
13		Acct Pay— OK Supplies	C3		30000	30000				13
14	10	Act Pay – OK Supplies	C3		30000				30000	14
15	Aug12	✓	T12	✓			29500	29500		15

Prob. 3-1
Ruling 3

WORK TOGETHER (concluded)

R = Receipt

JOURNAL
PAGE 5

	DATE	ACCOUNT TITLE	DOC. NO.	POST. REF.	GENERAL DEBIT	GENERAL CREDIT	SALES CREDIT	CASH DEBIT	CASH CREDIT	
1	Apr 12	Rent Expense	C4		1 000 00				1 000 00	1
2	13	✓	T13	✓			2 500 00	2 500 00		2
3	14	Acc. Receiv – L. Rohe	S1		510 00		510 00			3
4	19	Utilitie Expense	C5		148 00				148 00	4
5	20	Acc. Receiv L. Rohe	R1		25 00			255 00		5
6	21	Norm Denep Drawing	C6		1 000 00				1 000 00	6
7										7
8										8
9										9
10										10
11										11
12										12
13										13
14										14
15										15

Prove page 1 of the journal:

Column	Debit Column Totals	Credit Column Totals
General	_____	_____
Sales	_____	_____
Cash	_____	_____
Totals	_____	_____

Prove page 2 of the journal:

Column	Debit Column Totals	Credit Column Totals
General	_____	_____
Sales	_____	_____
Cash	_____	_____
Totals	_____	_____

Prove cash:

Cash on hand at the beginning of the month .... _____
Plus total cash received during the month .... _____
Equals Total .... _____
Less total cash paid during the month .... _____
Equals cash balance at the end of the month .... _____
Checkbook balance on the next unused check stub .... _____

3-1, 3-2, 3-3, and 3-4 ON YOUR OWN, pp. 62, 66, 72, 78

3-1 Journalizing entries in a five-column journal
3-2 Journalizing entries in a five-column journal
3-3 Journalizing transactions that affect owner's equity in a five-column journal
3-4 Proving and ruling a journal

P. 72 3-3
on your own 3-3

JOURNAL

	DATE	ACCOUNT TITLE	DOC. NO.	POST. REF.	GENERAL DEBIT	GENERAL CREDIT	SALES CREDIT	CASH DEBIT	CASH CREDIT
1	Jun 11	Rent Exp.	C4		52500				
2	12	A/R - C. Lord.	S1		70000		70000		
3	16	✓	T16	✓			230000	230000	
4	17	Miscell. Expense	C5		3700				3700
5	19	A/R - C. Lord.	R22			35000		35000	
6	20	C. Lord, Drawing	C6		85000				85000
7	23	A/R - L. Rohe	S2		37500		37500		
8	27	Norm Deiner, Drawing	C7		50000				50000
9	27	Carried Forward		✓	495800	225500	338500	425500	357300
10									
11									
12									
13									
14									
15									

PAGE 5

P. 78
3-4 on your own.

JOURNAL

PAGE 5

	DATE	ACCOUNT TITLE	DOC. NO.	POST. REF.	GENERAL DEBIT	GENERAL CREDIT	SALES CREDIT	CASH DEBIT	CASH CREDIT	
1	Jan 23	A/R — C. Loyd	92		40000					1
2	26									2
3	26									3
4										4
5										5
6										6
7										7
8										8
9										9
10										10
11										11
12										12
13										13
14										14
15										15

Prove page 1 of the journal:

Column	Debit Column Totals	Credit Column Totals
General		
Sales		
Cash		
Totals		

Prove page 2 of the journal:

Column	Debit Column Totals	Credit Column Totals
General		
Sales		
Cash		
Totals		

Prove cash:

Cash on hand at the beginning of the month . . . .
Plus total cash received during the month . . . .
Equals Total . . . .
Less total cash paid during the month . . . .
Equals cash balance at the end of the month . . . .
Checkbook balance on the next unused check stub . . . .

Name __Mayra Flores__ Date __2/25/13__ Class __1A__

3-1, 3-2, 3-3, and 3-4 APPLICATION PROBLEMS, pp. 80, 81

3-1 Journalizing transactions in a five-column journal
3-2 Journalizing buying insurance and buying and paying on account in a five-column journal
3-3 Journalizing transactions that affect owner's equity and receiving cash on account
3-4 Proving and ruling a journal

JOURNAL PAGE ①

	DATE	ACCOUNT TITLE	DOC. NO.	POST. REF.	GENERAL DEBIT	GENERAL CREDIT	SALES CREDIT	CASH DEBIT	CASH CREDIT
1	Feb 1	Dennis Gilbert Capital	R1			1000000		1000000	
2	4	Supplies	C1		300000				300000
3	5	Supplies	C2		25000				25000
4	Feb 6	Prepaid Insurance	C3		60000				60000
5	7	Supplies	M1		200000				
6		A/P – Scott Supply				200000			
7	8	A/P – Scott Supply	C4		100000				100000
8	12	A/R – Scott Supply	C5		100000	100700		100700	100000
9	Feb 12	Rent Expense	C6		80000				80000
10	13	✓	T13	✓			50000	50000	
11	14	A/R – Covey Company	S1		45000		45000		
12	15	Utilities Expense	C7		38000				38000
13	15	Dennis Gilbert Drawing	C8	✓	280000				280000
14	18	✓	T18	✓			27800	27800	
15	19	Miscellaneous Expense	C9		6400				6400
16	21	A/R – Covey Company	R2			25000		25000	
17	22	✓	T22	✓			70000	70000	
18	22	Utilities Expense	C10		33900				33900
19	25	Supplies–Scott Supplies	M2		34600				
20		A/P – Covey Company				34000			
21	Feb 25	A/P – Covey Company	R3			20000		20000	
22	25	Miscellaneous Expense	C11		2500				2500
23	26	A/R – Covey Company	S2		8000		80000		
24	26	Carrying Forward		✓	1383800	1379000	2 323000	2 1837800	1024800
25									

3-1
pp 80

JOURNAL

PAGE 5

	DATE	ACCOUNT TITLE	DOC. NO.	POST. REF.	GENERAL DEBIT	GENERAL CREDIT	SALES CREDIT	CASH DEBIT	CASH CREDIT
1	Feb 26	Brought Forward		✓	1283800	1379000	82800	1287800	924800
2	26	Supplies	C12		4400				4400
3	27	Rent Expense	C13		20000				20000
4	27	Miscellaneous Expense	C14		3700				3700
5	28		T28	✓		136500	136500	136500	
6	28	Dennis Gilbert-Drawing	C15		80000				80000
7	28	Totals			1491900	1277900	409300	1329300	1132900
8									
9									
10									
11									
12									
13									
14									
15									

Prove page 1 of the journal:

Column	Debit Column Totals	Credit Column Totals
General	13,882.00	12,790.00
Sales		2,728.00
Cash	11,928.00	10,292.00
Totals	25,810.00	25,810.00

Prove page 2 of the journal:

Column	Debit Column Totals	Credit Column Totals
General	14,919.00	12,790.00
Sales		4,093.00
Cash	13,293.00	11,329.00
Totals	28,212.00	28,212.00

Prove cash:

Cash on hand at the beginning of the month	10.8
Plus total cash received during the month	13,293.00
Equals Total	13,293.00
Less total cash paid during the month	11,329.00
Equals cash balance at the end of the month	1,964.00
Checkbook balance on the next unused check stub	1,964.00

Name __Mayra Flores__ Date __2/26/13__ Class __1A__

3-5 APPLICATION PROBLEM, p. 81

Journalizing transactions and proving and ruling a five-column journal

(pg. 81 / 3-5)

JOURNAL PAGE 1

DATE	ACCOUNT TITLE	DOC. NO.	POST. REF.	GENERAL DEBIT	GENERAL CREDIT	SALES CREDIT	CASH DEBIT	CASH CREDIT
Apr 1	Hans Schultz, Capital	R1			250000		250000	
3	Supplies	C1		10500				10500
4	Prepaid Insurance	C2		24000				24000
5	Supplies	M1		7500				
	A/P - Midwest Supplies				7500			
11	A/P - Midwest Supplies	C3		7500				7500
12	Utilities	C4		6500				6500
15	Hans Schultz, Drawing	C5		70000				70000
16	Frank Morris	S1		35800		35800		
17	✓	T17	✓			128700	128700	
18	Advertising	C6		39000				39000
25	A/R - Frank Morris	R2			35800		35800	
25	Totals			170800	293300	169500	414500	127500

3. *Prove the journal:*

Column	Debit Column Totals	Credit Column Totals
General	1,708.00	2,933.00
Sales		1,695.00
Cash	4,145.00	1,275.00
Totals	5,853.00	5,853.00

4. *Prove cash:*

Cash on hand at the beginning of the month	0.00
Plus total cash received during the month	4,145.00
Equals Total	4,145.00
Less total cash paid during the month	1,275.00
Equals cash balance at the end of the month	2,870.00
Checkbook balance on the next unused check stub	2,870.00

Journalizing transactions and proving and ruling a five-column journal

JOURNAL PAGE 5

Date	Account Title	Doc. No.	Post. Ref.	General Debit (1)	General Credit (2)	Sales Credit (3)	Cash Debit (4)	Cash Credit (5)
Jun 01	Jane Fernandez, Capital	R1			1600000		1600000	
02	Supplies	C1		30000				30000
03	Rent Expense	C2		90000				90000
04	Supplies	M1		170000				
	A/P - Atkin Supplies				170000			
05	Utilities	C3		14600				14600
08	A/P - Atkin Supplies	C4		100000				100000
08	✓	T8	✓			98000	98000	
08	A/R - Tony's Limo	S1		45000		45000		
09	Prepaid Insurance	C5		120000				120000
10	Miscellaneous Expense	C6		38800				38800
10	✓	T10	✓			47600	47600	
11	Miscellaneous Expense	C7		1500				1500
11	✓	T11	✓			63000	63000	
12	✓	T12	✓			9000	9000	
15	Jane Fernandez - Drawing	C8		40000				40000
15	✓	T15	✓			85000	85000	
16	Supplies	C9		110000				110000
17	A/R - Tony's Limo	R2			22500		22500	
17	Supplies	M2		60000				
	A/P - Pine Supplies				60000			
17	✓	T17	✓			50000	50000	
18	✓	T18	✓			80000	80000	
19	✓	T19	✓			65000	65000	
19	Carrying Forward		✓	819900	1852500	623600	2201100	5449100

3-6 MASTERY PROBLEM (concluded)

JOURNAL PAGE 2 ②

	DATE	ACCOUNT TITLE	DOC. NO.	POST. REF.	GENERAL DEBIT	GENERAL CREDIT	SALES CREDIT	CASH DEBIT	CASH CREDIT
1	June 19	Brought Forward		✓	819900	1852500	623600	2201160	54900
2	22	Supplies	M3		600				
3		A/P-Fire Supplies				600			
4	22		T22	✓			61000	61000	
5	23	Utilities	C10		8500				8500
6	23	A/R-Tony's Limo	S2		58200		58200		
7	24	Miscellaneous	C11		12500				12500
8	24		T24	✓			3000	3000	
9	25		T25	✓			7700	7700	
10	26	Supplies	C12		9000				9000
11	26		T26	✓			3000	3000	
12	29	A/R-Tony's Limo	R3			35000	35000	35000	
13	30	Jane Fernandez, Drawing	C13		45000				45000
14	30		T30	✓			5000	5000	
15	30	Totals			959100	1893500	929800	2284100	619900

Prove page 1 of the journal:

Column	Debit Column Totals	Credit Column Totals
General	8,199.00	18,525.00
Sales		6,236.00
Cash	22,011.00	5,449.00
Totals	30,210.00	30,210.00

Prove page 2 of the journal:

Column	Debit Column Totals	Credit Column Totals
General	9,591.00	18,935.00
Sales		9,298.00
Cash	24,841.00	6,199.00
Totals	34,432.00	34,432.00

Prove cash:

Cash on hand at the beginning of the month	0.00
Plus total cash received during the month	24,841.00
Equals Total	24,841.00
Less total cash paid during the month	6,199.00
Equals cash balance at the end of the month	18,642.00
Checkbook balance on the next unused check stub	18,642.00

Journalizing transactions using a variation of the five-column journal

JOURNAL

PAGE 5

DATE	ACCOUNT TITLE	DOC. NO.	POST. REF.	GENERAL DEBIT	GENERAL CREDIT	SALES CREDIT	CASH DEBIT	CASH CREDIT	
20-- June 1	Tony Wirth, Capital	R1			17000000		17000000		1
2	Prepaid Insurance	C1		-300000				300000	2
3	Supplies	M1		-25000					3
4	Accounts P - Marker Supplies	C2			250000				4
	Supplies			-140000					5
8	Account P - Marker Supplies	C3							6
9	Rent Expense	C4							7
12		T12	✓						8
15	A/R - Amy's Uniforms	S1							9
16	Utilities Expense	C5							10
22	A/R - Amy's Uniforms	R2							11
25	Tony Wirth, Drawing	C6							12
30	Totals			10 27000	1980000	850000	1785000	747000	13
									14
									15
									16
									17
									18

3. *Prove the journal:*

Column	Debit Column Totals	Credit Column Totals
General	10,270.00	19,800.00
Sales		850.00
Cash	17,850.00	7470.00
Totals	28,120.00	28,120.00

4. *Prove cash:*

Cash on hand at the beginning of the month 0.00
Plus total cash received during the month 17,850.00
Equals Total 17,850.00
Less total cash paid during the month 7470.00
Equals cash balance at the end of the month 10,380.00
Checkbook balance on the next unused check stub 10,380.00

USING SOURCE DOCUMENTS, p. 85

Journalizing transactions and proving and ruling a journal

Receipt No. __1__		Receipt No. __1__	Form __1__
Date _May 1_, 20--		Date _May 1_ 20--	
From _Cy Sawyer_		Rec'd from _Cy Sawyer_	
For _Investment_		For _Investment_	
		Five Thousand & ⁿᵒ/100 Dollars	
$ 5,000 00		Amount $ 5,000 00	
		_CS_	
		Received by	

NO. __1__	Form __2__
Date: _5/3_ 20 -- $200.00	
To: _National Supply Co._	
For: _Supplies_	

BAL. BRO'T. FOR'D		0 00
AMT. DEPOSITED	5—1	5000 00
SUBTOTAL		5000 00
AMT. THIS CHECK		200 00
BAL. CAR'D. FOR'D		4800 00

NO. __2__	Form __3__
Date: _5/5_ 20 -- $500.00	
To: _SW Management Co._	
For: _May Rent_	

BAL. BRO'T. FOR'D	4800 00
AMT. DEPOSITED	
SUBTOTAL	4800 00
AMT. THIS CHECK	500 00
BAL. CAR'D. FOR'D	4300 00

No. __1__	Form __4__

MEMORANDUM

Bought supplies on account from
Atlas Supplies, $550.00

Signed: _CS_   Date: _5/8/--_

NO. *3*   Form ___*5*___
Date: *5/9*   20 - - $ *75.00*
To: *City Electric*

For: *Electric bill*

BAL. BRO'T. FOR'D	4300 00
AMT. DEPOSITED	
SUBTOTAL	4300 00
AMT. THIS CHECK	75 00
BAL. CAR'D. FOR'D	4225 00

NO. *4*   Form ___*6*___
Date: *5/11*   20 - - $ *350.00*
To: *Atlas Supplies*

For: *Payment on*
       account

BAL. BRO'T. FOR'D	4225 00
AMT. DEPOSITED	
SUBTOTAL	4225 00
AMT. THIS CHECK	350 00
BAL. CAR'D. FOR'D	3875 00

Form ___*7*___
0.00 *

May 12, 20- -
T12   200.00 +
                     450.00 +
                     650.00 *

CRS
Cy's Repair Service   Sold to: _____*J. Hutton*_____   No. ___*1*___   Form ___*8*___
4814 Central Avenue   _____*199 Park Drive*_____   Date ___*5/15/- -*___
Great Falls, MT 59405-6184   *Great Falls, MT 59401-9043*   Terms *2/10, n/30*

Description	Amount
Repair condenser unit	500.00
Repair motor	300.00
Repair generator	400.00
Total	1,200.00

USING SOURCE DOCUMENTS (continued)

NO. 5   Form 9
Date: 5/16   20 -- $ 175.00
To: Pineridge
     Insurance Co.
For: Insurance

BAL. BRO'T. FOR'D		3875	00
AMT. DEPOSITED	5—12	650	00
SUBTOTAL		4525	00
AMT. THIS CHECK		175	00
BAL. CAR'D. FOR'D		4350	00

                                    Form 10
                                    0.00 *
May 19, 20--
T19   150.00 +
                 214.00 +
                 294.00 +
                 658.00 *

NO. 6   Form 11
Date: 5/23   20 -- $ 45.00
To: Sunset Delivery Co.

For: Miscellaneous
      Expense

BAL. BRO'T. FOR'D		4350	00
AMT. DEPOSITED	5—19	658	00
SUBTOTAL		5008	00
AMT. THIS CHECK		45	00
BAL. CAR'D. FOR'D		4963	00

                                    Form 12
                                    0.00 *
May 26, 20--
T26   307.00 +
                 323.00 +
                 630.00 *

NO. 7   Form 13
Date: 5/29   20 -- $ 20.00
To: Foothills Cleaning Co.

For: Miscellaneous
      Expense

BAL. BRO'T. FOR'D		4963	00
AMT. DEPOSITED	5—26	630	00
SUBTOTAL		5593	00
AMT. THIS CHECK		20	00
BAL. CAR'D. FOR'D		5573	00

Receipt No. _2_

Date _May 29_ , 20--

From _J. Hutton_

For _On Account_

_____

$ 1,000 | 00

Receipt No. _2_   Form _14_

Date _May 29_ _____ 20--

Rec'd from _J. Hutton_

For _On Account_

One thousand & no/100 _____ Dollars

Amount $ 1,000 | 00

_CS_

Received by

NO. _8_   Form _15_

Date: _5/29_ 20 -- $ _50.00_ _____

To: _Great Falls Telephone_
Company

For: _Telephone_
bill

BAL. BRO'T. FOR'D		5573	00
AMT. DEPOSITED	5—29	1000	00
SUBTOTAL		6573	00
AMT. THIS CHECK		50	00
BAL. CAR'D. FOR'D		6523	00

NO. _9_   Form _16_

Date: _5/30_ 20 -- $ _1500.00_

To: _Cy Sawyer_

For: _Owner_
withdrawal

BAL. BRO'T. FOR'D		6523	00
AMT. DEPOSITED			
SUBTOTAL		6523	00
AMT. THIS CHECK		1500	00
BAL. CAR'D. FOR'D		5023	00

Form _17_

0.00 *

May 31, 20--
_T31_

200.00+

200.00 *

NO. _10_   Form _18_

Date: _____ 20 -- $ _____

To: _____

For: _____

BAL. BRO'T. FOR'D		5023	00
AMT. DEPOSITED	5—31	200	00
SUBTOTAL		5223	00
AMT. THIS CHECK			
BAL. CAR'D. FOR'D			

USING SOURCE DOCUMENTS (concluded)

JOURNAL

PAGE 5

DATE	ACCOUNT TITLE	DOC. NO.	POST. REF.	GENERAL DEBIT 1	GENERAL CREDIT 2	SALES CREDIT 3	CASH DEBIT 4	CASH CREDIT 5
1								
2								
3								
4								
5								
6								
7								
8								
9								
10								
11								
12								
13								
14								
15								
16								
17								
18								
19								

2. *Prove the journal:*

Column	*Debit Column Totals*	*Credit Column Totals*
General	_____	_____
Sales	_____	_____
Cash	_____	_____
Totals	_____	_____

3. *Prove cash:*

Cash on hand at the beginning of the month . . . . _____

Plus total cash received during the month . . . . _____

Equals Total . . . . _____

Less total cash paid during the month . . . . _____

Equals cash balance at the end of the month . . . . _____

Checkbook balance on the next unused check stub . . . . _____

Study Guide 4

Name		Perfect Score	Your Score
	Identifying Accounting Terms	7 Pts.	
	Identifying Accounting Concepts and Practices	15 Pts.	
	Analyzing Posting from a Journal to a General Ledger	13 Pts.	
	Total	35 Pts.	

Part One—Identifying Accounting Terms

Directions: Select the one term in Column I that best fits each definition in Column II. Print the letter identifying your choice in the Answers column.

Column I	Column II	Answers
A. account number ✓	**1.** A group of accounts. (p. 92) *Ledger*	1. _E_
B. correcting entry	**2.** A ledger that contains all accounts needed to prepare financial statements. (p. 92) *General Ledger.*	2. _D_
C. file maintenance ✓	**3.** The number assigned to an account. (p. 92) *Account number.*	3. _A_
D. general ledger ✓	**4.** The procedure for arranging accounts in a general ledger, assigning account numbers, and keeping records current. (p. 93) *file Maintenance*	4. _C_
E. ledger ✓	**5.** Writing an account title and number on the heading of an account. (p. 94) *Opening an account.*	5. _F_
F. opening an account ✓	**6.** Transferring information from a journal entry to a ledger account. (p. 96) *Posting*	6. _G_
G. posting ✓	**7.** A journal entry made to correct an error in a previous journal entry. (p. 108) *correcting entry.*	7. _B_

Part Two—Identifying Accounting Concepts and Practices

Directions: Place a *T* for True or an *F* for False in the Answers column to show whether each of the following statements is true or false.

1. Because an account form has columns for the debit and credit balance of an account, it is often referred to as the balance-ruled account form. (p. 91) **1.** T

2. The asset division accounts for TechKnow Consulting are numbered in the 100s. (p. 92) **2.** T

3. The cash account is the first asset account and is numbered 100. (p. 92) **3.** F

4. The second division of TechKnow Consulting's chart of accounts is the owner's equity division. (p. 92) **4.** F

5. The first digit of account numbers for accounts in the owner's equity ledger division is 3. (p. 92) **5.** T

6. The last two digits in a 3-digit account number indicate the general ledger division of the account. (p. 93) **6.** F

7. When adding a new expense account between accounts numbered 510 and 520, the new account is assigned the account number 515. (p. 93) **7.** T

8. TechKnow Consulting arranges expense accounts in chronological order in its general ledger. (p. 93) **8.** F

9. The two steps for opening an account are writing the account title and recording the balance. (p. 94) **9.** F

10. Separate amounts in special amount columns are posted individually. (p. 96) **10.** F

11. Separate amounts in general amount columns are not posted individually. (p. 96) **11.** F

12. The only reason for the Post. Ref. columns of the journal and general ledger is to indicate which entries in the journal still need to be posted if posting is interrupted. (p. 97) **12.** F

13. A check mark in parentheses below a General Debit column total indicates that the total is not posted. (p. 100) **13.** T

14. The totals of special amount columns in a journal are not posted. (p. 101) **14.** F

15. With the exception of the totals lines, the Post. Ref. column is completely filled in with either an account number or a check mark. (p. 105) **15.** T

Name _____Mayra Flores_____ Date _____ Class _____

Part Three—Analyzing Posting from a Journal to a General Ledger

Directions: In the journal below, some items are identified with capital letters. In the general ledger accounts, locations to which items are posted are identified with numbers. For each number in a general ledger account, select the letter in the journal that will be posted to the account. Print the letter identifying your choice in the Answers column.

JOURNAL PAGE 1 **A**

	DATE	ACCOUNT TITLE	DOC. NO.	POST. REF.	GENERAL DEBIT	GENERAL CREDIT	SALES CREDIT	CASH DEBIT	CASH CREDIT	
1	20-- May 2	J. Nichols, Capital	R1		1 0 0 0 00				1 0 0 0 00	1
2	4	Supplies	C1		2 0 0 00	**B**			2 0 0 00	2
3	6	✓	T6	✓			8 0 0 00	**C**	8 0 0 00	3
25	31	Totals			2 0 5 5 00	5 0 0 00	3 4 0 0 00	3 9 0 0 00	2 0 5 5 00	25
26	**D** **E**			**F**	**G**	**H**	**I**	**J**	**K**	26

General ledger. (handwritten)

ACCOUNT Cash   ACCOUNT NO. 110

A through F (pp. 96–100)

DATE	ITEM	POST. REF.	DEBIT	CREDIT	BALANCE DEBIT	BALANCE CREDIT
1 2		3	4			
				5		

G through K (pp. 101–104)

ACCOUNT Supplies   120

6 DATE 7	ITEM 8 9	POST. REF.	DEBIT	CREDIT

Bold Numbers in Ledger Accounts / **Answers**

ACCOUNT Sales   ACCOUNT NO. 410

DATE	ITEM	POST. REF.	DEBIT	CREDIT	BALANCE DEBIT	BALANCE CREDIT
10 11		12		13		

Bold Numbers	Answers
1.	D
2.	E
3.	A
4.	J
5.	K
6.	D
7.	E
8.	A
9.	B
10.	D
11.	E
12.	A
13.	I

we debit cash first (handwritten)

4-1 WORK TOGETHER, p. 95

Foto.

Preparing a chart of accounts and opening an account

1.

Ross Company
Chart of Accounts.

Balance Sheet Accounts.	Income Stat. Accounts.
(100) Assets	(400) Revenue.
110 Cash.	410 Sales.
120 A/R - Megan Alvarez	(500) Expenses
130 A/R - Tyler Link.	510 Automobile. Exp
140 Supplies.	520 Insurance Exp
150 Prepaid Insurance.	530 Miscellan. Exp.
(200) Liabilities	540 Rent Exp.
210 A/P - Mid City Supplies.	550 Supplies Exp.
220 A/P - Sherer Supplies.	
(300) Owner's Equity	
310 Clara Ross, Capital.	
320 Clara Ross, Drawing.	

2.

New Accounts

Account Number	Account Title
535	Postage Expense.
560	Utilities. Expense.

3.

ACCOUNT CASH   ACCOUNT NO. 110

DATE	ITEM	POST. REF.	DEBIT	CREDIT	BALANCE DEBIT	BALANCE CREDIT

Preparing a chart of accounts and opening an account

1.

Roen's Hair Care
Chart of Accounts

Balance Sheet Accounts	Income Statement Accounts
(100) Assets	(400) Revenue
110- Cash	410- Sales
120- A/R - M. Waller	(500) Expenses
130- A/R - Superior Supplies	510- Delivery
140- Supplies	520- Insurance
150- Prepaid Insurance	530- Supplies
	540- Telephone
(200) Liabilities	
210- A/P - Milton Company	
220- A/P - North Star	
(300) Owner's Equity	
310- Erin Roen, Capital	
320- Eric Roen, Drawing	

2.

Account number	Account title
(515)	Gasoline Exp
(550)	Water Exp.

3.

ACCOUNT						ACCOUNT NO.	
DATE	ITEM	POST. REF.	DEBIT	CREDIT	BALANCE		
					DEBIT	CREDIT	

4-2 and 4-3 WORK TOGETHER, pp. 99, 104

4-2 Posting separate amounts to a general ledger
4-3 Posting column totals to a general ledger

JOURNAL

PAGE 1

	DATE	ACCOUNT TITLE	DOC. NO.	POST. REF.	GENERAL DEBIT	GENERAL CREDIT	SALES CREDIT	CASH DEBIT	CASH CREDIT	
1	Mar. 1	Leonard Witkowski, Capital	R1			5000 00		5000 00		1
2	3	Prepaid Insurance	C1		660 00				660 00	2
3	4	Supplies	M1		78 00					3
4		Accts. Payable—Joshua's Supplies				78 00				4
5	8	✓	T8	✓			675 00	675 00		5
6	9	Accts. Receivable—Danielle Braastad	S1		163 00		163 00			6
7	12	Rent Expense	C2		375 00				375 00	7
8	15	Accts. Payable—Joshua's Supplies	C3		50 00				50 00	8
9	16	Accts. Receivable—Danielle Braastad	R2			100 00		100 00		9
10	25	Leonard Witkowski, Drawing	C4		1000 00				1000 00	10
11	31	Totals			2326 00	5178 00	838 00	5775 00	2085 00	11
12					(✓)	(✓)				12
13										13
14										14
15										15
16										16
17										17
18										18
19										19
20										20
21										21
22										22
23										23

GENERAL LEDGER

ACCOUNT Cash   ACCOUNT NO. 110

DATE	ITEM	POST. REF.	DEBIT	CREDIT	BALANCE DEBIT	BALANCE CREDIT
Mar 31		1	575000		577500	
31		1		208500	369000	

ACCOUNT Accounts Receivable—Danielle Braastad   ACCOUNT NO. 120

DATE	ITEM	POST. REF.	DEBIT	CREDIT	BALANCE DEBIT	BALANCE CREDIT
Mar 9		1	16300		16300	
16		1		10000	6300	

ACCOUNT Supplies   ACCOUNT NO. 130

DATE	ITEM	POST. REF.	DEBIT	CREDIT	BALANCE DEBIT	BALANCE CREDIT
Mar 4		1	7800		7800	

ACCOUNT Prepaid Insurance   ACCOUNT NO. 140

DATE	ITEM	POST. REF.	DEBIT	CREDIT	BALANCE DEBIT	BALANCE CREDIT
Mar 3		1	66000		66000	

ACCOUNT Accounts Payable—Joshua's Supplies   ACCOUNT NO. 210

DATE	ITEM	POST. REF.	DEBIT	CREDIT	BALANCE DEBIT	BALANCE CREDIT
Mar 4		1		7800		7800
15		1	5000			2800

4-2 and 4-3   WORK TOGETHER (concluded)

GENERAL LEDGER

ACCOUNT Leonard Witkowski, Capital   ACCOUNT NO. 310

DATE	ITEM	POST. REF.	DEBIT	CREDIT	BALANCE DEBIT	BALANCE CREDIT
Mar 1		1		5 000 00		5 000 00

ACCOUNT Leonard Witkowski, Drawing   ACCOUNT NO. 320

DATE	ITEM	POST. REF.	DEBIT	CREDIT	BALANCE DEBIT	BALANCE CREDIT
Mar 25		1	1 000 00		1 000 00	

ACCOUNT Sales   ACCOUNT NO. 410

DATE	ITEM	POST. REF.	DEBIT	CREDIT	BALANCE DEBIT	BALANCE CREDIT
Mar 31		1		8 38 00		8 38 00

ACCOUNT Rent Expense   ACCOUNT NO. 510

DATE	ITEM	POST. REF.	DEBIT	CREDIT	BALANCE DEBIT	BALANCE CREDIT
Mar 12		1	375 00		375 00	

ACCOUNT   ACCOUNT NO.

DATE	ITEM	POST. REF.	DEBIT	CREDIT	BALANCE DEBIT	BALANCE CREDIT

4-2 Posting separate amounts to a general ledger
4-3 Posting column totals to a general ledger

JOURNAL

PAGE 1

	DATE	ACCOUNT TITLE	DOC. NO.	POST. REF.	GENERAL DEBIT	GENERAL CREDIT	SALES CREDIT	CASH DEBIT	CASH CREDIT	
1	20-- Sept. 1	Heather Hasley, Capital	R1			4 5 0 0 00		4 5 0 0 00		1
2	4	Supplies	M1		6 7 00					2
3		Accounts Payable—Bodden Company				6 7 00				3
4	7	Prepaid Insurance	C1		3 0 0 00				3 0 0 00	4
5	10	Accounts Receivable—Ken Garlie	S1		1 9 5 00		1 9 5 00			5
6	13		T13	✔			1 2 0 0 00	1 2 0 0 00		6
7	18	Advertising Expense	C2		4 9 00				4 9 00	7
8	21	Accounts Payable—Bodden Company	C3		3 5 00				3 5 00	8
9	27	Accounts Receivable—Ken Garlie	R2			1 0 0 00		1 0 0 00		9
10	30	Heather Hasley, Drawing	C4		1 3 0 0 00				1 3 0 0 00	10
11	30	Totals			1 9 4 6 00	4 6 6 7 00	1 3 9 5 00	5 8 0 0 00	1 6 8 4 00	11
12					(✔)	(✔)				12
13										13
14										14
15										15
16										16
17										17
18										18
19										19
20										20
21										21
22										22
23										23

4-2 and 4-3 ON YOUR OWN (continued)

GENERAL LEDGER

ACCOUNT Cash   ACCOUNT NO. 110

DATE	ITEM	POST. REF.	DEBIT	CREDIT	BALANCE DEBIT	BALANCE CREDIT
Sept 30		1	5 800 00		5 800 00	
30		1		1 684 00	4 116 00	

ACCOUNT Accounts Receivable—Ken Garlie   ACCOUNT NO. 120

DATE	ITEM	POST. REF.	DEBIT	CREDIT	BALANCE DEBIT	BALANCE CREDIT
Sept 10		1	1 95 00		1 95 00	
		1		1 00 00	1 95 00	

ACCOUNT Supplies   ACCOUNT NO. 130

DATE	ITEM	POST. REF.	DEBIT	CREDIT	BALANCE DEBIT	BALANCE CREDIT
Sept 4		2	67 00		67 00	

ACCOUNT Prepaid Insurance   ACCOUNT NO. 140

DATE	ITEM	POST. REF.	DEBIT	CREDIT	BALANCE DEBIT	BALANCE CREDIT
Sept 7		1	3 000 00		3 000 00	

ACCOUNT Accounts Payable—Bodden Company   ACCOUNT NO. 210

DATE	ITEM	POST. REF.	DEBIT	CREDIT	BALANCE DEBIT	BALANCE CREDIT
Sept 4		1		67 00		67 00
		1	35 00			32 00

GENERAL LEDGER

account Heather Hasley, Capital   ACCOUNT NO. 310

DATE	ITEM	POST. REF.	DEBIT	CREDIT	BALANCE DEBIT	BALANCE CREDIT
Sept 1		1		450000		450000

account Heather Hasley, Drawing   ACCOUNT NO. 320

DATE	ITEM	POST. REF.	DEBIT	CREDIT	BALANCE DEBIT	BALANCE CREDIT
Sept 30		1	130000		130000	

account Sales   ACCOUNT NO. 410

DATE	ITEM	POST. REF.	DEBIT	CREDIT	BALANCE DEBIT	BALANCE CREDIT
Sept 30		1		139500		139500

account Advertising Expense   ACCOUNT NO. 510

DATE	ITEM	POST. REF.	DEBIT	CREDIT	BALANCE DEBIT	BALANCE CREDIT
Sept 8		1	4900		4900	

account   ACCOUNT NO.

DATE	ITEM	POST. REF.	DEBIT	CREDIT	BALANCE DEBIT	BALANCE CREDIT

4-4 WORK TOGETHER, p. 109

Journalizing correcting entries

JOURNAL PAGE 21

	DATE	ACCOUNT TITLE	DOC. NO.	POST. REF.	GENERAL DEBIT	GENERAL CREDIT	SALES CREDIT	CASH DEBIT	CASH CREDIT	
1	Nov. 1	Supplies	M15		6000					1
2		Prepaid Insurance				6000				2
3	1	Rent Expense	M16		55000					3
4		Repair Expense				55000				4
5										5
6										6
7										7
8										8
9										9
10										10
11										11
12										12
13										13
14										14
15										15
16										16
17										17
18										18
19										19
20										20
21										21
22										22
23										23
24										24

Journalizing correcting entries

JOURNAL

PAGE 11

DATE	ACCOUNT TITLE	DOC. NO.	POST. REF.	GENERAL DEBIT	GENERAL CREDIT	SALES CREDIT	CASH DEBIT	CASH CREDIT	
Jun 1	Supplies	C123		15000					1
	Prepaid Insurance				15000				2
1	Utilities Expense	C124		85000					3
	Miscellaneous Expense				85000				4
									5
									6
									7
									8
									9
									10
									11
									12
									13
									14
									15
									16
									17
									18
									19
									20
									21
									22
									23
									24

4-1 APPLICATION PROBLEM, p. 111

Preparing a chart of accounts and opening an account

1.

Deters Duplicating
Chart of Accounts

Balance Sheet Accounts	Income Statement Accounts
(100) Assets	(400) Revenue
110 Cash	410 Sales
120 Accounts Re— Austin Kirnyczuk	(500) Expenses
130 A/R — Teegan Walters	510 Advertising Expense
140 Supplies	520 Charitable Expense
150 Prepaid Insurance	530 Postage Expense
(200) Liabilities	540 Rent Expense
210 A/P — Dakota Company	
220 A/P — Falls Supply	
(300) Owner's Equity	
310 Lillian Deters, Capital	
320 Lillian Deters, Drawing	

2.

New Accounts

Account #	Account title
525	Delivery Exp.
550	Thelephone Exp.

3.

ACCOUNT						ACCOUNT NO.		
DATE	ITEM	POST. REF.	DEBIT	CREDIT	BALANCE			
					DEBIT	CREDIT		

ACCOUNT						ACCOUNT NO.		
DATE	ITEM	POST. REF.	DEBIT	CREDIT	BALANCE			
					DEBIT	CREDIT		

4-2 Posting separate amounts to a general ledger
4-3 Posting column totals to a general ledger

JOURNAL

PAGE 1

DATE		ACCOUNT TITLE	DOC. NO.	POST. REF.	GENERAL DEBIT	GENERAL CREDIT	SALES CREDIT	CASH DEBIT	CASH CREDIT	
20-- Oct.	1	Alta Komoko, Capital	R1			2 0 0 0 00		2 0 0 0 00		1
	4	Prepaid Insurance	C1		3 0 0 00				3 0 0 00	2
	10	Supplies	M1		9 0 00	9 0 00				3
		Accts. Pay.—Bay Bridge Supply								4
	12		T12	✔			4 8 2 00	4 8 2 00		5
	15	Accts. Rec.—Melanie Ford	S1		7 5 00		7 5 00			6
	19	Advertising Expense	C2		1 2 5 00				1 2 5 00	7
	20	Accts. Pay.—Bay Bridge Supply	C3		6 0 00				6 0 00	8
	27	Accts. Rec.—Melanie Ford	R2			5 0 00		5 0 00		9
	31	Alta Komoko, Drawing	C4		4 0 0 00				4 0 0 00	10
	31	Totals			1 0 5 0 00	2 1 4 0 00	5 5 7 00	2 5 3 2 00	8 8 5 00	11
					(✔)	(✔)	(410)	(110)	(110)	12
										13
										14
										15
										16
										17
										18
										19
										20
										21
										22
										23

4-2 and 4-3 APPLICATION PROBLEMS (continued)

GENERAL LEDGER

ACCOUNT Cash   ACCOUNT NO. 110

DATE		ITEM	POST. REF.	DEBIT	CREDIT	BALANCE	
						DEBIT	CREDIT
Oct	31		1	2532 00		2532 00	
	31		1		885 00	1647 00	

ACCOUNT Accounts Receivable—Melanie Ford   ACCOUNT NO. 120

DATE		ITEM	POST. REF.	DEBIT	CREDIT	BALANCE	
						DEBIT	CREDIT
Oct	15		1	75 00		75 00	
	27		1		50 00	25 00	

ACCOUNT Supplies   ACCOUNT NO. 130

DATE		ITEM	POST. REF.	DEBIT	CREDIT	BALANCE	
						DEBIT	CREDIT
Oct	10		1	90 00		90 00	

ACCOUNT Prepaid Insurance   ACCOUNT NO. 140

DATE		ITEM	POST. REF.	DEBIT	CREDIT	BALANCE	
						DEBIT	CREDIT
Oct	4		1	300 00		300 00	

ACCOUNT Accounts Payable—Bay Bridge Supply   ACCOUNT NO. 210

DATE		ITEM	POST. REF.	DEBIT	CREDIT	BALANCE	
						DEBIT	CREDIT
Oct	10		1		90 00		90 00
	20		1	60 00			30 00

GENERAL LEDGER

ACCOUNT Alta Komoko, Capital   ACCOUNT NO. 310

DATE	ITEM	POST. REF.	DEBIT	CREDIT	BALANCE DEBIT	BALANCE CREDIT
Oct 1		1	2 000 00			2 000 00

ACCOUNT Alta Komoko, Drawing   ACCOUNT NO. 320

DATE	ITEM	POST. REF.	DEBIT	CREDIT	BALANCE DEBIT	BALANCE CREDIT
Oct 31		1	400 00		400 00	

ACCOUNT Sales   ACCOUNT NO. 410

DATE	ITEM	POST. REF.	DEBIT	CREDIT	BALANCE DEBIT	BALANCE CREDIT
Oct 31		1		557 00		557 00

ACCOUNT Advertising Expense   ACCOUNT NO. 510

DATE	ITEM	POST. REF.	DEBIT	CREDIT	BALANCE DEBIT	BALANCE CREDIT
Oct 19		1	125 00		125 00	

ACCOUNT   ACCOUNT NO.

DATE	ITEM	POST. REF.	DEBIT	CREDIT	BALANCE DEBIT	BALANCE CREDIT

4-4 APPLICATION PROBLEM, p. 111

Journalizing correcting entries

JOURNAL

PAGE 7

	DATE	ACCOUNT TITLE	DOC. NO.	POST. REF.	GENERAL DEBIT	GENERAL CREDIT	SALES CREDIT	CASH DEBIT	CASH CREDIT	
1	Apr 1	Utilities Expense	M66		26500					1
2		Repairs Expense				26500				2
3	5	Sales	M67		60000					3
4		Manuel Ricardo, Capital				60000				4
5										5
6										6
7										7
8										8
9										9
10										10
11										11
12										12
13										13
14										14
15										15
16										16
17										17
18										18
19										19
20										20
21										21
22										22
23										23
24										24

Journalizing transactions and posting to a general ledger

JOURNAL

pic in phone

DATE	ACCOUNT TITLE	DOC. NO.	POST. REF.	GENERAL DEBIT	GENERAL CREDIT	SALES CREDIT	CASH DEBIT	CASH CREDIT
Nov 1	Patrick O'Kalla, Capital							
	3 Supplies							

PAGE 5

3. *Prove the journal:*

Column	Debit Column Totals	Credit Column Totals
General		
Sales		
Cash		
Totals		

4. *Prove cash:*

Cash on hand at the beginning of the month ....

Plus total cash received during the month ....

Equals Total ....

Less total cash paid during the month ....

Equals cash balance at the end of the month ....

Checkbook balance on the next unused check stub ....

4-5 MASTERY PROBLEM (continued)

GENERAL LEDGER

ACCOUNT Cash　　　　　　　　　　　　　　　　　　　　ACCOUNT NO. 110

DATE	ITEM	POST. REF.	DEBIT	CREDIT	BALANCE DEBIT	BALANCE CREDIT
Nov 30		1	9 190 00		9 190 00	
30		1		2 293 00	6 897 00	

ACCOUNT Accounts Receivable—Merilda Domingo　　　　　　ACCOUNT NO. 120

DATE	ITEM	POST. REF.	DEBIT	CREDIT	BALANCE DEBIT	BALANCE CREDIT
Nov 6		1	280 00		280 00	
20		1		150 00	130 00	

ACCOUNT Supplies　　　　　　　　　　　　　　　　　　ACCOUNT NO. 130

DATE	ITEM	POST. REF.	DEBIT	CREDIT	BALANCE DEBIT	BALANCE CREDIT
Nov 3		1	400 00		400 00	
13		1	240 00		640 00	
25		1	150 00		790 00	
27		1	80 00		870 00	

ACCOUNT Accounts Payable—Park Supplies　　　　　　　ACCOUNT NO. 210

DATE	ITEM	POST. REF.	DEBIT	CREDIT	BALANCE DEBIT	BALANCE CREDIT
Nov 13		1		240 00		240 00
18		1	140 00			100 00

GENERAL LEDGER

ACCOUNT Patrick O'Kalla, Capital   ACCOUNT NO. 310

DATE	ITEM	POST. REF.	DEBIT	CREDIT	BALANCE DEBIT	BALANCE CREDIT
Nov 1		1		550000		550000

ACCOUNT Patrick O'Kalla, Drawing   ACCOUNT NO. 320

DATE	ITEM	POST. REF.	DEBIT	CREDIT	BALANCE DEBIT	BALANCE CREDIT
Nov 30		1	50000		50000	

ACCOUNT Sales   ACCOUNT NO. 410

DATE	ITEM	POST. REF.	DEBIT	CREDIT	BALANCE DEBIT	BALANCE CREDIT
Nov 30		1		382000		382000

ACCOUNT Advertising Expense   ACCOUNT NO. 510

DATE	ITEM	POST. REF.	DEBIT	CREDIT	BALANCE DEBIT	BALANCE CREDIT
Nov 16		1	14300		14300	

4-5 MASTERY PROBLEM (concluded)

GENERAL LEDGER

account **Miscellaneous Expense**   account no. 520

DATE	ITEM	POST. REF.	DEBIT	CREDIT	BALANCE DEBIT	BALANCE CREDIT
Nov 11		1	50 00		50 00	

account **Rent Expense**   account no. 530

DATE	ITEM	POST. REF.	DEBIT	CREDIT	BALANCE DEBIT	BALANCE CREDIT
Nov 9		1	600 00		600 00	

ACCOUNT   ACCOUNT NO.

DATE	ITEM	POST. REF.	DEBIT	CREDIT	BALANCE DEBIT	BALANCE CREDIT
Nov 20		1	230 00		230 00	

ACCOUNT   ACCOUNT NO.

DATE	ITEM	POST. REF.	DEBIT	CREDIT	BALANCE DEBIT	BALANCE CREDIT

Posting using a variation of the five-column journal

pic in phone ✕

JOURNAL   PAGE 5

Line	DEBIT CASH	DEBIT GENERAL	DATE	ACCOUNT TITLE	DOC. NO.	POST. REF.	CREDIT GENERAL	CREDIT SALES	CREDIT CASH
1	3000 00		Mar. 1	Frances Fessler, Capital	R1		3000 00		
2		850 00	3	Rent Expense	C1				850 00
3		5 00	5	Miscellaneous Expense	C2				5 00
4		250 00	9	Accounts Receivable—Joelle Chu	S1			250 00	
5		400 00	11	Supplies	C3				400 00
6	450 00		13	✔	T13	✔		450 00	
7		200 00	16	Supplies	M1				
8				Accounts Payable—Dollar Supplies			200 00		
9		150 00	18	Accounts Payable—Dollar Supplies	C4				150 00
10		60 00	19	Utilities Expense	C5				60 00
11	1100 00		20	✔	T20	✔		1100 00	
12		50 00	23	Advertising Expense	C6				50 00
13		150 00	23	Supplies	C7				150 00
14		150 00	27	Supplies	C8				150 00
15	1830 00		27	✔	T27	✔		1830 00	
16		1400 00	30	Frances Fessler, Drawing	C9				1400 00
17	410 00		31	✔	T31	✔		410 00	
18	6790 00	3665 00	31	Totals			3200 00	4040 00	3215 00
19		(✔)					(✔)		
20									
21									
22									
23									
24									

4-6 CHALLENGE PROBLEM (continued)

GENERAL LEDGER

ACCOUNT Cash — ACCOUNT NO. 110

DATE	ITEM	POST. REF.	DEBIT	CREDIT	BALANCE DEBIT	BALANCE CREDIT
Mar 31		5	6 79000		6 79000	
31		5		3 21500	3 57500	

ACCOUNT Accounts Receivable—Joelle Chu — ACCOUNT NO. 120

DATE	ITEM	POST. REF.	DEBIT	CREDIT	BALANCE DEBIT	BALANCE CREDIT
Mar 9		5	25000		25000	

ACCOUNT Supplies — ACCOUNT NO. 130

DATE	ITEM	POST. REF.	DEBIT	CREDIT	BALANCE DEBIT	BALANCE CREDIT
Mar 11		5	40000		40000	
16		5	20000		60000	
23		5	15000		75000	
27		5	15000		90000	

ACCOUNT Accounts Payable—Dollar Supplies — ACCOUNT NO. 210

DATE	ITEM	POST. REF.	DEBIT	CREDIT	BALANCE DEBIT	BALANCE CREDIT
Mar 16		5		20000		20000
18		5	15000			5000

ACCOUNT Frances Fessler, Capital — ACCOUNT NO. 310

DATE	ITEM	POST. REF.	DEBIT	CREDIT	BALANCE DEBIT	BALANCE CREDIT
Mar 1		5		300000		300000

GENERAL LEDGER

ACCOUNT Frances Fessler, Drawing ACCOUNT NO. 320

DATE	ITEM	POST. REF.	DEBIT	CREDIT	BALANCE DEBIT	BALANCE CREDIT
Mar 30		5	1 40 00 0		1 40 00 0	

ACCOUNT Sales ACCOUNT NO. 410

DATE	ITEM	POST. REF.	DEBIT	CREDIT	BALANCE DEBIT	BALANCE CREDIT
Mar 31		5		4 04 00 0		4 04 00 0

ACCOUNT Advertising Expense ACCOUNT NO. 510

DATE	ITEM	POST. REF.	DEBIT	CREDIT	BALANCE DEBIT	BALANCE CREDIT
Mar 23		5	5 00 0		5 00 0	

ACCOUNT Miscellaneous Expense ACCOUNT NO. 520

DATE	ITEM	POST. REF.	DEBIT	CREDIT	BALANCE DEBIT	BALANCE CREDIT
Mar 5		5	5 00		5 00	

ACCOUNT Rent Expense ACCOUNT NO. 530

DATE	ITEM	POST. REF.	DEBIT	CREDIT	BALANCE DEBIT	BALANCE CREDIT
Mar 3		5	85 0 00		85 0 00	

ACCOUNT Utilities Expense ACCOUNT NO. 540

DATE	ITEM	POST. REF.	DEBIT	CREDIT	BALANCE DEBIT	BALANCE CREDIT
Mar 19		5	6 00 0		6 00 0	

USING SOURCE DOCUMENTS, p. 114

Journalizing transactions and posting to a general ledger

Receipt No. _1_	Receipt No. _1_ Form _1_
Date _7/2_ , 20--	Date _July 2_ 20--
From _Darcia Tomzak_	Rec'd from _Darcia Tomzak_
For _Investment_	For _Investment_
	Seven Thousand & ^{no}/100 Dollars
$ 7,000 00	Amount $ 7,000 00
	LCB
	Received by

NO. _1_   Form _2_
Date: _7/3_   20 - - $ _1,000.00_
To: _Quincy Rental Agency_

For: _July Rent_

BAL. BRO'T. FOR'D		0 00
AMT. DEPOSITED	7—1	7000 00
SUBTOTAL		7000 00
AMT. THIS CHECK		1000 00
BAL. CAR'D. FOR'D		6000 00

No. _1_   Form _3_

MEMORANDUM

_Bought supplies on account
from Music Supply Co., $1,300.00_

Signed: _____ _LCB_ _____   Date: _7/6/- -_

USING SOURCE DOCUMENTS (continued)

NO. 2		Form 4
Date: 7/7 20-- $ 119.00		
To: City Telephone Company		
For: Telephone bill		

BAL. BRO'T. FOR'D	6000	00
AMT. DEPOSITED		
SUBTOTAL	6000	00
AMT. THIS CHECK	119	00
BAL. CAR'D. FOR'D	5881	00

Form 5

0.00 *

July 7, 20--
T7

175.00+
80.00+
475.00+
70.00+
800.00 *

Darcia's
School of Dance
313 King Street
Concord, NH 03303

Sold to: Kid's Stop
366 Park Street
Concord, NH 03303

Form 6
No. 1
Date 7/10/--
Terms 2/10, n/30

Description	Amount
Pre-School Dance class-1 Hr.	300.00
K-3 Dance class-1 Hr.	350.00
Total	650.00

NO. 3		Form 7
Date: 7/11 20-- $ 795.00		
To: Orion Insurance Company		
For: Insurance		

BAL. BRO'T. FOR'D		5881	00
AMT. DEPOSITED	7—7	800	00
SUBTOTAL		6681	00
AMT. THIS CHECK		795	00
BAL. CAR'D. FOR'D		5886	00

Form 8

0.00 *

July 14, 20--
T14

425.00+
525.00+
150.00+
1,100.00 *

USING SOURCE DOCUMENTS (continued)

NO. 4   Form __9__
Date: _7/16_   20 -- $ _325.00_
To: ____Prescott Media____

For: ____Advertising____

BAL. BRO'T. FOR'D	5886	00
AMT. DEPOSITED 7—14	1100	00
SUBTOTAL	6986	00
AMT. THIS CHECK	325	00
BAL. CAR'D. FOR'D	6661	00

Form __10__
0.00 *

July 21, 20--
T 21   575.00+
   275.00+

   850.00 *

NO. 5   Form __11__
Date: _7/23_   20 -- $ _850.00_
To: ____Music Supply____
         Company
For: __On account__

BAL. BRO'T. FOR'D	6661	00
AMT. DEPOSITED 7—21	850	00
SUBTOTAL	7511	00
AMT. THIS CHECK	850	00
BAL. CAR'D. FOR'D	6661	00

Receipt No. __2__
Date _7/24_ , 20--
From _Kid's Stop_
For _On account_
_____

$ 425 | 00

Receipt No. __2__   Form __12__
Date _July 24_ _____ 20--
Rec'd from _Kid's Stop_
For _On account_
     Four hundred twenty-five & $^{no}/100$ Dollars

Amount $ 425 | 00
_____LCB_____
Received by

USING SOURCE DOCUMENTS (continued)

NO. 6   Form 13

Date: 7/26   20-- $ 600.00

To: Columbus Supplies

For: Supplies

BAL. BRO'T. FOR'D		6661	00
AMT. DEPOSITED	7—24	425	00
SUBTOTAL		7086	00
AMT. THIS CHECK		600	00
BAL. CAR'D. FOR'D		6486	00

Form 14

0.00 *

July 28, 20--
T 28   500.00+

500.00 *

NO. 7   Form 15

Date: 7/30   20-- $ 110.00

To: Concord Electric
Company

For: Electric bill

BAL. BRO'T. FOR'D		6486	00
AMT. DEPOSITED	7—28	500	00
SUBTOTAL		6986	00
AMT. THIS CHECK		110	00
BAL. CAR'D. FOR'D		6876	00

Darcia's
School of Dance
313 King Street
Concord, NH 03303

Sold to: Kid's Stop   No.   Form 16 / 2

366 Park Street   Date 7/30/--

Concord, NH 03303   Terms 2/10, n/30

Description	Amount
K-3 Dance class–1 Hr.	350.00
Consultation–1 Hr.	125.00
Total	475.00

USING SOURCE DOCUMENTS (continued)

Form _17_

0.00 *

July 31, 20- -
T31

225.00+
225.00+
250.00+
700.00 *

NO. _8_   Form _18_

Date: _7/31_ 20 - - $ _1000.00_

To: _Darcia Tomzak_

For: _Withdrawal_

BAL. BRO'T. FOR'D		6876	00
AMT. DEPOSITED	7—31	700	00
SUBTOTAL		7576	00
AMT. THIS CHECK		1000	00
BAL. CAR'D. FOR'D		6576	00

NO. _9_   Form _19_

Date: _____ 20 - - $ _____

To: _____

For: _____

BAL. BRO'T. FOR'D	6576	00
AMT. DEPOSITED		
SUBTOTAL		
AMT. THIS CHECK		
BAL. CAR'D. FOR'D		

Copy on phone

JOURNAL

PAGE 5

	DATE	ACCOUNT TITLE	DOC. NO.	POST. REF.	GENERAL DEBIT 1	GENERAL CREDIT 2	SALES CREDIT 3	CASH DEBIT 4	CASH CREDIT 5	
1										1
2										2
3										3
4										4
5										5
6										6
7										7
8										8
9										9
10										10
11										11
12										12
13										13
14										14
15										15
16										16
17										17
18										18
19										19
20										20
21										21

2. *Prove the journal:*

Column	Debit Column Totals	Credit Column Totals
General	_____	_____
Sales		_____
Cash	_____	_____
Totals	_____	_____

3. *Prove cash:*

Cash on hand at the beginning of the month . . . . _____
Plus total cash received during the month . . . . _____
Equals Total . . . . _____
Less total cash paid during the month . . . . _____
Equals cash balance at the end of the month . . . . _____
Checkbook balance on the next unused check stub . . . . _____

USING SOURCE DOCUMENTS (continued)

GENERAL LEDGER

ACCOUNT Cash   ACCOUNT NO. 110

DATE	ITEM	POST. REF.	DEBIT	CREDIT	BALANCE DEBIT	BALANCE CREDIT
Jul 31		1	11 375 00		11 375 00	
31		1		4 799 00	6 576 00	

ACCOUNT Accounts Receivable—Kid's Stop   ACCOUNT NO. 120

DATE	ITEM	POST. REF.	DEBIT	CREDIT	BALANCE DEBIT	BALANCE CREDIT
Jul 10		1	650 00		650 00	
24		1		425 00	225 00	
30		1	475 00		700 00	

ACCOUNT Supplies   ACCOUNT NO. 130

DATE	ITEM	POST. REF.	DEBIT	CREDIT	BALANCE DEBIT	BALANCE CREDIT
Jul 6		1	1 300 00		1 300 00	
26		1	600 00		1 900 00	

ACCOUNT Prepaid Insurance   ACCOUNT NO. 140

DATE	ITEM	POST. REF.	DEBIT	CREDIT	BALANCE DEBIT	BALANCE CREDIT
Jul 11		1	795 00		795 00	

USING SOURCE DOCUMENTS (continued)

GENERAL LEDGER

ACCOUNT Accounts Payable—Music Supply Company   ACCOUNT NO. 210

DATE	ITEM	POST. REF.	DEBIT	CREDIT	BALANCE DEBIT	BALANCE CREDIT
Jul 6		1		1 3 0 0 00		1 3 0 0 00
23		1	8 5 0 00			4 5 0 00

ACCOUNT Darcia Tomzak, Capital   ACCOUNT NO. 310

DATE	ITEM	POST. REF.	DEBIT	CREDIT	BALANCE DEBIT	BALANCE CREDIT
Jul 2		1		7 0 0 0 00		7 0 0 0 00

ACCOUNT Darcia Tomzak, Drawing   ACCOUNT NO. 320

DATE	ITEM	POST. REF.	DEBIT	CREDIT	BALANCE DEBIT	BALANCE CREDIT
Jul 31		1	1 0 0 0 00		1 0 0 0 00	

ACCOUNT Sales   ACCOUNT NO. 410

DATE	ITEM	POST. REF.	DEBIT	CREDIT	BALANCE DEBIT	BALANCE CREDIT
Jul 31		1		5 0 7 5 00		5 0 7 5 00

USING SOURCE DOCUMENTS (concluded)

GENERAL LEDGER

ACCOUNT Advertising Expense   ACCOUNT NO. 510

DATE	ITEM	POST. REF.	DEBIT	CREDIT	BALANCE DEBIT	BALANCE CREDIT
Jul 16		1	32500		32500	

ACCOUNT Rent Expense   ACCOUNT NO. 520

DATE	ITEM	POST. REF.	DEBIT	CREDIT	BALANCE DEBIT	BALANCE CREDIT
Jul 3		1	100000		100000	

ACCOUNT Utilities Expense   ACCOUNT NO. 530

DATE	ITEM	POST. REF.	DEBIT	CREDIT	BALANCE DEBIT	BALANCE CREDIT
Jul 7		1	11900		11900	
30		1	11900		22900	

ACCOUNT   ACCOUNT NO.

DATE	ITEM	POST. REF.	DEBIT	CREDIT	BALANCE DEBIT	BALANCE CREDIT

Name	Mayra Flores	Perfect Score	Your Score
	Identifying Accounting Terms	13 Pts.	
	Analyzing Transactions in a Cash Control System	12 Pts.	
	Identifying Accounting Concepts and Practices	20 Pts.	
	Total	45 Pts.	

Part One—Identifying Accounting Terms

Directions: Select the one term in Column I that best fits each definition in Column II. Print the letter identifying your choice in the Answers column.

Column I	Column II	Answers
A. bank statement	1. A statement that guides the ethical behavior of a company and its employees. (p. 118)	1. D
B. blank endorsement	2. A bank account from which payments can be ordered by a depositor. (p. 119)	2. C
C. checking account	3. A signature or stamp on the back of a check, transferring ownership. (p. 120)	3. H
D. code of conduct	4. An endorsement consisting only of the endorser's signature. (p. 120)	4. B
E. debit card	5. An endorsement indicating a new owner of a check. (p. 120)	5. M
F. dishonored check	6. An endorsement restricting further transfer of a check's ownership. (p. 120)	6. L
G. electric funds transfer	7. A check with a future date on it. (p. 121)	7. K
H. endorsement	8. A report of deposits, withdrawals, and bank balances sent to a depositor by a bank. (p. 124)	8. A
I. petty cash	9. A check that a bank refuses to pay. (p. 129)	9. F
J. petty cash slip	10. A computerized cash payments system that transfers funds without the use of checks, currency, or other paper documents. (p. 131)	10. G
K. postdated check	11. A bank card that automatically deducts that amount of a purchase from the checking account of the cardholder. (p. 132)	11. E
L. restrictive endorsement	12. An amount of cash kept on hand and used for making small payments. (p. 134)	12. I
M. special endorsement	13. A form showing proof of a petty cash payment. (p. 135)	13. J

Part Two—Analyzing Transactions in a Cash Control System

Directions: Analyze each of the following transactions into debit and credit parts. Print the letters identifying your choices in the proper Answers columns.

Account Titles

A. Cash
B. Petty Cash
C. Accounts Receivable—R. Sandell

D. Supplies
E. Accounts Payable—Suburban Office Supplies
F. Miscellaneous Expense

	Transactions	Answers Debit	Credit
1–2.	Received bank statement showing bank service charge. (p. 127)	1. _F_	2. _A_
3–4.	Received notice from a bank of a dishonored check from R. Sandell. (p. 130)	3. _C_	4. _A_
5–6.	Paid cash on account to Suburban Office Supplies using EFT. (p. 131)	5. _E_	6. _A_
7–8.	Purchased supplies using a debit card. (p. 132)	7. _D_	8. _A_
9–10.	Paid cash to establish a petty cash fund. (p. 134)	9. _B_	10. _A_
11–12.	Paid cash to replenish a petty cash fund: $12.00, supplies; $3.50, miscellaneous expense, $8.50. (p. 136)	11. _F_	12. _A_

Part Three—Identifying Accounting Concepts and Practices

Directions: Place a *T* for True or an *F* for False in the Answers column to show whether each of the following statements is true or false.

Answers

1. Because cash transactions occur more frequently than other transactions, the chances for making recording errors affecting cash are less. (p. 118)

1. *F*

2. When a deposit is made in a bank account, the bank issues a receipt. (p. 119)

2. *T*

3. There are four types of endorsements commonly used: blank, special, original, and restrictive. (p. 120)

3. *T*

4. A check with a blank endorsement can be cashed by anyone who has possession of the check. (p. 120)

4. *T*

5. When writing a check, the first step is to prepare the check stub. (p. 121)

5. *T*

6. Most banks do not look at the date the check is written and will withdraw money from the depositor's account anytime. (p. 121)

6. *F*

7. The amount of a check is written twice on each check. (p. 121)

7. *T*

8. A check that contains errors must be marked with the word VOID and another check must be written. (p. 122)

8. *T*

9. An important aspect of cash control is verifying that the information on a bank statement and a checkbook are in agreement. (p. 125)

9. _____

10. An outstanding check is one that has been issued but not yet reported on a bank statement by the bank. (p. 125)

10. _____

11. Banks deduct service charges from customers' checking accounts without requiring customers to write a check for the amount. (p. 126)

11. _____

12. Not only do banks charge a fee for handling a dishonored check, but they also deduct the amount of the check from the account as well. (p. 129)

12. _____

13. The journal entry for a payment on account using electronic funds transfer is exactly the same as when the payment is made by check. (p. 131)

13. _____

14. The source document for an electronic funds transfer is a memorandum. (p. 131)

14. _____

15. The source document for a debit card purchase is a memorandum. (p. 132)

15. _____

16. TechKnow Consulting maintains a petty cash fund for making large cash payments without writing checks. (p. 134)

16. _____

17. Businesses use petty cash when writing a check is not time or cost effective. (p. 134)

17. _____

18. A memorandum is the source document for the entry to record establishing a petty cash fund. (p. 134)

18. _____

19. Anytime a payment is made from the petty cash fund, a petty cash slip is prepared showing proof of a petty cash payment. (p. 135)

19. _____

20. When the petty cash fund is replenished, the balance of the petty cash account increases. (p. 136)

20. _____

5-1 WORK TOGETHER, p. 123

Endorsing and writing checks

1. a.

ENDORSE HERE

x _Mayra Flores_

DO NOT WRITE, STAMP, OR SIGN BELOW THIS LINE
RESERVED FOR FINANCIAL INSTITUTION USE

b.

ENDORSE HERE

x _Pay to the order._
to Kelsey Sather
Mayra Flores

DO NOT WRITE, STAMP, OR SIGN BELOW THIS LINE
RESERVED FOR FINANCIAL INSTITUTION USE

c.

ENDORSE HERE

x _For Deposit only for_
account of Balsam
Lake Accounting.
Mayra Flores

DO NOT WRITE, STAMP, OR SIGN BELOW THIS LINE
RESERVED FOR FINANCIAL INSTITUTION USE

2., 3., 4a.

NO. **78** $ _162.00_		
Date: _October 30,_ 20 _13_		
To: _Corner Garage_		
For: _Repairs_		
BAL. BRO'T. FOR'D.	1805	75
AMT. DEPOSITED .... _10/30/13_ Date	489	00
SUBTOTAL		
OTHER:		
SUBTOTAL	2,294	75
AMT. THIS CHECK	162	00
BAL. CAR'D. FOR'D.	2,132	75

Balsam Lake Accounting   NO. **78**   93-109 / 918
154 Main Street
Balsam Lake, WI 54810-3982   _October 30,_ 20 _13_

PAY TO THE ORDER OF _Corner Garage_ $ _162.00_

one hundred sixty two and $^{no}/_{100}$ — DOLLARS

Peoples national bank   For Classroom Use Only
Balsam Lake, WI 54810

FOR _Repairs._   _Mayra Flores_

⑆091004329⑆ 291⑈36118⑈

4b.

NO. **79** $ _92.00_		
Date: _October 30,_ 20 _13_		
To: _St. Croix Supply_		
For: _Supplies_		
BAL. BRO'T. FOR'D.	2132	75
AMT. DEPOSITED .... Date		
SUBTOTAL	2132	75
OTHER:		
SUBTOTAL	2132	75
AMT. THIS CHECK	92	00
BAL. CAR'D. FOR'D.	2040	75

Balsam Lake Accounting   NO. **79**   93-109 / 918
154 Main Street
Balsam Lake, WI 54810-3982   _October 30,_ 20 _13_

PAY TO THE ORDER OF _St. Croix Supply_ $ _92.00_

ninety two and $^{no}/_{100}$ — DOLLARS

Peoples national bank   For Classroom Use Only
Balsam Lake, WI 54810

FOR _Supplies_   _Mayra Flores_

⑆091004329⑆ 291⑈36118⑈

Endorsing and writing checks

1. a.

ENDORSE HERE
x *Pay to the order of*
Kenneth Burleson.
Mayra Flores.
DO NOT WRITE, STAMP, OR SIGN BELOW THIS LINE
RESERVED FOR FINANCIAL INSTITUTION USE

b.

ENDORSE HERE
x *For Deposit only*
for the Account of
Centuria Hair Care
Mayra Flores
DO NOT WRITE, STAMP, OR SIGN BELOW THIS LINE
RESERVED FOR FINANCIAL INSTITUTION USE

2., 3., 4a.

NO. 345	$ 355.00
Date: May 31 20__	
To: _____	
For: _____	

BAL. BRO'T. FOR'D.	2106	53
AMT. DEPOSITED 5/31/13	456	25
SUBTOTAL	2562	78
OTHER:		
SUBTOTAL	$ 2562	78
AMT. THIS CHECK	355	00
BAL. CAR'D. FOR'D.	$ 2,207	78

CENTURIA HAIR CARE   NO. **345**   79-1058 / 918
1250 State Street
Centuria, WI 54824-7264

May 31 20 13

PAY TO THE ORDER OF *Uniforms Plus* $ 355 00

Three hundred fifty five and NO/100 DOLLARS

For Classroom Use Only

County Bank
Dresser, WI 54009

FOR *Uniform Rental*   *Mayra Flores*

⑆091004329⑆ 291⑈36118⑈

4b.

NO. 346	$ 412.00
Date: May 31 20 13	
To: Hairworld	
For: Supplies.	

BAL. BRO'T. FOR'D.	2,207	78
AMT. DEPOSITED Date	—	
SUBTOTAL	2,207	78
OTHER:		
SUBTOTAL	2,207	78
AMT. THIS CHECK	412	00
BAL. CAR'D. FOR'D.	1,795	78

CENTURIA HAIR CARE   NO. **346**   79-1058 / 918
1250 State Street
Centuria, WI 54824-7264

May 31 20 13

PAY TO THE ORDER OF *Hairworld* $ 412.00

four hundred twelve and NO/100 DOLLARS

For Classroom Use Only

County Bank
Dresser, WI 54009

FOR *Supplies*   *Mayra Flores*

⑆091004329⑆ 291⑈36118⑈

Name _Mayra Flores_ Date _____ Class _____

5-2 **WORK TOGETHER, p. 128**

Reconciling a bank statement and recording a bank service charge

1.

RECONCILIATION OF BANK STATEMENT

July 29, 2013
(Date)

Balance On Check Stub No. _106_	$1,575 00	Balance On Bank Statement	$1,528 00

DEDUCT BANK CHARGES:

Description	Amount
Service Ch.	$ 2 00

ADD OUTSTANDING DEPOSITS:

Date	Amount
July 28	$ 150 00

Total outstanding deposits ▶   150 00

Total bank charges ▶   2 00

SUBTOTAL $1,678 00

DEDUCT OUTSTANDING CHECKS:

Ck. No.	Amount	Ck. No.	Amount
103	70 00		
105	35 00		

Total outstanding checks ▶   105 00

Adjusted Check Stub Balance $1,573 00

Adjusted Bank Balance $1,573 00

2.

NO. **106**	$ _____	
Date: _____	20 - -	
To: _____		
For: _____		
BAL. BRO'T. FOR'D.	1575	00
AMT. DEPOSITED . . . . [Date]		
SUBTOTAL	1575	00
OTHER Serv. CHarge	2	00
SUBTOTAL	1573	00
AMT. THIS CHECK		
BAL. CAR'D. FOR'D.	1573	00

3.

JOURNAL   PAGE 1

DATE	ACCOUNT TITLE	DOC. NO.	POST. REF.	GENERAL DEBIT	GENERAL CREDIT	SALES CREDIT	CASH DEBIT	CASH CREDIT	
14	29 Misc	M44		2 00				2 00	14
15									15
16									16

Reconciling a bank statement and recording a bank service charge

1.

RECONCILIATION OF BANK STATEMENT

April 30, 2013
(Date)

Balance On Check Stub No. 119	$3606	00

DEDUCT BANK CHARGES:

Description	Amount	
Service charge	$ 15	00

Total bank charges ▶ 15 00

Balance On Bank Statement	$3184	00

ADD OUTSTANDING DEPOSITS:

Date	Amount	
4/29	$ 360	00
4/30	510	00

Total outstanding deposits ▶ 870 00

SUBTOTAL $4054 00

DEDUCT OUTSTANDING CHECKS:

Ck. No.	Amount	Ck. No.	Amount
115	70 00		
117	313 00		
118	80 00		

Total outstanding checks ▶ 463 00

Adjusted Check Stub Balance	$3591	00

Adjusted Bank Balance	$3591	00

2.

NO. 119	$ _____
Date: _____ 20 - -	
To: _____	
For: _____	

BAL. BRO'T. FOR'D.	3606	00
AMT. DEPOSITED .... Date		
SUBTOTAL	3606	00
OTHER: Service charge	15	00
_____		
SUBTOTAL	3,591	00
AMT. THIS CHECK		
BAL. CAR'D. FOR'D.	3,591	00

3.

JOURNAL   PAGE 8

	DATE	ACCOUNT TITLE	DOC. NO.	POST. REF.	GENERAL DEBIT	GENERAL CREDIT	SALES CREDIT	CASH DEBIT	CASH CREDIT	
17	30	Misc Exp.	M84		15 00				15 00	17
18										18
19										19

5-3 WORK TOGETHER, p. 133

Recording dishonored checks, electronic funds transfers, and debit card purchases

JOURNAL

PAGE 6

	DATE	ACCOUNT TITLE	DOC. NO.	POST. REF.	GENERAL DEBIT	GENERAL CREDIT	SALES CREDIT	CASH DEBIT	CASH CREDIT	
3	15	A/R- Christopher Ikola	M121		7300				7300	3
4	16	A/P- Spinoza Enterprize	M122		13500				13500	4
5	17	Supplies	M123		3100				3100	5
6										6
7										7
8										8
9										9
10										10
11										11
12										12
13										13
14										14
15										15
16										16
17										17
18										18

Recording dishonored checks, electronic funds transfers, and debit card purchases

JOURNAL   PAGE 12

	DATE	ACCOUNT TITLE	DOC. NO.	POST. REF.	GENERAL DEBIT	GENERAL CREDIT	SALES CREDIT	CASH DEBIT	CASH CREDIT	
15	Jun 12	A/R — Thomas Hofski	M54		9500				9500	15
16	13	A/P — Alfonso Co.	M55		24300				24300	16
17	14	Supplies	M56		6500				6500	17
18										18
19										19
20										20
21										21
22										22
23										23
24										24
25										25
26										26
27										27
28										28
29										29
30										30

5-4 WORK TOGETHER, p. 137

Establishing and replenishing a petty cash fund

JOURNAL PAGE

	DATE	ACCOUNT TITLE	DOC. NO.	POST. REF.	GENERAL DEBIT	GENERAL CREDIT	SALES CREDIT	CASH DEBIT	CASH CREDIT	
1	July 3	Petty Cash	C57		25000				25000	1
2	31	Supplies	C97		2500				7800	2
3		Miscellaneous Exp.			800					3
4		Repairs Exp.			4500					4
5										5
6										6
7										7
8										8
9										9
10										10
11										11
12										12
13										13
14										14
15										15
16										16
17										17

Establishing and replenishing a petty cash fund

JOURNAL   PAGE

	DATE	ACCOUNT TITLE	DOC. NO.	POST. REF.	GENERAL DEBIT	GENERAL CREDIT	SALES CREDIT	CASH DEBIT	CASH CREDIT	
1	Aug 1	Petty Cash.	C114		200 00				200 00	1
2	31	Supplies.	C157		72 00				145 00	2
3		Advertising Exp.			40 00					3
4		Miscellaneous Exp.			33 00					4
5										5
6										6
7										7
8										8
9										9
10										10
11										11
12										12
13										13
14										14
15										15
16										16
17										17

5-1 APPLICATION PROBLEM, p. 140

Endorsing and writing checks

1. **a.**

ENDORSE HERE

X *Karla Calderon*

_____

_____

DO NOT WRITE, STAMP, OR SIGN BELOW THIS LINE
RESERVED FOR FINANCIAL INSTITUTION USE

b.

ENDORSE HERE

X *Pay to the order*

of Vu Kim

Karla Calderon

DO NOT WRITE, STAMP, OR SIGN BELOW THIS LINE
RESERVED FOR FINANCIAL INSTITUTION USE

c.

ENDORSE HERE

X *For Deposit only*

in the account of

Accounting Tutors

Karla Calderon

DO NOT WRITE, STAMP, OR SIGN BELOW THIS LINE
RESERVED FOR FINANCIAL INSTITUTION USE

Extra forms

ENDORSE HERE

X

_____

_____

_____

DO NOT WRITE, STAMP, OR SIGN BELOW THIS LINE
RESERVED FOR FINANCIAL INSTITUTION USE

ENDORSE HERE

X

_____

_____

_____

DO NOT WRITE, STAMP, OR SIGN BELOW THIS LINE
RESERVED FOR FINANCIAL INSTITUTION USE

2., 3., 4a.

NO. **390**	$ 945.=
Date: 9-30- 20 13	
To: Williamson Street Supplies	
For: Supplies	

BAL. BRO'T. FOR'D.	6	711	62
AMT. DEPOSITED 9 30 13		124	25
SUBTOTAL	7	955	87
OTHER:			
SUBTOTAL	7	955	87
AMT. THIS CHECK		945	00
BAL. CAR'D. FOR'D.	7	010	87

Accounting Tutors
707 Oak Street
Minneapolis, MN 55447

NO. **390** $\frac{17\text{-}432}{910}$

9-30 20 13

PAY TO THE ORDER OF Williamson Street Supplies $ 945⁰⁰

nine hundred fourty five & NO/100 ——— DOLLARS

For Classroom Use Only

First National Bank
Minneapolis, MN 55447

FOR Supplies   Karla Calderon

⑆091004329⑆ 291⑈36118⑈

4b.

NO. **391**	$ 112.00
Date: 9-30- 20 13	
To: Street Park Tribune	
For: Advertising	

BAL. BRO'T. FOR'D.	7	010	87
AMT. DEPOSITED			
SUBTOTAL	7	010	87
OTHER:			
SUBTOTAL	7	010	87
AMT. THIS CHECK		112	00
BAL. CAR'D. FOR'D.	6	898	87

Accounting Tutors
707 Oak Street
Minneapolis, MN 55447

NO. **391** $\frac{17\text{-}432}{910}$

9-30 20 13

PAY TO THE ORDER OF Spring Park Tribune $ 112.—

one hundred twelve & NO/100 — DOLLARS

For Classroom Use Only

First National Bank
Minneapolis, MN 55447

FOR Advertising   Karla Calderon

⑆091004329⑆ 291⑈36118⑈

4c.

NO. **392**	$ 250.00
Date: 9-30 20 13	
To: Bryce Wilton	
For: Rent	

BAL. BRO'T. FOR'D.	6	898	87
AMT. DEPOSITED			
SUBTOTAL			
OTHER:			
SUBTOTAL	6	898	87
AMT. THIS CHECK		250	00
BAL. CAR'D. FOR'D.	6	648	87

Accounting Tutors
707 Oak Street
Minneapolis, MN 55447

NO. **392** $\frac{17\text{-}432}{910}$

9-30 20 13

PAY TO THE ORDER OF Bryce Wilton $ 250.=

two hundred fifty & NO/100 — DOLLARS

For Classroom Use Only

First National Bank
Minneapolis, MN 55447

FOR Rent   Karla Calderon

⑆091004329⑆ 291⑈36118⑈

5-2 APPLICATION PROBLEM, p. 140

Reconciling a bank statement and recording a bank service charge

1.

RECONCILIATION OF BANK STATEMENT

May 30, 2013
(Date)

Balance On Check Stub No. 312	$2130 99

DEDUCT BANK CHARGES:

Description	Amount
Service Charge	$ 20 00

Total bank charges ▶ 20.00

Adjusted Check Stub Balance $2110 99

Balance On Bank Statement	$1927 00

ADD OUTSTANDING DEPOSITS:

Date	Amount
May – 30	$756.25

Total outstanding deposits ▶ 756.25

SUBTOTAL 2683 25

DEDUCT OUTSTANDING CHECKS:

Ck. No.	Amount	Ck. No.	Amount
310	421.76		
311	150.50		

Total outstanding checks ▶ 571 26

Adjusted Bank Balance $2,111 99

2.

NO. 312	$ _____	
Date: _____ 20__		
To: _____		
For: _____		
BAL. BRO'T. FOR'D.	2,130	99
AMT. DEPOSITED .... Date		
SUBTOTAL	2,130	99
OTHER: Serr. CH.		
_____	20	00
SUBTOTAL	2,110	99
AMT. THIS CHECK		
BAL. CAR'D. FOR'D.	2,110	99

3.

JOURNAL   PAGE 10

	DATE	ACCOUNT TITLE	DOC. NO.	POST. REF.	GENERAL DEBIT	GENERAL CREDIT	SALES CREDIT	CASH DEBIT	CASH CREDIT	
1	May 30	Misc. Expense	M58		20 00				20 00	1
2										2
3										3
4										4

Recording dishonored checks, electronic funds transfers, and debit card purchases

JOURNAL   PAGE 8

	DATE	ACCOUNT TITLE	DOC. NO.	POST. REF.	GENERAL DEBIT	GENERAL CREDIT	SALES CREDIT	CASH DEBIT	CASH CREDIT	
7	Jan 25	A/R - Ralston Eubanks	M333		1 55 00				1 55 00	7
8	26	A/P - Reed Rosman	M334		2 89 00				2 89 00	8
9	27	Supplies	M335		5 4 00				5 4 00	9
10										10
11										11
12										12
13										13
14										14
15										15
16										16
17										17
18										18
19										19
20										20
21										21
22										22

5-4 APPLICATION PROBLEM, p. 141

Establishing and replenishing a petty cash fund

JOURNAL   PAGE 22

	DATE	ACCOUNT TITLE	DOC. NO.	POST. REF.	GENERAL DEBIT	GENERAL CREDIT	SALES CREDIT	CASH DEBIT	CASH CREDIT	
4	Nov 5	Petty Cash	C527		30000				30000	4
5	30	Supplies	C555		5700				16500	5
6		Misc Exp			5800					6
7		Postage Exp			1000					7
8										8
9										9
10										10
11										11
12										12
13										13
14										14
15										15
16										16
17										17
18										18
19										19
20										20

Reconciling a bank statement; journalizing a bank service charge, a dishonored check, and petty cash transactions

JOURNAL — PAGE 20

	DATE	ACCOUNT TITLE	DOC. NO.	POST. REF.	GENERAL DEBIT	GENERAL CREDIT	SALES CREDIT	CASH DEBIT	CASH CREDIT	
1	Ag 21	Petty Cash	C110		30000				30000	1
2	24	Repairs Exp.	C111		16500				16500	2
3	26	Supplies	C112		6000				6000	3
4	27	A/R- Bruce Kassola	MB3		17500				17500	4
5	28	Misc. Exp.	C113		3100				3100	5
6	31	James Astrup-Drawing	C114	320	40000				40000	6
7	31	Supplies Exp.	C115		12500				25500	7
8		Miscell. Exp.			13000					8
9		✓	T31				35000			9
10	31	Miscell. Exp			1500				1500	10
11										11
12										12
13										13
14										14
15										15

RECONCILIATION OF BANK STATEMENT

Aug- 31 -13
(Date)

Balance On Check Stub No. 116 .... $2,431 00

DEDUCT BANK CHARGES:

Description	Amount
S. CH	$ 15.00

Total bank charges ▶ 15 00

Adjusted Check Stub Balance $2,416 00

Balance On Bank Statement $2,721 00

ADD OUTSTANDING DEPOSITS:

Date	Amount
Aug. 31	$ 350 00

Total outstanding deposits ▶ 350 00

SUBTOTAL $3,071 00

DEDUCT OUTSTANDING CHECKS:

Ck. No.	Amount	Ck. No.	Amount
114			
115			

Total outstanding checks ▶ _____

Adjusted Bank Balance .... $

5-6 CHALLENGE PROBLEM, p. 142

Reconciling a bank statement and recording a bank service charge

1., 2.

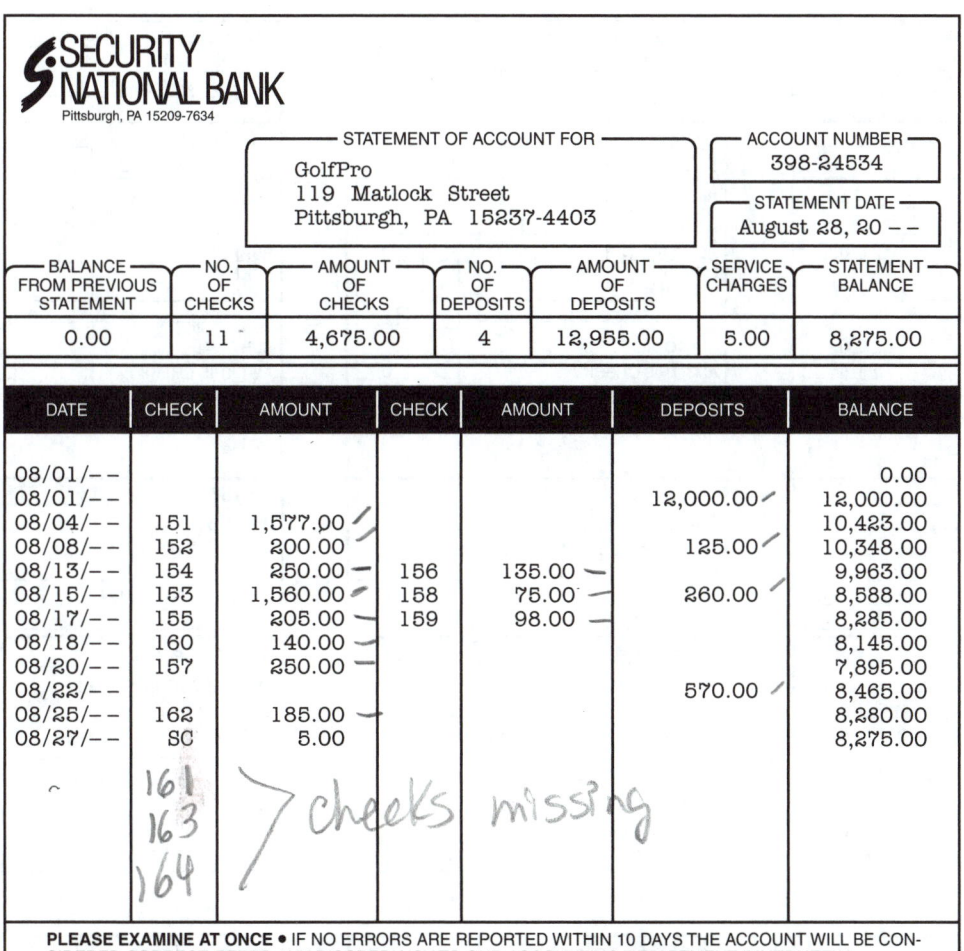

SECURITY NATIONAL BANK
Pittsburgh, PA 15209-7634

STATEMENT OF ACCOUNT FOR

GolfPro
119 Matlock Street
Pittsburgh, PA 15237-4403

ACCOUNT NUMBER
398-24534

STATEMENT DATE
August 28, 20 – –

BALANCE FROM PREVIOUS STATEMENT	NO. OF CHECKS	AMOUNT OF CHECKS	NO. OF DEPOSITS	AMOUNT OF DEPOSITS	SERVICE CHARGES	STATEMENT BALANCE
0.00	11	4,675.00	4	12,955.00	5.00	8,275.00

DATE	CHECK	AMOUNT	CHECK	AMOUNT	DEPOSITS	BALANCE
08/01/––						0.00
08/01/––					12,000.00	12,000.00
08/04/––	151	1,577.00				10,423.00
08/08/––	152	200.00			125.00	10,348.00
08/13/––	154	250.00	156	135.00		9,963.00
08/15/––	153	1,560.00	158	75.00	260.00	8,588.00
08/17/––	155	205.00	159	98.00		8,285.00
08/18/––	160	140.00				8,145.00
08/20/––	157	250.00				7,895.00
08/22/––					570.00	8,465.00
08/25/––	162	185.00				8,280.00
08/27/––	SC	5.00				8,275.00

161
163 7 checks missing
164

PLEASE EXAMINE AT ONCE • IF NO ERRORS ARE REPORTED WITHIN 10 DAYS THE ACCOUNT WILL BE CONSIDERED CORRECT. REFER ANY DISCREPANCY TO OUR ACCOUNTING DEPARTMENT IMMEDIATELY.

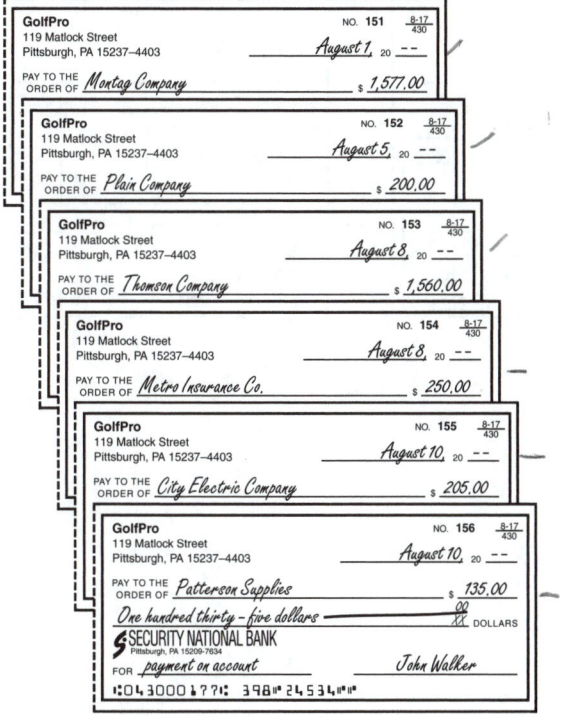

GolfPro
119 Matlock Street
Pittsburgh, PA 15237–4403
NO. 151   8-17/430
August 1, 20 – –
PAY TO THE ORDER OF *Montag Company* $ 1,577.00

GolfPro
119 Matlock Street
Pittsburgh, PA 15237–4403
NO. 152   8-17/430
August 5, 20 – –
PAY TO THE ORDER OF *Plain Company* $ 200.00

GolfPro
119 Matlock Street
Pittsburgh, PA 15237–4403
NO. 153   8-17/430
August 8, 20 – –
PAY TO THE ORDER OF *Thomson Company* $ 1,560.00

GolfPro
119 Matlock Street
Pittsburgh, PA 15237–4403
NO. 154   8-17/430
August 8, 20 – –
PAY TO THE ORDER OF *Metro Insurance Co.* $ 250.00

GolfPro
119 Matlock Street
Pittsburgh, PA 15237–4403
NO. 155   8-17/430
August 10, 20 – –
PAY TO THE ORDER OF *City Electric Company* $ 205.00

GolfPro
119 Matlock Street
Pittsburgh, PA 15237–4403
NO. 156   8-17/430
August 10, 20 – –
PAY TO THE ORDER OF *Patterson Supplies* $ 135.00
One hundred thirty – five dollars   00/XX DOLLARS
SECURITY NATIONAL BANK
Pittsburgh, PA 15209-7634
FOR *payment on account*   John Walker
⑆043000177⑆ 398⑈ 24534⑈

GolfPro
119 Matlock Street
Pittsburgh, PA 15237–4403
NO. 157   8-17/430
August 13, 20 – –
PAY TO THE ORDER OF *John Walker* $ 250.00

GolfPro
119 Matlock Street
Pittsburgh, PA 15237–4403
NO. 158   8-17/430
August 14, 20 – –
PAY TO THE ORDER OF *Pennsylvania Telephone Co.* $ 75.00

GolfPro
119 Matlock Street
Pittsburgh, PA 15237–4403
NO. 159   8-17/430
August 15, 20 – –
PAY TO THE ORDER OF *Ace Cleaning Company* $ 98.00

GolfPro
119 Matlock Street
Pittsburgh, PA 15237–4403
NO. 160   8-17/430
August 15, 20 – –
PAY TO THE ORDER OF *Tri-State Agency* $ 140.00

GolfPro
119 Matlock Street
Pittsburgh, PA 15237–4403
NO. 162   8-17/430
August 22, 20 – –
PAY TO THE ORDER OF *Dowd Company* $ 185.00
One hundred eighty – five dollars   00/XX DOLLARS
SECURITY NATIONAL BANK
Pittsburgh, PA 15209-7634
FOR *payment on account*   John Walker
⑆043000177⑆ 398⑈ 24534⑈

1., 2., 4.

NO. **151**	$ 1,577.00	
Date: *August 1,*		20 - -
To: *Montag Company*		
For: *Supplies*		

BAL. BRO'T. FOR'D.	0	00
AMT. DEPOSITED . . . . 8 1 -- *Date*	12,000	00
SUBTOTAL	12,000	00
OTHER:		
SUBTOTAL	12,000	00
AMT. THIS CHECK	1,577	00
BAL. CAR'D. FOR'D.	10,423	00

NO. **152**	$ 200.00	
Date: *August 5,*		20 - -
To: *Plain Company*		
For: *Rent*		

BAL. BRO'T. FOR'D.	10,423	00
AMT. DEPOSITED . . . . *Date*		
SUBTOTAL	10,423	00
OTHER:		
SUBTOTAL	10,423	00
AMT. THIS CHECK	200	00
BAL. CAR'D. FOR'D.	10,223	00

NO. **153**	$ 1,560.00	
Date: *August 8,*		20 - -
To: *Thomson Company*		
For: *Supplies*		

BAL. BRO'T. FOR'D.	10,223	00
AMT. DEPOSITED . . . . 8 8 -- *Date*	125	00
SUBTOTAL	10,348	00
OTHER:		
SUBTOTAL	10,348	00
AMT. THIS CHECK	1,560	00
BAL. CAR'D. FOR'D.	8,788	00

NO. **154**	$ 250.00	
Date: *August 8,*		20 - -
To: *Metro Insurance Company*		
For: *Insurance*		

BAL. BRO'T. FOR'D.	8,788	00
AMT. DEPOSITED . . . . *Date*		
SUBTOTAL	8,788	00
OTHER:		
SUBTOTAL	8,788	00
AMT. THIS CHECK	250	00
BAL. CAR'D. FOR'D.	8,538	00

NO. **155**	$ 205.00	
Date: *August 10,*		20 - -
To: *City Electric Company*		
For: *Utilities*		

BAL. BRO'T. FOR'D.	8,538	00
AMT. DEPOSITED . . . . *Date*		
SUBTOTAL	8,538	00
OTHER:		
SUBTOTAL	8,538	00
AMT. THIS CHECK	205	00
BAL. CAR'D. FOR'D.	8,333	00

NO. **156**	$ 135.00	
Date: *August 10,*		20 - -
To: *Patterson Supplies*		
For: *Payment on account*		

BAL. BRO'T. FOR'D.	8,333	00
AMT. DEPOSITED . . . . *Date*		
SUBTOTAL	8,333	00
OTHER:		
SUBTOTAL	8,333	00
AMT. THIS CHECK	135	00
BAL. CAR'D. FOR'D.	8,198	00

NO. **157**	$ 250.00	
Date: *August 13,*		20 - -
To: *John Walker*		
For: *Owner's withdrawal*		

BAL. BRO'T. FOR'D.	8,198	00
AMT. DEPOSITED . . . . *Date*		
SUBTOTAL	8,198	00
OTHER:		
SUBTOTAL	8,198	00
AMT. THIS CHECK	250	00
BAL. CAR'D. FOR'D.	7,948	00

NO. **158**	$ 75.00	
Date: *August 14,*		20 - -
To: *Pennsylvania Telephone Company*		
For: *Utilities*		

BAL. BRO'T. FOR'D.	7,948	00
AMT. DEPOSITED . . . . *Date*		
SUBTOTAL	7,948	00
OTHER:		
SUBTOTAL	7,948	00
AMT. THIS CHECK	75	00
BAL. CAR'D. FOR'D.	7,873	00

NO. **159**	$ 98.00	
Date: *August 15,*		20 - -
To: *Ace Cleaning Company*		
For: *Cleaning*		

BAL. BRO'T. FOR'D.	7,873	00
AMT. DEPOSITED . . . . *Date*		
SUBTOTAL	7,873	00
OTHER:		
SUBTOTAL	7,873	00
AMT. THIS CHECK	98	00
BAL. CAR'D. FOR'D.	7,775	00

5-6 CHALLENGE PROBLEM (continued)

1., 2., 4.

NO. **160**	$ *140.00*	
Date: *August 15,*	20 - -	
To: *Tri-State Agency*		
For: *Miscellaneous*		

BAL. BRO'T. FOR'D.	7,775	00
AMT. DEPOSITED . . . . *8* *15* - -	260	00
SUBTOTAL	8,035	00
OTHER:		
SUBTOTAL	8,035	00
AMT. THIS CHECK	140	00
BAL. CAR'D. FOR'D.	7,895	00

NO. **161**	$ *375.00*	
Date: *August 19,*	20 - -	
To: *Pittsburgh Enquirer*		
For: *Advertising*		

BAL. BRO'T. FOR'D.	7,895	00
AMT. DEPOSITED		
SUBTOTAL	7,895	00
OTHER:		
SUBTOTAL	7,895	00
AMT. THIS CHECK	375	00
BAL. CAR'D. FOR'D.	7,520	00

NO. **162**	$ *185.00*	
Date: *August 22,*	20 - -	
To: *Dowd Company*		
For: *Payment on account*		

BAL. BRO'T. FOR'D.	7,520	00
AMT. DEPOSITED . . . . *8* *22* - -	570	00
SUBTOTAL	8,090	00
OTHER:		
SUBTOTAL	8,090	00
AMT. THIS CHECK	185	00
BAL. CAR'D. FOR'D.	7,905	00

NO. **163**	$ *17.00*	
Date: *August 23,*	20 - -	
To: *Jason North*		
For: *Miscellaneous*		

BAL. BRO'T. FOR'D.	7,905	00
AMT. DEPOSITED		
SUBTOTAL	7,905	00
OTHER:		
SUBTOTAL	7,905	00
AMT. THIS CHECK	17	00
BAL. CAR'D. FOR'D.	7,888	00

NO. **164**	$ *250.00*	
Date: *August 28,*	20 - -	
To: *John Walker*		
For: *Owner's withdrawal*		

BAL. BRO'T. FOR'D.	7,888	00
AMT. DEPOSITED . . . . *8* *28* - -	430	00
SUBTOTAL	8,318	00
OTHER:		
SUBTOTAL	8,318	00
AMT. THIS CHECK	250	00
BAL. CAR'D. FOR'D.	8,068	00

NO. **165**	$ _____	
Date:	20 - -	
To:		
For:		

BAL. BRO'T. FOR'D.	8,068	00
AMT. DEPOSITED		
SUBTOTAL	8,068	00
OTHER: S.CH	5	00
SUBTOTAL		
AMT. THIS CHECK		
BAL. CAR'D. FOR'D.	8,063	00

2.

RECONCILIATION OF BANK STATEMENT

Aug. 29, 2013
(Date)

Balance On Check Stub No. ____ .... $ 8,068 00

DEDUCT BANK CHARGES:

Description	Amount	
S.C	$	

Total bank charges ▶   5 00

Adjusted Check Stub Balance .... $ 8063 00

Balance On Bank Statement .... $

ADD OUTSTANDING DEPOSITS:

Date	Amount	
	$	

Total outstanding deposits ▶

SUBTOTAL .... $

DEDUCT OUTSTANDING CHECKS:

Ck. No.	Amount	Ck. No.	Amount

Total outstanding checks ▶

Adjusted Bank Balance .... $

3.

JOURNAL   PAGE

	DATE	ACCOUNT TITLE	DOC. NO.	POST. REF.	GENERAL DEBIT	GENERAL CREDIT	SALES CREDIT	CASH DEBIT	CASH CREDIT	
1	Sep 1	Misc. Exp.	M25		500				500	1
2	1	A/R - Sheldon Mart	M26		17500					2
3										3
4										4
5										5
6										6
7										7
8										8
9										9
10										10
11										11
12										12
13										13
14										14
15										15
16										16

REINFORCEMENT ACTIVITY 1

PART A, p. 147

An Accounting Cycle for a Proprietorship: Journalizing and Posting Transactions
1., 2., 3.

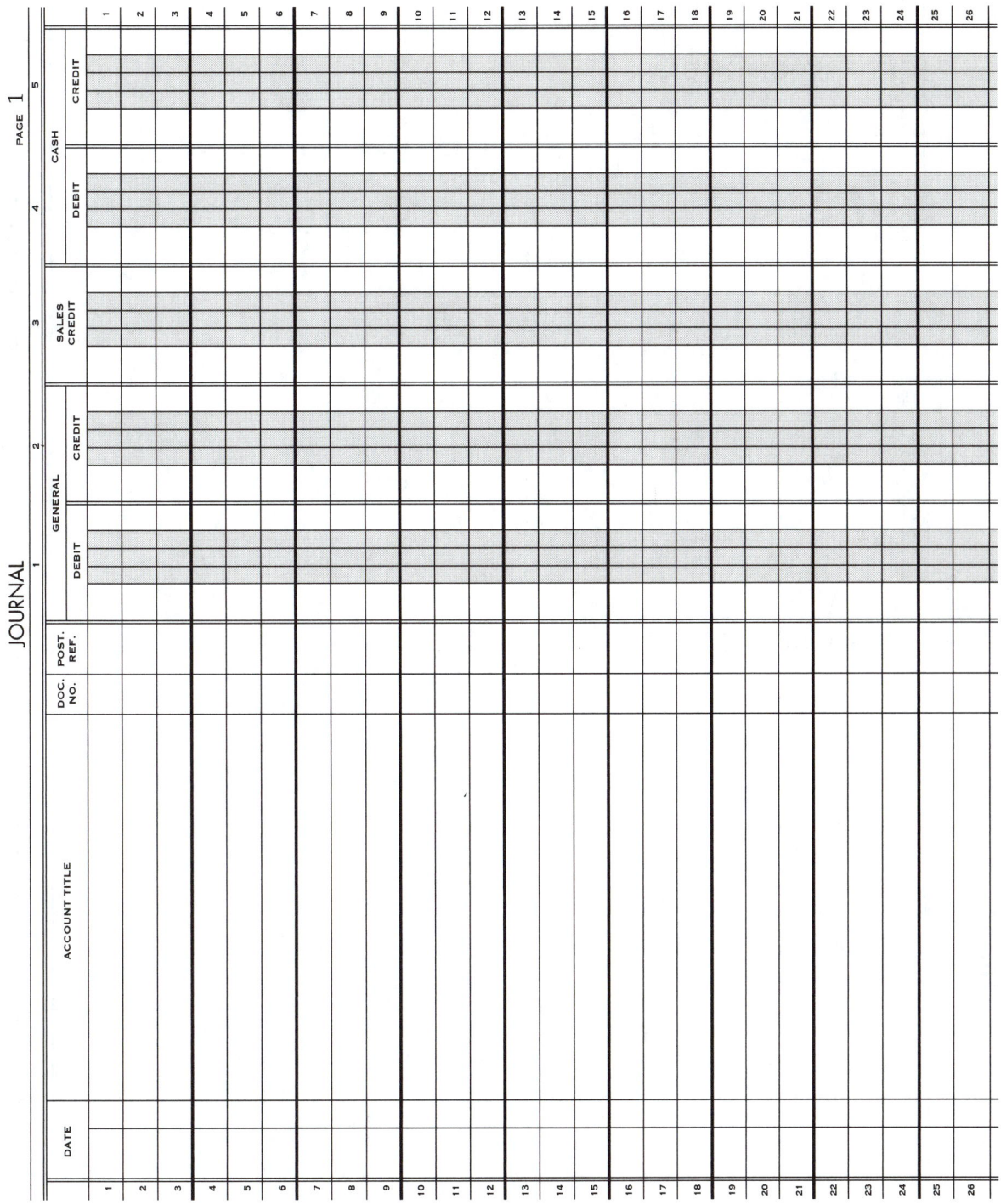

JOURNAL

PAGE 1

	DATE	ACCOUNT TITLE	DOC. NO.	POST. REF.	GENERAL DEBIT	GENERAL CREDIT	SALES CREDIT	CASH DEBIT	CASH CREDIT	
1										1
2										2
3										3
4										4
5										5
6										6
7										7
8										8
9										9
10										10
11										11
12										12
13										13
14										14
15										15
16										16
17										17
18										18
19										19
20										20
21										21
22										22
23										23
24										24
25										25
26										26

PART A (continued)

2., 4., 6., 7., 9., 10., 11.

JOURNAL

PAGE 2

DATE	ACCOUNT TITLE	DOC. NO.	POST. REF.	GENERAL DEBIT	GENERAL CREDIT	SALES CREDIT	CASH DEBIT	CASH CREDIT
				1	2	3	4	5

REINFORCEMENT ACTIVITY 1

PART A (continued)

5.

RECONCILIATION OF BANK STATEMENT

_____
(Date)

Balance On Check Stub No. ___ . . . . $ |

DEDUCT BANK CHARGES:

Description	Amount
	$

Total bank charges ▶

Adjusted Check Stub Balance . . . . $ |

Balance On Bank Statement . . . . $ |

ADD OUTSTANDING DEPOSITS:

Date	Amount
	$

Total outstanding deposits ▶

SUBTOTAL . . . . $ |

DEDUCT OUTSTANDING CHECKS:

Ck. No.	Amount	Ck. No.	Amount

Total outstanding checks ▶

Adjusted Bank Balance . . . . $ |

6. *Prove page 1 of the journal:*

Column	Debit Column Totals	Credit Column Totals
General		
Sales		
Cash		
Totals		

7. *Prove page 2 of the journal:*

Column	Debit Column Totals	Credit Column Totals
General		
Sales		
Cash		
Totals		

8. *Prove cash:*

Cash on hand at the beginning of the month . . . . _____

Plus total cash received during the month . . . . _____

Equals Total . . . . _____

Less total cash paid during the month . . . . _____

Equals cash balance at the end of the month . . . . _____

Checkbook balance on the next unused check stub . . . . _____

REINFORCEMENT ACTIVITY 1

PART A (continued)

The general ledger prepared in Reinforcement Activity 1, Part A, is needed to complete Reinforcement Activity 1, Part B.

3., 10., 11., 19., 20. GENERAL LEDGER

NOTE: May 31 postings from page 3 of the journal are part of the solution to Part B.

ACCOUNT Cash ACCOUNT NO. 110

DATE	ITEM	POST. REF.	DEBIT	CREDIT	BALANCE DEBIT	BALANCE CREDIT

ACCOUNT Petty Cash ACCOUNT NO. 120

DATE	ITEM	POST. REF.	DEBIT	CREDIT	BALANCE DEBIT	BALANCE CREDIT

ACCOUNT Accounts Receivable—Matterhorn University ACCOUNT NO. 130

DATE	ITEM	POST. REF.	DEBIT	CREDIT	BALANCE DEBIT	BALANCE CREDIT

ACCOUNT Accounts Receivable—Midwest College ACCOUNT NO. 140

DATE	ITEM	POST. REF.	DEBIT	CREDIT	BALANCE DEBIT	BALANCE CREDIT

ACCOUNT Supplies ACCOUNT NO. 150

DATE	ITEM	POST. REF.	DEBIT	CREDIT	BALANCE DEBIT	BALANCE CREDIT

ACCOUNT Prepaid Insurance ACCOUNT NO. 160

DATE	ITEM	POST. REF.	DEBIT	CREDIT	BALANCE DEBIT	BALANCE CREDIT

REINFORCEMENT ACTIVITY 1
PART A (continued)
3., 10., 11., 19., 20.   GENERAL LEDGER

NOTE: May 31 postings from page 3 of the journal are part of the solution to Part B.

ACCOUNT Accounts Payable—Dunn Supplies   ACCOUNT NO. 210

DATE	ITEM	POST. REF.	DEBIT	CREDIT	BALANCE DEBIT	BALANCE CREDIT

ACCOUNT Accounts Payable—Greenway Supplies   ACCOUNT NO. 220

DATE	ITEM	POST. REF.	DEBIT	CREDIT	BALANCE DEBIT	BALANCE CREDIT

ACCOUNT Brian Dawson, Capital   ACCOUNT NO. 310

DATE	ITEM	POST. REF.	DEBIT	CREDIT	BALANCE DEBIT	BALANCE CREDIT

ACCOUNT Brian Dawson, Drawing   ACCOUNT NO. 320

DATE	ITEM	POST. REF.	DEBIT	CREDIT	BALANCE DEBIT	BALANCE CREDIT

ACCOUNT Income Summary   ACCOUNT NO. 330

DATE	ITEM	POST. REF.	DEBIT	CREDIT	BALANCE DEBIT	BALANCE CREDIT

ACCOUNT Sales   ACCOUNT NO. 410

DATE	ITEM	POST. REF.	DEBIT	CREDIT	BALANCE DEBIT	BALANCE CREDIT

ACCOUNT Advertising Expense   ACCOUNT NO. 510

DATE	ITEM	POST. REF.	DEBIT	CREDIT	BALANCE DEBIT	BALANCE CREDIT

REINFORCEMENT ACTIVITY 1
PART A (concluded)
The general ledger prepared in Reinforcement Activity 1, Part A, is needed to complete Reinforcement Activity 1, Part B.

3., 10., 11., 19., 20.   **GENERAL LEDGER**

ACCOUNT Insurance Expense   ACCOUNT NO. 520

DATE	ITEM	POST. REF.	DEBIT	CREDIT	BALANCE DEBIT	BALANCE CREDIT

ACCOUNT Miscellaneous Expense   ACCOUNT NO. 530

DATE	ITEM	POST. REF.	DEBIT	CREDIT	BALANCE DEBIT	BALANCE CREDIT

ACCOUNT Rent Expense   ACCOUNT NO. 540

DATE	ITEM	POST. REF.	DEBIT	CREDIT	BALANCE DEBIT	BALANCE CREDIT

ACCOUNT Repair Expense   ACCOUNT NO. 550

DATE	ITEM	POST. REF.	DEBIT	CREDIT	BALANCE DEBIT	BALANCE CREDIT

ACCOUNT Supplies Expense   ACCOUNT NO. 560

DATE	ITEM	POST. REF.	DEBIT	CREDIT	BALANCE DEBIT	BALANCE CREDIT

ACCOUNT Utilities Expense   ACCOUNT NO. 570

DATE	ITEM	POST. REF.	DEBIT	CREDIT	BALANCE DEBIT	BALANCE CREDIT

NOTE: May 31 postings from page 3 of the journal are part of the solution to Part B.

Study Guide 6

Name		Perfect Score	Your Score
Identifying Accounting Terms		8 Pts.	
Analyzing Accounting Practices Related to a Work Sheet		17 Pts.	
Analyzing the Preparation of a Trial Balance on a Work Sheet		16 Pts.	
Analyzing Adjustments and Extending Account Balances on a Work Sheet		16 Pts.	
	Total	57 Pts.	

Part One—Identifying Accounting Terms

Directions: Select the one term in Column I that best fits each definition in Column II. Print the letter identifying your choice in the Answers column.

Column I	Column II	Answers
A. adjustments	1. The length of time for which a business summarizes and reports financial information. (p. 153) *Fiscal Period*	1. _C_
B. balance sheet	2. A columnar accounting form used to summarize the general ledger information needed to prepare financial statements. (p. 153) *work sheet*	2. _H_
C. fiscal period	3. A proof of equality of debits and credits in a general ledger. (p. 154) *Trial Balance*	3. _G_
D. income statement	4. Changes recorded on a work sheet to update general ledger accounts at the end of a fiscal period. (p. 157) *Adjustments*	4. _A_
E. net income	5. A financial statement that reports assets, liabilities, and owner's equity on a specific date. (p. 162) *Balance Sheet*	5. _B_
F. net loss	6. A financial statement showing the revenue and expenses for a fiscal period. (p. 163) *Income Statement*	6. _D_
G. trial balance	7. The difference between total revenue and total expenses when total revenue is greater. (p. 164) *Net Income*	7. _E_
H. work sheet	8. The difference between total revenue and total expenses when total expenses are greater. (p. 165) *Net loss*	8. _F_

Revenue.— is income that a company receives from its normal business activities

Part Two—Analyzing Accounting Practices Related to a Work Sheet

Directions: Place a *T* for True or an *F* for False in the Answers column to show whether each of the following statements is true or false.

1. The accounting concept Consistent Reporting is being applied when a delivery business reports the number of deliveries made one year and the amount of revenue received for deliveries made the next year. (p. 152)

    1.   F

2. An accounting period is also known as a fiscal period. (p. 153)

    2.   T

3. Journals, ledgers, and work sheets are considered permanent records. (p. 153)

    3.   F

4. All general ledger account titles are listed on a trial balance in the same order as listed on the chart of accounts. (p. 154)

    4.   T

5. The four questions asked when analyzing an adjustment are: Why? Where? When? and How? (p. 158)

    5.   F

6. The two accounts affected by the adjustment for supplies are Supplies and Supplies Expense. (p. 158)

    6.   T

7. The two accounts affected by the adjustment for insurance are Prepaid Insurance Expense and Insurance. (p. 159)

    7.   F

8. Totaling and ruling the Adjustments columns of a work sheet is necessary to prove the equality of debits and credits. (p. 160)

    8.   T

9. Two financial statements are prepared from the information on the work sheet. (p. 162)

    9.   T

10. Net income on a work sheet is calculated by subtracting the Income Statement Credit column total from the Income Statement Debit column total. (p. 164)

    10.   F

11. If errors are found on a work sheet, they must be erased and corrected before any further work is completed. (p. 167)

    11.   T

12. When two column totals are not in balance on the work sheet, the difference between the two totals is calculated and checked. (p. 167)

    12.   T

13. If the difference between the totals of Debit and Credit columns on a work sheet can be evenly divided by 9, then the error is most likely in addition. (p. 167)

    13.   F

14. If there are errors in the work sheet's Trial Balance columns, it might be because not all general ledger account balances were copied in the Trial Balance column correctly. (p. 168)

    14.   T

15. Errors in general ledger accounts should never be erased. (p. 169)

    15.   T

16. Most errors occur in doing arithmetic. (p. 169)

    16.   T

17. The best way to prevent errors is to use a calculator. (p. 169)

    17.   F

Name _____Mayra Flores_____ Date _____ Class _____

Part Three—Analyzing the Preparation of a Trial Balance on a Work Sheet

Directions: For each account title listed below, decide whether the account balance is recorded in the Trial Balance Debit or Trial Balance Credit column. Place a check mark in the proper Answers column identifying your choice. Do not check either column if the account should not have a balance in the Trial Balance columns. (p. 154)

a heading of a worksheet consist in a 3 lines, contains the name of the business, name of the report, and the date of the report.

	Trial Balance Debit	Credit
1. Cash	✓	
2. Petty Cash	✓	
3. Accounts Receivable—Imagination Station	✓	
4. Supplies	✓	
5. Prepaid Insurance	✓	C
6. Accounts Payable—Suburban Office Supplies	C	✓
7. J. Nichols, Capital	D	✓
8. J. Nichols, Drawing	✓	
9. Income Summary		
10. Sales	C	✓
11. Advertising Expense	✓	
12. Insurance Expense		
13. Miscellaneous Expense	✓	
14. Rent Expense	✓	
15. Supplies Expense	D	
16. Utilities Expense	✓	

Part Four—Analyzing Adjustments and Extending Account Balances on a Work Sheet

Directions: For each account listed below, determine in which work sheet column(s) an amount typically will be written. Place a check mark in the proper Answers column to show your answer.

	Adjustments Debit Credit (pp. 157–160)		Income Statement Debit Credit (p. 163)		Balance Sheet Debit Credit (p. 162)	
1. Cash						
2. Petty Cash						
3. Accounts Receivable— Imagination Station					X	
4. Supplies						
5. Prepaid Insurance						
6. Accounts Payable— Suburban Office Supplies					X	
7. J. Nichols, Capital						
8. J. Nichols, Drawing						
9. Income Summary						
10. Sales						
11. Advertising Expense						
12. Insurance Expense						
13. Miscellaneous Expense						
14. Rent Expense						
15. Supplies Expense						
16. Utilities Expense						

(handwritten margin notes)
Working sheet = Balance Sheet and Income Statement
It is not a legal document, you can correct
It will tell you how many liabilities

6-1 Recording the trial balance on a work sheet
6-2 Planning adjustments on a work sheet
6-3 Completing a work sheet

Dabbo West
Work Sheet
For month ended December 31, 2013

	ACCOUNT TITLE	TRIAL BALANCE DEBIT	CREDIT	ADJUSTMENTS DEBIT	CREDIT	INCOME STATEMENT DEBIT	CREDIT	BALANCE SHEET DEBIT	CREDIT
1	Cash	6800 00						6800 00	
2	Petty Cash	7500						7500	
3	A/R - Burt Strong	149800						149800	
4	Supplies	23800			(a) 11800			12000	
5	Prepaid Insurance	32500			(b) 10000			22500	
6	A/P - Janet Dao		29800						29800
7	Dabbo West-Capital		744300						744300
8	Dabbo West-Drawing	70000						70000	
9	Income Summary								
10	Sales		414000				414000		
11	Advertising Exp.	45600				45600			
12	Insurance Exp.			(b) 10000		10000			
13	Misc. Exp.	18900				18900			
14	Supplies Exp.			(a) 11800		11800			
15	Utilities Exp.	6000				6000			
16		1188100	1188100	21800	21800	146300	414000	1041800	774100
17						267700			
18						414000	414000	1041800	1041800
19									

19 760.00 Balance

6-1, 6-2, and 6-3 ON YOUR OWN, pp. 156, 161, 166

6-1 Recording the trial balance on a work sheet
6-2 Planning adjustments on a work sheet
6-3 Completing a work sheet

Copa's Copies

ACCOUNT TITLE	TRIAL BALANCE DEBIT	TRIAL BALANCE CREDIT	ADJUSTMENTS DEBIT	ADJUSTMENTS CREDIT	INCOME STATEMENT DEBIT	INCOME STATEMENT CREDIT	BALANCE SHEET DEBIT	BALANCE SHEET CREDIT
1 Cash	8000						98000	
2							15000	
3 Acct/R – Ruby Rose							27950	
16	97600		38100	81800	279000	432000		
17					153000			
18					432000			

Name _____ Date 4/15/13 Class _____

6-4   WORK TOGETHER, p. 170

Finding and correcting errors in accounting records

1., 2.   **GENERAL LEDGER**

ACCOUNT Cash   ACCOUNT NO. 110

DATE	ITEM	POST. REF.	DEBIT	CREDIT	BALANCE DEBIT	BALANCE CREDIT
Sept. 1		1	4 000 00		4 000 00	
30		2	7 000 00		15 000 00	
30		2		6 750 00	8 000 00	

ACCOUNT Accounts Receivable—Sharon Mann   ACCOUNT NO. 120

DATE	ITEM	POST. REF.	DEBIT	CREDIT	BALANCE DEBIT	BALANCE CREDIT
Sept. 12		1	1 000 00		1 000 00	

ACCOUNT Supplies   ACCOUNT NO. 130

DATE	ITEM	POST. REF.	DEBIT	CREDIT	BALANCE DEBIT	BALANCE CREDIT
Sept. 2		1	600 00		600 00	
25		2	425 00		1 025 00 725 00	

ACCOUNT Prepaid Insurance   ACCOUNT NO. 140

DATE	ITEM	POST. REF.	DEBIT	CREDIT	BALANCE DEBIT	BALANCE CREDIT
Sept. 3		1	150 00		150 00	
20		2	150 00		400 00	

ACCOUNT Accounts Payable—Powers Supply   ACCOUNT NO. 210

DATE	ITEM	POST. REF.	DEBIT	CREDIT	BALANCE DEBIT	BALANCE CREDIT
Sept. 4		1		300 00		300 00
15		2	150 00			150 00

ACCOUNT Paul Coty, Capital   ACCOUNT NO. 310

DATE	ITEM	POST. REF.	DEBIT	CREDIT	BALANCE DEBIT	BALANCE CREDIT
Sept. 1		1		5 000 00		5 000 00

1., 2.   **GENERAL LEDGER**

ACCOUNT Paul Coty, Drawing   ACCOUNT NO. 320

DATE		ITEM	POST. REF.	DEBIT	CREDIT	BALANCE	
						DEBIT	CREDIT
Sept.	30		2	3 0 0 00		3 0 0 00	

ACCOUNT Income Summary   ACCOUNT NO. 330

DATE		ITEM	POST. REF.	DEBIT	CREDIT	BALANCE	
						DEBIT	CREDIT

ACCOUNT Sales   ACCOUNT NO. 410

DATE		ITEM	POST. REF.	DEBIT	CREDIT	BALANCE	
						DEBIT	CREDIT
Sept.	30		2		1 9 0 0 00		1 8 7 5 00

ACCOUNT Insurance Expense   ACCOUNT NO. 510

DATE		ITEM	POST. REF.	DEBIT	CREDIT	BALANCE	
						DEBIT	CREDIT

ACCOUNT Miscellaneous Expense   ACCOUNT NO. 520

DATE		ITEM	POST. REF.	DEBIT	CREDIT	BALANCE	
						DEBIT	CREDIT
Sept.	9		1	1 5 0 00		1 5 0 00	
	27		2	2 5 00		1 2 5 00	

ACCOUNT Supplies Expense   ACCOUNT NO. 530

DATE		ITEM	POST. REF.	DEBIT	CREDIT	BALANCE	
						DEBIT	CREDIT

6-4 WORK TOGETHER (continued)

1.   **ERRORS**

IN General Ledger Accounts.

1.

_____

_____

_____

_____

_____

_____

_____

_____

_____

_____

_____

_____

_____

_____

_____

_____

_____

_____

_____

_____

_____

_____

_____

_____

_____

_____

_____

_____

_____

_____

_____

_____

_____

1.

LeafyLift

Work Sheet

For Month Ended September 30, 20 – –

	ACCOUNT TITLE	TRIAL BALANCE DEBIT	TRIAL BALANCE CREDIT	ADJUSTMENTS DEBIT	ADJUSTMENTS CREDIT	INCOME STATEMENT DEBIT	INCOME STATEMENT CREDIT	BALANCE SHEET DEBIT	BALANCE SHEET CREDIT	
1	Cash	8000.00						8000.00		1
2	Accts. Rec.—Sharon Mann	1000.00						1000.00		2
3	Supplies	725.00		(a) 390.00				1115.00		3
4	Prepaid Insurance	400.00		(b) 95.00				495.00		4
5	Accts. Pay.—Powers Supply		150.00						150.00	5
6	Paul Coty, Capital		5000.00						5000.00	6
7	Paul Coty, Drawing	300.00							300.00	7
8	Income Summary									8
9	Sales		1875.00				1875.00			9
10	Insurance Expense				(b) 95.00		95.00			10
11	Miscellaneous Expense	125.00				152.00				11
12	Supplies Expense				(a) 390.00		390.00			12
13		10550.00	7025.00	485.00	485.00	152.00	2360.00	10610.00	5450.00	13
14	Net Income					2208.00			5160.00	14
15						2360.00	2360.00	10610.00	10610.00	15
16										16
17										17
18										18
19										19
20										20
21										21

6-4 WORK TOGETHER (concluded)

3.

ACCOUNT TITLE	TRIAL BALANCE		ADJUSTMENTS		INCOME STATEMENT		BALANCE SHEET	
	1 DEBIT	2 CREDIT	3 DEBIT	4 CREDIT	5 DEBIT	6 CREDIT	7 DEBIT	8 CREDIT
1								
2								
3								
4								
5								
6								
7								
8								
9								
10								
11								
12								
13								
14								
15								
16								
17								
18								
19								
20								
21								

Finding and correcting errors in accounting records

1., 2. GENERAL LEDGER

ACCOUNT Cash   ACCOUNT NO. 110

DATE		ITEM	POST. REF.	DEBIT	CREDIT	BALANCE DEBIT	BALANCE CREDIT
20-- Nov.	1		1	12 000 00		12 000 00	
	30		2	6 495 00		18 945 00	
	30		2		5 550 00	13 395 00	

ACCOUNT Supplies   ACCOUNT NO. 120

DATE		ITEM	POST. REF.	DEBIT	CREDIT	BALANCE DEBIT	BALANCE CREDIT
20-- Nov.	2		1	3 00 00		3 00 00	
	25		2	1 00 00		1 30 00	

ACCOUNT Prepaid Insurance   ACCOUNT NO. 130

DATE		ITEM	POST. REF.	DEBIT	CREDIT	BALANCE DEBIT	BALANCE CREDIT
20-- Nov.	3		1	3 50 00		5 30 00	

ACCOUNT Accounts Payable—NW Electric   ACCOUNT NO. 210

DATE		ITEM	POST. REF.	DEBIT	CREDIT	BALANCE DEBIT	BALANCE CREDIT
20-- Nov.	4		1		4 00 00		4 00 00
	15		2	1 50 00			5 50 00

ACCOUNT Nadine Fritz, Capital   ACCOUNT NO. 310

DATE		ITEM	POST. REF.	DEBIT	CREDIT	BALANCE DEBIT	BALANCE CREDIT
20-- Nov.	1		1		12 000 00		12 000 00

6-4 ON YOUR OWN (continued)

1., 2.   **GENERAL LEDGER**

ACCOUNT Nadine Fritz, Drawing   ACCOUNT NO. 320

DATE	ITEM	POST. REF.	DEBIT	CREDIT	BALANCE DEBIT	BALANCE CREDIT
Nov. 30		2	300 00		300 00	

ACCOUNT Income Summary   ACCOUNT NO. 330

DATE	ITEM	POST. REF.	DEBIT	CREDIT	BALANCE DEBIT	BALANCE CREDIT

ACCOUNT Sales   ACCOUNT NO. 410

DATE	ITEM	POST. REF.	DEBIT	CREDIT	BALANCE DEBIT	BALANCE CREDIT
Nov. 30		2		1 950 00		1 950 00

ACCOUNT Insurance Expense   ACCOUNT NO. 510

DATE	ITEM	POST. REF.	DEBIT	CREDIT	BALANCE DEBIT	BALANCE CREDIT

ACCOUNT Miscellaneous Expense   ACCOUNT NO. 520

DATE	ITEM	POST. REF.	DEBIT	CREDIT	BALANCE DEBIT	BALANCE CREDIT
Nov. 9		1	150 00		150 00	
27		2	55 00		95 00	

ACCOUNT Supplies Expense   ACCOUNT NO. 530

DATE	ITEM	POST. REF.	DEBIT	CREDIT	BALANCE DEBIT	BALANCE CREDIT

1.   **ERRORS**

6-4 ON YOUR OWN (continued)

2.

Your Personal Trainer

Work Sheet

For Month Ended November 30, 20 – –

	ACCOUNT TITLE	TRIAL BALANCE DEBIT	TRIAL BALANCE CREDIT	ADJUSTMENTS DEBIT	ADJUSTMENTS CREDIT	INCOME STATEMENT DEBIT	INCOME STATEMENT CREDIT	BALANCE SHEET DEBIT	BALANCE SHEET CREDIT
1	Cash	13395.00						13395.00	
2	Supplies	130.00		(a) 90.00				220.00	
3	Prepaid Insurance	530.00		(b) 104.00				643.00	
4	Accts. Pay.—NW Electric		550.00						550.00
5	Nadine Fritz, Capital		12000.00						12000.00
6	Nadine Fritz, Drawing	300.00							300.00
7	Income Summary								
8	Sales		1950.00				1950.00		
9	Insurance Expense				(b) 104.00		104.00		
10	Miscellaneous Expense	95.00				59.00			
11	Supplies Expense				(a) 90.00		90.00		
12		14450.00	14500.00	194.00	194.00	59.00	2144.00	14258.00	12850.00
13	Net Income					2085.00			1408.00
14						2144.00	2144.00	14258.00	14258.00
15									
16									
17									
18									
19									
20									
21									
22									

3.

ACCOUNT TITLE	TRIAL BALANCE		ADJUSTMENTS		INCOME STATEMENT		BALANCE SHEET	
	DEBIT	CREDIT	DEBIT	CREDIT	DEBIT	CREDIT	DEBIT	CREDIT
1								
2								
3								
4								
5								
6								
7								
8								
9								
10								
11								
12								
13								
14								
15								
16								
17								
18								
19								
20								
21								

6-1, 6-2, and 6-3 APPLICATION PROBLEMS, p. 172

6-1 Recording the trial balance on a work sheet
6-2 Planning adjustments on a work sheet
6-3 Completing a work sheet

ACCOUNT TITLE	TRIAL BALANCE DEBIT	TRIAL BALANCE CREDIT	ADJUSTMENTS DEBIT	ADJUSTMENTS CREDIT	INCOME STATEMENT DEBIT	INCOME STATEMENT CREDIT	BALANCE SHEET DEBIT	BALANCE SHEET CREDIT
	155500	155100	59000	59000	147600	227000	1907500	
					79400			
					827000			

6-4 APPLICATION PROBLEM, p. 173

complete ✓

Finding and correcting errors in accounting records

1., 2.   **GENERAL LEDGER**

ACCOUNT Cash   ACCOUNT NO. 110

DATE		ITEM	POST. REF.	DEBIT	CREDIT	BALANCE DEBIT	BALANCE CREDIT
20-- Apr.	1		1	8 5 0 0 00		8 5 0 0 00	
	30		2	1 5 3 5 00		*10 035 00* 10 3 0 5 00	
	30		2		2 3 4 0 00	*2695 00* 7 9 6 5 00	

ACCOUNT Supplies   ACCOUNT NO. 120

DATE		ITEM	POST. REF.	DEBIT	CREDIT	BALANCE DEBIT	BALANCE CREDIT
20-- Apr.	2		1	5 0 0 00		5 0 0 00	

ACCOUNT Prepaid Insurance   ACCOUNT NO. 130

DATE		ITEM	POST. REF.	DEBIT	CREDIT	BALANCE DEBIT	BALANCE CREDIT
20-- Apr.	3		1	6 3 0 00		6 3 0 00	

ACCOUNT Accounts Payable—Archer Supplies   ACCOUNT NO. 210

DATE		ITEM	POST. REF.	DEBIT	CREDIT	BALANCE DEBIT	BALANCE CREDIT
20-- Apr.	4		1		7 0 0 00		7 0 0 00
	15		2	2 0 0 00			5 0 0 00

ACCOUNT Ervin Watkins, Capital   ACCOUNT NO. 310

DATE		ITEM	POST. REF.	DEBIT	CREDIT	BALANCE DEBIT	BALANCE CREDIT
20-- Apr.	1		1		8 5 0 0 00		*8 500 00* 5 8 0 0 00

6-4 **APPLICATION PROBLEM (continued)**

1., 2.   **GENERAL LEDGER**

ACCOUNT Ervin Watkins, Drawing   ACCOUNT NO. 320

DATE	ITEM	POST. REF.	DEBIT	CREDIT	BALANCE DEBIT	BALANCE CREDIT
20-- Apr. 30		2	6 0 0 00		6 0 0 00	

ACCOUNT Income Summary   ACCOUNT NO. 330

DATE	ITEM	POST. REF.	DEBIT	CREDIT	BALANCE DEBIT	BALANCE CREDIT

ACCOUNT Sales   ACCOUNT NO. 410

DATE	ITEM	POST. REF.	DEBIT	CREDIT	BALANCE DEBIT	BALANCE CREDIT
20-- Apr. 30		2		9 0 0 00		9 0 0 00

ACCOUNT Insurance Expense   ACCOUNT NO. 510

DATE	ITEM	POST. REF.	DEBIT	CREDIT	BALANCE DEBIT	BALANCE CREDIT

ACCOUNT Miscellaneous Expense   ACCOUNT NO. 520

DATE	ITEM	POST. REF.	DEBIT	CREDIT	BALANCE DEBIT	BALANCE CREDIT
20-- Apr. 9		1	3 5 0 00		3 5 0 00	3 5 0 00
27		2	1 2 5 00			2 2 5 00

ACCOUNT Supplies Expense   ACCOUNT NO. 530

DATE	ITEM	POST. REF.	DEBIT	CREDIT	BALANCE DEBIT	BALANCE CREDIT

1.   **ERRORS**

6-4 APPLICATION PROBLEM (continued)

1.

Ever Clean

Work Sheet

For Month Ended April 30, 20 – –

#	ACCOUNT TITLE	TRIAL BALANCE DEBIT	TRIAL BALANCE CREDIT	ADJUSTMENTS DEBIT	ADJUSTMENTS CREDIT	INCOME STATEMENT DEBIT	INCOME STATEMENT CREDIT	BALANCE SHEET DEBIT	BALANCE SHEET CREDIT
1	Cash	7965 00						7956 00	
2	Supplies	50 00			(b) 30 00				250 00
3	Prepaid Insurance	630 00			(b) 210 00			240 00	
4	Accts. Pay.—Archer Supplies		500 00						500 00
5	Ervin Watkins, Capital		5800 00						5800 00
6	Ervin Watkins, Drawing	600 00						600 00	
7	Income Summary								
8	Sales		990 00				990 00		
9	Insurance Expense			(b) 210 00		210 00			
10	Miscellaneous Expense	225 00				225 00			
11	Supplies Expense			(b) 30 00		30 00			
12		9470 00	7290 00			525 00	1200 00	8796 00	6550 00
13	Net Income					675 00			2246 00
14						1200 00	1200 00	8796 00	8796 00
15									
16									
17									
18									
19									
20									
21									

Ever Clean.

3.

ACCOUNT TITLE	TRIAL BALANCE		ADJUSTMENTS		INCOME STATEMENT		BALANCE SHEET	
	DEBIT	CREDIT	DEBIT	CREDIT	DEBIT	CREDIT	DEBIT	CREDIT
	1	2	3	4	5	6	7	8
1								
2								
3								
4								
5								
6								
7								
8								
9								
10								
11								
12								
13								
14								
15								
16								
17								
18								
19								
20								
21								

6-5 **MASTERY PROBLEM, p. 173**

Completing a work sheet

ACCOUNT TITLE	TRIAL BALANCE		ADJUSTMENTS		INCOME STATEMENT		BALANCE SHEET	
	DEBIT 1	CREDIT 2	DEBIT 3	CREDIT 4	DEBIT 5	CREDIT 6	DEBIT 7	CREDIT 8
1								
2								
3								
4								
5								
6								
7								
8								
9								
10								
11								
12								
13								
14								
15								
16								
17								
18								
19								
20								
21								

Completing a work sheet

Lawn Pro Company
Work Sheet
For Month Ended November 30, 2013

ACCOUNT TITLE	TRIAL BALANCE		ADJUSTMENTS		INCOME STATEMENT		BALANCE SHEET	
	DEBIT	CREDIT	DEBIT	CREDIT	DEBIT	CREDIT	DEBIT	CREDIT
Supplies								
Don.								
658400	658400	6500	6500					

Name	Perfect Score	Your Score
Identifying Accounting Concepts and Practices	20 Pts.	
Analyzing an Income Statement	15 Pts.	
Analyzing Income Statement Procedures	5 Pts.	
Total	40 Pts.	

Part One—Identifying Accounting Concepts and Practices

Directions: Place a *T* for True or an *F* for False in the Answers column to show whether each of the following statements is true or false.

Answers

1. The Adequate Disclosure accounting concept is applied when financial statements contain all information necessary to understand a business's financial condition. (p. 180) — 1. *T*

2. Stakeholders are any persons or groups who will be affected by an action. (p. 181) — 2. *T*

3. An income statement reports information over a period of time, indicating the financial progress of a business in earning a net income or a net loss. (p. 182) — 3. *T*

4. The Matching Expenses with Revenue accounting concept is applied when the revenue earned and the expenses incurred to earn that revenue are reported in the same fiscal period. (p. 182) — 4. *T*

5. Information needed to prepare an income statement comes from the trial balance columns and the income statement columns of a work sheet. (p. 182) — 5. _____

6. The income statement for a service business has five sections: heading, revenue, expenses, net income or loss, and capital. (p. 182) — 6. _____

7. The income statement's account balances are obtained from the work sheet's Income Statement columns. (p. 182) — 7. _____

8. The net income on an income statement is verified by checking the balance sheet. (p. 183) — 8. _____

9. Single lines ruled across an amount column of an income statement indicate that amounts are to be added. (p. 183) — 9. _____

10. A component percentage is the percentage relationship between one financial statement item and the total that includes that item. (p. 184) — 10. _____

11. Component percentages on an income statement are calculated by dividing sales and total expenses by net income. (p. 184) — 11. _____

12. All companies should have a total expenses component percentage that is not more than 80.0%. (p. 184) — 12. _____

13. When a business has two different sources of revenue, a separate income statement should be prepared for each kind of revenue. (p. 185) — 13. _____

14. An amount written in parentheses on a financial statement indicates an estimate. (p. 185) — 14. _____

15. A balance sheet reports financial information on a specific date and includes the assets, liabilities, and owner's equity. (p. 187) — 15. _____

16. A balance sheet reports information about the elements of the accounting equation. (p. 188) — 16. _____

17. The owner's capital amount reported on a balance sheet is calculated as: capital account balance plus drawing account balance, less net income. (p. 189) — 17. _____

18. The position of the total asset line on the balance sheet is determined after the equities section is prepared. (p. 189) — 18. _____

19. Double lines are ruled across the balance sheet columns to show that the column totals have been verified as correct. (p. 189) — 19. _____

20. The owner's equity section of a balance sheet may report different kinds of details about owner's equity, depending on the need of the business. (p. 190) — 20. _____

Part Two—Analyzing an Income Statement

Directions: The parts of the income statement below are identified with capital letters. Decide the location of each of the following items. Print the letter identifying your choice in the Answers column.

	A
	B
	C

				% OF SALES
D				
E		F		N
G				
H		I		
J		K		O
L		M		P

(pp. 182–185)

		Answers
1.	Date of the income statement.	1. _____
2.	The amount of net income or net loss.	2. _____
3.	Business name.	3. _____
4.	Expense account balances.	4. _____
5.	Expense account titles.	5. _____
6.	Heading of expense section.	6. _____
7.	Heading of revenue section.	7. _____
8.	Net income or net loss component percentage.	8. _____
9.	Revenue account title.	9. _____
10.	Sales component percentage.	10. _____
11.	Statement name.	11. _____
12.	Total amount of revenue.	12. _____
13.	Total expenses component percentage.	13. _____
14.	Words *Net Income* or *Net Loss*.	14. _____
15.	Words *Total Expenses*.	15. _____

CENTURY 21 ACCOUNTING, 8TH EDITION

Part Three—Analyzing Income Statement Procedures

Directions: For each of the following items, select the choice that best completes the statement. Print the letter identifying your choice in the Answers column.

Answers

1. The date on a monthly income statement prepared on July 31 is written as (A) For Month Ended July 31, 20-- (B) July 31, 20-- (C) 20--, July 31 (D) none of the above. (p. 182)

1. _____

2. Information needed to prepare an income statement's revenue section is obtained from a work sheet's Account Title column and (A) Income Statement Debit column (B) Income Statement Credit column (C) Balance Sheet Debit column (D) Balance Sheet Credit column. (p. 183)

2. _____

3. Information needed to prepare an income statement's expense section is obtained from a work sheet's Account Title column and (A) Income Statement Debit column (B) Income Statement Credit column (C) Balance Sheet Debit column (D) Balance Sheet Credit column. (p. 183)

3. _____

4. The amount of net income calculated on an income statement is correct if (A) it is the same as net income shown on the work sheet (B) debits equal credits (C) it is the same as the balance sheet (D) none of the above. (p. 183)

4. _____

5. The formula for calculating the net income component percentage is (A) net income divided by total sales equals net income component percentage (B) total sales divided by total expenses equals net income component percentage (C) total sales minus total expenses divided by net income equals total net income percentage (D) none of the above. (p. 184)

5. _____

7-1 WORK TOGETHER, p. 186

Preparing an income statement

	ACCOUNT TITLE	INCOME STATEMENT		BALANCE SHEET		
		5 DEBIT	6 CREDIT	7 DEBIT	8 CREDIT	
11	Sales		5 5 1 1 00			11
12	Advertising Expense	8 2 1 00				12
13	Insurance Expense	3 0 0 00				13
14	Miscellaneous Expense	3 4 7 00				14
15	Supplies Expense	7 1 3 00				15
16		2 1 8 1 00	5 5 1 1 00	11 0 6 0 00	7 7 3 0 00	16
17	Net Income	3 3 3 0 00			3 3 3 0 00	17
18		5 5 1 1 00	5 5 1 1 00	11 0 6 0 00	11 0 6 0 00	18
19						19
20						20
21						21
22						22

			% OF SALES

Preparing an income statement

	ACCOUNT TITLE	INCOME STATEMENT DEBIT (5)	INCOME STATEMENT CREDIT (6)	BALANCE SHEET DEBIT (7)	BALANCE SHEET CREDIT (8)	
12	Sales		3 8 4 7 00			12
13	Insurance Expense	2 5 0 00				13
14	Miscellaneous Expense	9 8 00				14
15	Supplies Expense	3 7 7 00				15
16	Utilities Expense	1 2 2 0 00				16
17		1 9 4 5 00	3 8 4 7 00	8 4 0 6 00	6 5 0 4 00	17
18	Net Income	1 9 0 2 00			1 9 0 2 00	18
19		3 8 4 7 00	3 8 4 7 00	8 4 0 6 00	8 4 0 6 00	19
20						20
21						21
22						22
23						23

			% OF SALES

7-2 WORK TOGETHER, p. 192

Preparing a balance sheet

	ACCOUNT TITLE	BALANCE SHEET DEBIT	BALANCE SHEET CREDIT	
1	Cash	9 5 0 0 00		1
2	Petty Cash	1 0 0 00		2
3	Accts. Rec.—Betsy Russell	1 6 5 0 00		3
4	Accts. Rec.—Charles Healy	1 4 0 3 00		4
5	Supplies	2 2 0 00		5
6	Prepaid Insurance	6 4 0 00		6
7	Accts. Pay.—Lindgren Supply		5 4 8 00	7
8	Accts. Pay.—Taxes By Thomas		1 1 1 00	8
9	Ken Cherniak, Capital		11 8 1 0 00	9
10	Ken Cherniak, Drawing	8 5 5 00		10
11	Income Summary			11
18		14 3 6 8 00	12 4 6 9 00	18
19	Net Income		1 8 9 9 00	19
20		14 3 6 8 00	14 3 6 8 00	20
21				21
22				22

Preparing a balance sheet

	ACCOUNT TITLE		7 BALANCE SHEET DEBIT	8 CREDIT	
1	Cash		5 3 0 0 00		1
2	Petty Cash		2 5 0 00		2
3	Accts. Rec.—K. Hartwood		5 5 2 00		3
4	Accts. Rec.—Ruth Kabila		1 8 7 00		4
5	Supplies		3 4 3 00		5
6	Prepaid Insurance		9 0 0 00		6
7	Accts. Pay.—Sam's Supply			1 6 5 00	7
8	Accts. Pay.—Ella's on Eaton			1 6 0 00	8
9	Anne Olson, Capital			6 2 1 0 00	9
10	Anne Olson, Drawing		1 2 0 0 00		10
16			8 7 3 2 00	6 5 3 5 00	16
17	Net Income			2 1 9 7 00	17
18			8 7 3 2 00	8 7 3 2 00	18
19					19
20					20
21					21

7-1   APPLICATION PROBLEM, p. 194

Preparing an income statement

							% OF SALES

Preparing a balance sheet

7-3   MASTERY PROBLEM, p. 195

Preparing financial statements with a net loss

1., 2.

				% OF SALES

3.

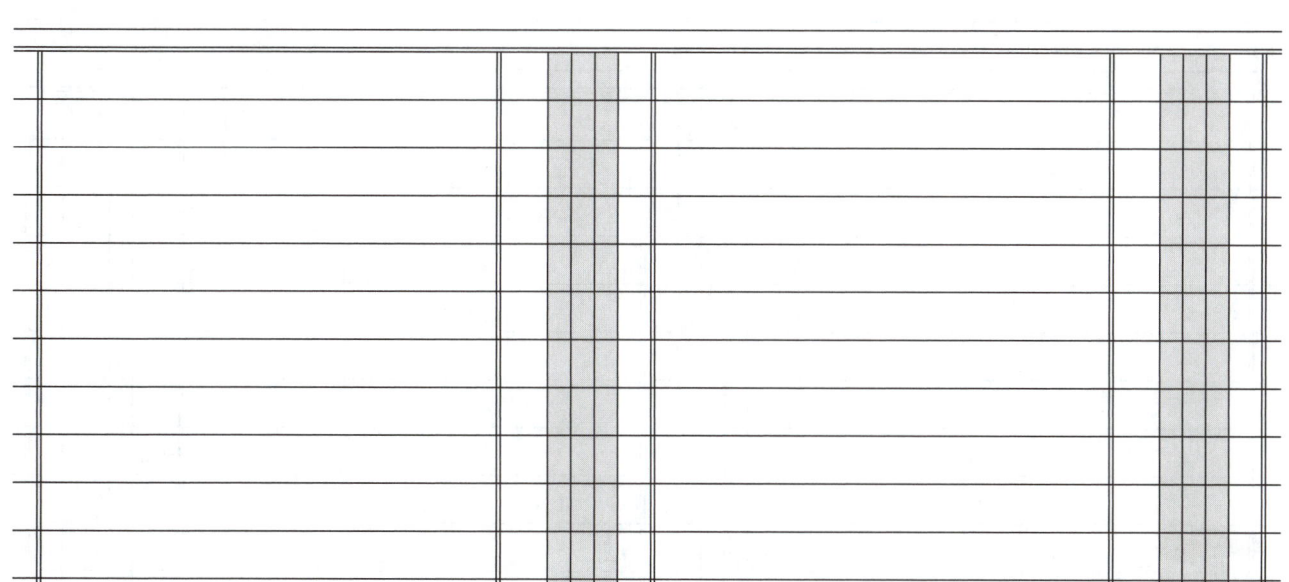

Preparing financial statements with two sources of revenue and a net loss

1., 2.

			% OF SALES

3.

Study Guide 8

Name	Perfect Score	Your Score
Identifying Accounting Terms	6 Pts.	
Analyzing Accounts Affected by Adjusting and Closing Entries	14 Pts.	
Analyzing Accounts After Closing Entries Are Posted	16 Pts.	
Analyzing Adjusting and Closing Entries	9 Pts.	
Identifying the Accounting Cycle for a Service Business	8 Pts.	
Total	53 Pts.	

Part One—Identifying Accounting Terms

Directions: Select the one term in Column I that best fits each definition in Column II. Print the letter identifying your choice in the Answers column.

Column I	Column II	Answers
A. accounting cycle	**1.** Journal entries recorded to update general ledger accounts at the end of a fiscal period. (p. 202)	1. _____
B. adjusting entries	**2.** Accounts used to accumulate information from one fiscal period to the next. (p. 206)	2. _____
C. closing entries	**3.** Accounts used to accumulate information until it is transferred to the owner's capital account. (p. 206)	3. _____
D. permanent accounts	**4.** Journal entries used to prepare temporary accounts for a new fiscal period. (p. 206)	4. _____
E. post-closing trial balance	**5.** A trial balance prepared after the closing entries are posted. (p. 216)	5. _____
F. temporary accounts	**6.** The series of accounting activities included in recording financial information for a fiscal period. (p. 217)	6. _____

Part Two—Analyzing Accounts Affected by Adjusting and Closing Entries

Directions: Use the partial chart of accounts given below. For each adjusting or closing entry described, decide which accounts are debited and credited. Write the account numbers identifying your choice in the proper Answers column.

Account Title	Acct. No.
Supplies	150
Prepaid Insurance	160
J. Nichols, Capital	310
J. Nichols, Drawing	320
Income Summary	330
Sales	410
Advertising Expense	510
Insurance Expense	520
Supplies Expense	550

	Accounts to Be	
	Debited	Credited
1–2. Adjusting entry for Supplies. (p. 203)	1. _____	2. _____
3–4. Adjusting entry for Prepaid Insurance. (p. 204)	3. _____	4. _____
5–6. Closing entry for Sales. (p. 208)	5. _____	6. _____
7–8. Closing entry for all expense accounts. (p. 209)	7. _____	8. _____
9–10. Closing entry for Income Summary with a net income. (p. 210)	9. _____	10. _____
11–12. Closing entry for Income Summary with a net loss. (p. 210)	11. _____	12. _____
13–14. Closing entry for owner's drawing account. (p. 211)	13. _____	14. _____

Part Three—Analyzing Accounts After Closing Entries Are Posted (p. 216)

Directions: For each account listed below, decide whether the account will normally appear on a post-closing trial balance. Place a check mark in the proper Answers column to show your answer.

Appears on a Post-Closing Trial Balance

	Yes	No
1. Accounts Receivable—Imagination Station	1. _____	_____
2. Supplies Expense	2. _____	_____
3. Sales	3. _____	_____
4. Miscellaneous Expense	4. _____	_____
5. Prepaid Insurance	5. _____	_____
6. Petty Cash	6. _____	_____
7. Accounts Payable—Suburban Office Supplies	7. _____	_____
8. Rent Expense	8. _____	_____
9. J. Nichols, Drawing	9. _____	_____
10. Supplies	10. _____	_____
11. Cash	11. _____	_____
12. Advertising Expense	12. _____	_____
13. Insurance Expense	13. _____	_____
14. J. Nichols, Capital	14. _____	_____
15. Income Summary	15. _____	_____
16. Utilities Expense	16. _____	_____

Part Four—Analyzing Adjusting and Closing Entries

Directions: For each of the following items, select the choice that best completes the statement. Print the letter identifying your choice in the Answers column.

Answers

1. Which accounting concept applies when a work sheet is prepared at the end of each fiscal cycle to summarize the general ledger information needed to prepare financial statements? (A) Business Entity (B) Accounting Period Cycle (C) Adequate Disclosure (D) Consistent Reporting (p. 202)

    1. _____

2. Which accounting concept applies when expenses are reported in the same fiscal period that they are used to produce revenue? (A) Business Entity (B) Going Concern (C) Matching Expenses with Revenue (D) Adequate Disclosure (p. 203)

    2. _____

3. Information needed for journalizing the adjusting entries is obtained from the (A) general ledger account Balance columns (B) income statement (C) work sheet's Adjustments columns (D) balance sheet (p. 203)

    3. _____

4. After adjusting entries are posted, the supplies account balance will be equal to (A) the cost of supplies used during the fiscal period (B) the cost of the supplies on hand at the end of the fiscal period (C) zero (D) none of these. (p. 203)

    4. _____

5. When revenue is greater than total expenses, resulting in a net income, the income summary account has a (A) debit balance (B) credit balance (C) normal debit balance (D) normal credit balance. (p. 207)

    5. _____

6. Information needed for recording the closing entries is obtained from the (A) general ledger accounts' Debit Balance columns (B) work sheet's Income Statement and Balance Sheet columns (C) balance sheet (D) income statement. (p. 207)

    6. _____

7. Income Summary is (A) an asset account (B) a liability account (C) a temporary account (D) a permanent account. (p. 207)

    7. _____

8. After the closing entries are posted, the owner's capital account balance should be the same as (A) shown on the balance sheet for the fiscal period (B) shown in the work sheet's Balance Sheet Debit column (C) shown in the work sheet's Balance Sheet Credit column (D) shown in the work sheet's Income Statement Debit column. (p. 211)

    8. _____

9. The accounts listed on a post-closing trial balance are (A) general ledger accounts with balances after the closing entries are posted (B) all general ledger accounts (C) those that have no balances after adjusting and closing entries (D) those that appear in the work sheet's Trial Balance columns. (p. 216)

    9. _____

Part Five—Identifying the Accounting Cycle for a Service Business

Directions: Arrange the series of accounting activities listed below for the accounting cycle for a service business. Indicate the sequence of the steps by writing a number from 1 to 8 to the left of each activity. (p. 217)

Answers

1. _____ A work sheet, including a trial balance, is prepared from the general ledger.

2. _____ Transactions, from information on source documents, are recorded in a journal.

3. _____ Source documents are checked for accuracy, and transactions are analyzed into debit and credit parts.

4. _____ Adjusting and closing entries are posted to the general ledger.

5. _____ Financial statements are prepared from the work sheet.

6. _____ Adjusting and closing entries are journalized from the work sheet.

7. _____ A post-closing trial balance of the general ledger is prepared.

8. _____ Journal entries are posted to the general ledger.

8-1 and 8-2 WORK TOGETHER, pp. 205, 212

8-1 Journalizing and posting adjusting entries
8-2 Journalizing and posting closing entries

	ACCOUNT TITLE	ADJUSTMENTS DEBIT	ADJUSTMENTS CREDIT	INCOME STATEMENT DEBIT	INCOME STATEMENT CREDIT	BALANCE SHEET DEBIT	BALANCE SHEET CREDIT	
1	Cash					7350 00		1
2	Accts. Rec.—Romelle Woods					372 00		2
3	Accts. Rec.—Wyatt Ames					88 00		3
4	Supplies		(a) 713 00			250 00		4
5	Prepaid Insurance		(b) 300 00			900 00		5
6	Accts. Pay.—Colin Gas						975 00	6
7	Accts. Pay.—Grand Uniforms						212 00	7
8	Darlene Wong, Capital						6543 00	8
9	Darlene Wong, Drawing					2100 00		9
10	Income Summary							10
11	Sales				5511 00			11
12	Advertising Expense			821 00				12
13	Insurance Expense	(b) 300 00		300 00				13
14	Miscellaneous Expense			347 00				14
15	Supplies Expense	(a) 713 00		713 00				15
16		1013 00	1013 00	2181 00	5511 00	11060 00	7730 00	16
17	Net Income			3330 00			3330 00	17
18				5511 00	5511 00	11060 00	11060 00	18
19								19
20								20
21								21
22								22
23								23

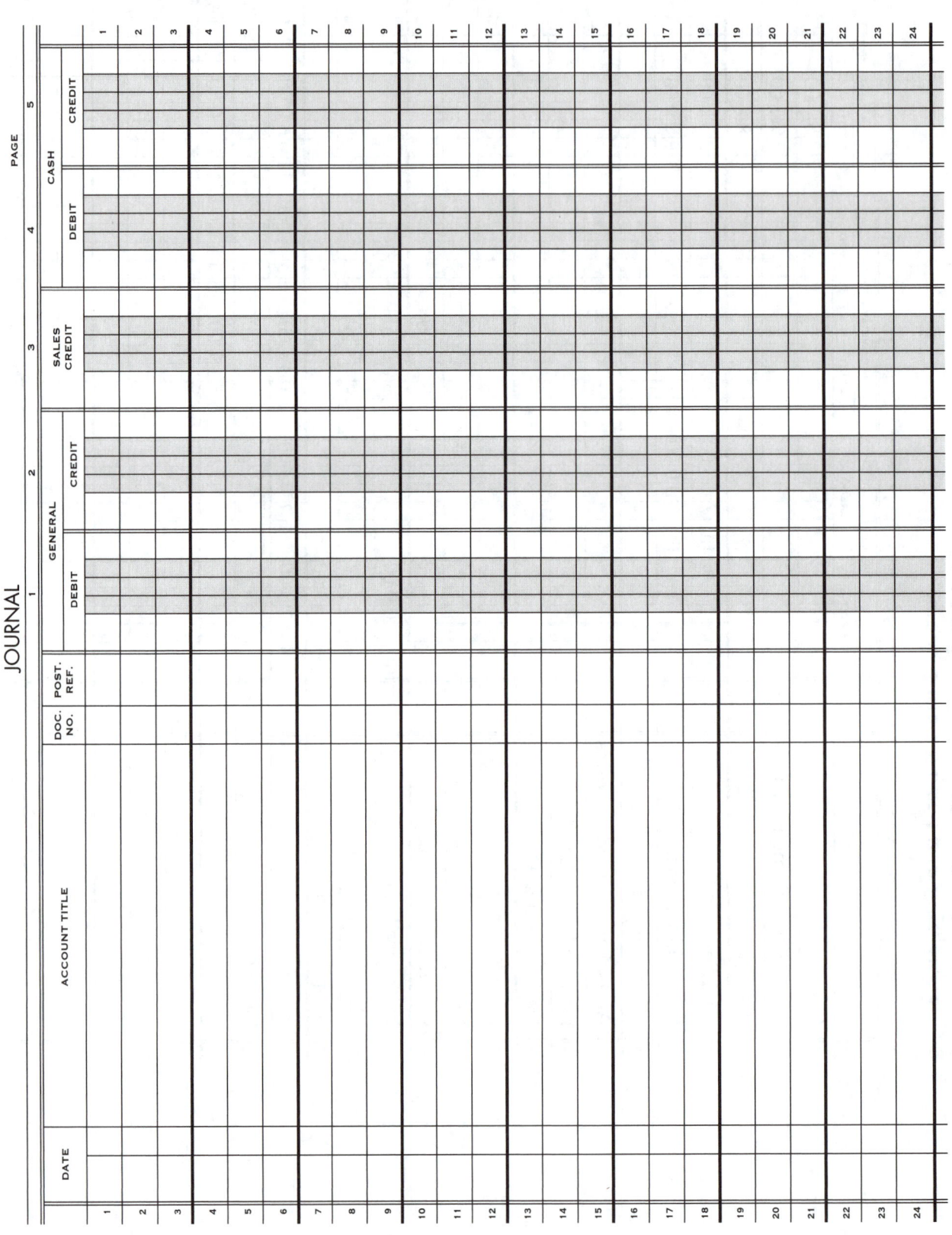

8-1 and 8-2   WORK TOGETHER (continued)

GENERAL LEDGER

ACCOUNT Cash   ACCOUNT NO. 110

DATE	ITEM	POST. REF.	DEBIT	CREDIT	BALANCE DEBIT	BALANCE CREDIT
July 20-- 31	Balance	✔			7 3 5 0 00	

ACCOUNT Accounts Receivable—Romelle Woods   ACCOUNT NO. 120

DATE	ITEM	POST. REF.	DEBIT	CREDIT	BALANCE DEBIT	BALANCE CREDIT
July 20-- 31	Balance	✔			3 7 2 00	

ACCOUNT Accounts Receivable—Wyatt Ames   ACCOUNT NO. 130

DATE	ITEM	POST. REF.	DEBIT	CREDIT	BALANCE DEBIT	BALANCE CREDIT
July 20-- 31	Balance	✔			8 8 00	

ACCOUNT Supplies   ACCOUNT NO. 140

DATE	ITEM	POST. REF.	DEBIT	CREDIT	BALANCE DEBIT	BALANCE CREDIT
July 20-- 31	Balance	✔			9 6 3 00	

ACCOUNT Prepaid Insurance   ACCOUNT NO. 150

DATE	ITEM	POST. REF.	DEBIT	CREDIT	BALANCE DEBIT	BALANCE CREDIT
July 20-- 31	Balance	✔			1 2 0 0 00	

ACCOUNT Accounts Payable—Colin Gas   ACCOUNT NO. 210

DATE	ITEM	POST. REF.	DEBIT	CREDIT	BALANCE DEBIT	BALANCE CREDIT
July 20-- 31	Balance	✔				9 7 5 00

GENERAL LEDGER

ACCOUNT Accounts Payable—Grand Uniforms   ACCOUNT NO. 220

DATE		ITEM	POST. REF.	DEBIT	CREDIT	BALANCE DEBIT	BALANCE CREDIT
July 20--	31	Balance	✔				2 1 2 00

ACCOUNT Darlene Wong, Capital   ACCOUNT NO. 310

DATE		ITEM	POST. REF.	DEBIT	CREDIT	BALANCE DEBIT	BALANCE CREDIT
July 20--	31	Balance	✔				6 5 4 3 00

ACCOUNT Darlene Wong, Drawing   ACCOUNT NO. 320

DATE		ITEM	POST. REF.	DEBIT	CREDIT	BALANCE DEBIT	BALANCE CREDIT
July 20--	31	Balance	✔			2 1 0 0 00	

ACCOUNT Income Summary   ACCOUNT NO. 330

DATE		ITEM	POST. REF.	DEBIT	CREDIT	BALANCE DEBIT	BALANCE CREDIT

ACCOUNT Sales   ACCOUNT NO. 410

DATE		ITEM	POST. REF.	DEBIT	CREDIT	BALANCE DEBIT	BALANCE CREDIT
July 20--	31	Balance	✔				5 5 1 1 00

ACCOUNT Advertising Expense   ACCOUNT NO. 510

DATE		ITEM	POST. REF.	DEBIT	CREDIT	BALANCE DEBIT	BALANCE CREDIT
July 20--	31	Balance	✔			8 2 1 00	

8-1 and 8-2   WORK TOGETHER (concluded)

GENERAL LEDGER

ACCOUNT Insurance Expense   ACCOUNT NO. 520

DATE	ITEM	POST. REF.	DEBIT	CREDIT	BALANCE DEBIT	BALANCE CREDIT

ACCOUNT Miscellaneous Expense   ACCOUNT NO. 530

DATE	ITEM	POST. REF.	DEBIT	CREDIT	BALANCE DEBIT	BALANCE CREDIT
July 31 20--	Balance	✔			3 4 7 00	

ACCOUNT Supplies Expense   ACCOUNT NO. 540

DATE	ITEM	POST. REF.	DEBIT	CREDIT	BALANCE DEBIT	BALANCE CREDIT

ACCOUNT   ACCOUNT NO.

DATE	ITEM	POST. REF.	DEBIT	CREDIT	BALANCE DEBIT	BALANCE CREDIT

ACCOUNT   ACCOUNT NO.

DATE	ITEM	POST. REF.	DEBIT	CREDIT	BALANCE DEBIT	BALANCE CREDIT

ACCOUNT   ACCOUNT NO.

DATE	ITEM	POST. REF.	DEBIT	CREDIT	BALANCE DEBIT	BALANCE CREDIT

8-1 Journalizing and posting adjusting entries
8-2 Journalizing and posting closing entries

#	ACCOUNT TITLE	ADJUSTMENTS DEBIT	ADJUSTMENTS CREDIT	INCOME STATEMENT DEBIT	INCOME STATEMENT CREDIT	BALANCE SHEET DEBIT	BALANCE SHEET CREDIT
1	Cash					6116 00	
2	Petty Cash					200 00	
3	Accts. Rec.—Jodi Ford					317 00	
4	Accts. Rec.—Midville Center					148 00	
5	Supplies		(a) 377 00			225 00	
6	Prepaid Insurance		(b) 250 00			400 00	
7	Accts. Pay.—Beauty Supply Co.						422 00
8	Accts. Pay.—Midwest Towel						182 00
9	Kelley Cooper, Capital						5900 00
10	Kelley Cooper, Drawing					1000 00	
11	Income Summary						
12	Sales				3847 00		
13	Insurance Expense	(b) 250 00		250 00			
14	Miscellaneous Expense			98 00			
15	Supplies Expense	(a) 377 00		377 00			
16	Utilities Expense			1220 00			
17		627 00	627 00	1945 00	3847 00	8406 00	6504 00
18	Net Income			1902 00			1902 00
19				3847 00	3847 00	8406 00	8406 00
20							
21							
22							

8-1 and 8-2   ON YOUR OWN (continued)

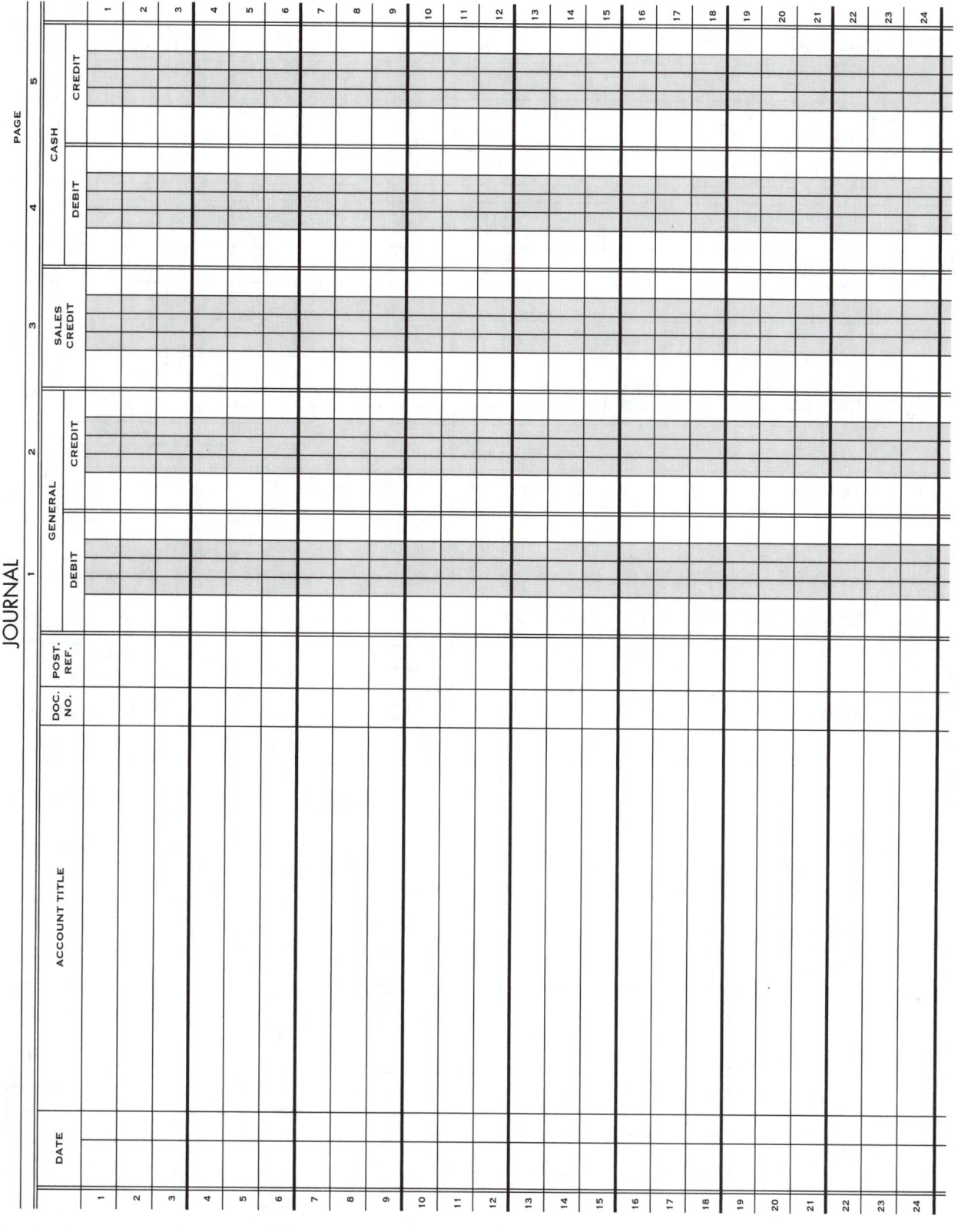

GENERAL LEDGER

ACCOUNT Cash   ACCOUNT NO. 110

DATE	ITEM	POST. REF.	DEBIT	CREDIT	BALANCE DEBIT	BALANCE CREDIT
Feb. 28	Balance	✔			6 1 1 6 00	

ACCOUNT Petty Cash   ACCOUNT NO. 120

DATE	ITEM	POST. REF.	DEBIT	CREDIT	BALANCE DEBIT	BALANCE CREDIT
Feb. 28	Balance	✔			2 0 0 00	

ACCOUNT Accounts Receivable—Jodi Ford   ACCOUNT NO. 130

DATE	ITEM	POST. REF.	DEBIT	CREDIT	BALANCE DEBIT	BALANCE CREDIT
Feb. 28	Balance	✔			3 1 7 00	

ACCOUNT Accounts Receivable—Midville Center   ACCOUNT NO. 140

DATE	ITEM	POST. REF.	DEBIT	CREDIT	BALANCE DEBIT	BALANCE CREDIT
Feb. 28	Balance	✔			1 4 8 00	

ACCOUNT Supplies   ACCOUNT NO. 150

DATE	ITEM	POST. REF.	DEBIT	CREDIT	BALANCE DEBIT	BALANCE CREDIT
Feb. 28	Balance	✔			6 0 2 00	

ACCOUNT Prepaid Insurance   ACCOUNT NO. 160

DATE	ITEM	POST. REF.	DEBIT	CREDIT	BALANCE DEBIT	BALANCE CREDIT
Feb. 28	Balance	✔			6 5 0 00	

8-1 and 8-2 ON YOUR OWN (continued)

GENERAL LEDGER

ACCOUNT Accounts Payable—Beauty Supply Co.   ACCOUNT NO. 210

DATE	ITEM	POST. REF.	DEBIT	CREDIT	BALANCE DEBIT	BALANCE CREDIT
Feb. 28	Balance	✔				4 2 2 00

ACCOUNT Accounts Payable—Midwest Towel   ACCOUNT NO. 220

DATE	ITEM	POST. REF.	DEBIT	CREDIT	BALANCE DEBIT	BALANCE CREDIT
Feb. 28	Balance	✔				1 8 2 00

ACCOUNT Kelley Cooper, Capital   ACCOUNT NO. 310

DATE	ITEM	POST. REF.	DEBIT	CREDIT	BALANCE DEBIT	BALANCE CREDIT
Feb. 28	Balance	✔				5 9 0 0 00

ACCOUNT Kelley Cooper, Drawing   ACCOUNT NO. 320

DATE	ITEM	POST. REF.	DEBIT	CREDIT	BALANCE DEBIT	BALANCE CREDIT
Feb. 28	Balance	✔			1 0 0 0 00	

ACCOUNT Income Summary   ACCOUNT NO. 330

DATE	ITEM	POST. REF.	DEBIT	CREDIT	BALANCE DEBIT	BALANCE CREDIT

ACCOUNT Sales   ACCOUNT NO. 410

DATE	ITEM	POST. REF.	DEBIT	CREDIT	BALANCE DEBIT	BALANCE CREDIT
Feb. 28	Balance	✔				3 8 4 7 00

GENERAL LEDGER

ACCOUNT Insurance Expense   ACCOUNT NO. 510

DATE	ITEM	POST. REF.	DEBIT	CREDIT	BALANCE DEBIT	BALANCE CREDIT

ACCOUNT Miscellaneous Expense   ACCOUNT NO. 520

DATE	ITEM	POST. REF.	DEBIT	CREDIT	BALANCE DEBIT	BALANCE CREDIT
Feb. 28	Balance	✔			9 8 00	

ACCOUNT Supplies Expense   ACCOUNT NO. 530

DATE	ITEM	POST. REF.	DEBIT	CREDIT	BALANCE DEBIT	BALANCE CREDIT

ACCOUNT Utilities Expense   ACCOUNT NO. 540

DATE	ITEM	POST. REF.	DEBIT	CREDIT	BALANCE DEBIT	BALANCE CREDIT
Feb. 28	Balance	✔			1 2 2 0 00	

ACCOUNT   ACCOUNT NO.

DATE	ITEM	POST. REF.	DEBIT	CREDIT	BALANCE DEBIT	BALANCE CREDIT

ACCOUNT   ACCOUNT NO.

DATE	ITEM	POST. REF.	DEBIT	CREDIT	BALANCE DEBIT	BALANCE CREDIT

8-3 WORK TOGETHER, p. 219

Preparing a post-closing trial balance

ACCOUNT TITLE	DEBIT	CREDIT

Preparing a post-closing trial balance

ACCOUNT TITLE	DEBIT	CREDIT

8-1 and 8-2   APPLICATION PROBLEMS, p. 221

8-1 Journalizing and posting adjusting entries
8-2 Journalizing and posting closing entries

JOURNAL

PAGE

| | | | | | GENERAL | | SALES | CASH | |
DATE	ACCOUNT TITLE	DOC. NO.	POST. REF.		1 DEBIT	2 CREDIT	3 CREDIT	4 DEBIT	5 CREDIT
1										1
2										2
3										3
4										4
5										5
6										6
7										7
8										8
9										9
10										10
11										11
12										12
13										13
14										14
15										15
16										16
17										17
18										18
19										19
20										20
21										21
22										22

GENERAL LEDGER

ACCOUNT Cash   ACCOUNT NO. 110

DATE		ITEM	POST. REF.	DEBIT	CREDIT	BALANCE	
						DEBIT	CREDIT
20-- Apr.	30	Balance	✔			7 6 0 7 00	

ACCOUNT Accounts Receivable—Natasha Goodlad   ACCOUNT NO. 130

DATE		ITEM	POST. REF.	DEBIT	CREDIT	BALANCE	
						DEBIT	CREDIT
20-- Apr.	30	Balance	✔			7 0 0 00	

ACCOUNT Accounts Receivable—R. Henry   ACCOUNT NO. 140

DATE		ITEM	POST. REF.	DEBIT	CREDIT	BALANCE	
						DEBIT	CREDIT
20-- Apr.	30	Balance	✔			4 9 8 00	

ACCOUNT Supplies   ACCOUNT NO. 150

DATE		ITEM	POST. REF.	DEBIT	CREDIT	BALANCE	
						DEBIT	CREDIT
20-- Apr.	30	Balance	✔			8 8 1 00	

ACCOUNT Prepaid Insurance   ACCOUNT NO. 160

DATE		ITEM	POST. REF.	DEBIT	CREDIT	BALANCE	
						DEBIT	CREDIT
20-- Apr.	30	Balance	✔			4 0 0 00	

8-1 and 8-2   APPLICATION PROBLEMS (continued)

GENERAL LEDGER

ACCOUNT Accounts Payable—Tri-County Supplies   ACCOUNT NO. 210

DATE		ITEM	POST. REF.	DEBIT	CREDIT	BALANCE DEBIT	BALANCE CREDIT
20-- Apr.	30	Balance	✔				3 8 1 00

ACCOUNT Accounts Payable—West End Supply Co.   ACCOUNT NO. 220

DATE		ITEM	POST. REF.	DEBIT	CREDIT	BALANCE DEBIT	BALANCE CREDIT
20-- Apr.	30	Balance	✔				5 5 5 00

ACCOUNT Leonard Long, Capital   ACCOUNT NO. 310

DATE		ITEM	POST. REF.	DEBIT	CREDIT	BALANCE DEBIT	BALANCE CREDIT
20-- Apr.	30	Balance	✔				6 5 2 7 00

ACCOUNT Leonard Long, Drawing   ACCOUNT NO. 320

DATE		ITEM	POST. REF.	DEBIT	CREDIT	BALANCE DEBIT	BALANCE CREDIT
20-- Apr.	30	Balance	✔			1 0 0 0 00	

ACCOUNT Income Summary   ACCOUNT NO. 330

DATE		ITEM	POST. REF.	DEBIT	CREDIT	BALANCE DEBIT	BALANCE CREDIT

ACCOUNT Sales   ACCOUNT NO. 410

DATE		ITEM	POST. REF.	DEBIT	CREDIT	BALANCE DEBIT	BALANCE CREDIT
20-- Apr.	30	Balance	✔				6 2 3 3 00

GENERAL LEDGER

ACCOUNT Advertising Expense   ACCOUNT NO. 510

DATE	ITEM	POST. REF.	DEBIT	CREDIT	BALANCE DEBIT	BALANCE CREDIT
Apr. 30	Balance	✔			8 0 0 00	

ACCOUNT Insurance Expense   ACCOUNT NO. 520

DATE	ITEM	POST. REF.	DEBIT	CREDIT	BALANCE DEBIT	BALANCE CREDIT

ACCOUNT Miscellaneous Expense   ACCOUNT NO. 530

DATE	ITEM	POST. REF.	DEBIT	CREDIT	BALANCE DEBIT	BALANCE CREDIT
Apr. 30	Balance	✔			3 1 5 00	

ACCOUNT Supplies Expense   ACCOUNT NO. 540

DATE	ITEM	POST. REF.	DEBIT	CREDIT	BALANCE DEBIT	BALANCE CREDIT

ACCOUNT Utilities Expense   ACCOUNT NO. 550

DATE	ITEM	POST. REF.	DEBIT	CREDIT	BALANCE DEBIT	BALANCE CREDIT
Apr. 30	Balance	✔			1 4 9 5 00	

ACCOUNT   ACCOUNT NO.

DATE	ITEM	POST. REF.	DEBIT	CREDIT	BALANCE DEBIT	BALANCE CREDIT

8-3 APPLICATION PROBLEM, p. 222

Preparing a post-closing trial balance

ACCOUNT TITLE	DEBIT	CREDIT

Journalizing and posting adjusting and closing entries with a net loss; preparing a post-closing trial balance

1., 2.

JOURNAL

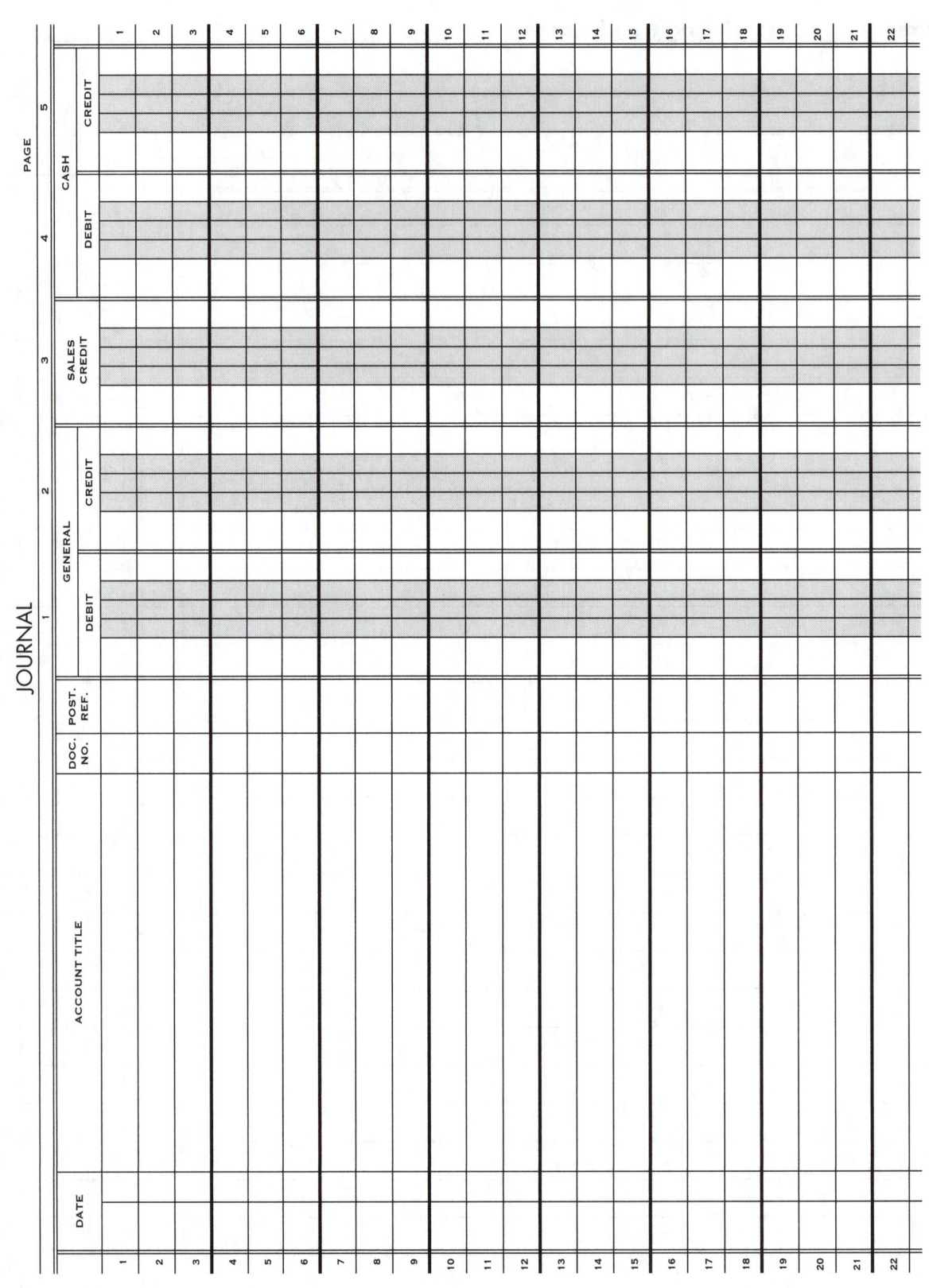

8-4 MASTERY PROBLEM (continued)

1., 2.   **GENERAL LEDGER**

ACCOUNT Cash   ACCOUNT NO. 110

DATE		ITEM	POST. REF.	DEBIT	CREDIT	BALANCE	
						DEBIT	CREDIT
Oct.	31	Balance	✓			6 9 5 8 00	

ACCOUNT Petty Cash   ACCOUNT NO. 120

DATE		ITEM	POST. REF.	DEBIT	CREDIT	BALANCE	
						DEBIT	CREDIT
Oct.	31	Balance	✓			1 5 0 00	

ACCOUNT Accounts Receivable—M. Hollerud   ACCOUNT NO. 130

DATE		ITEM	POST. REF.	DEBIT	CREDIT	BALANCE	
						DEBIT	CREDIT
Oct.	31	Balance	✓			1 9 7 00	

ACCOUNT Supplies   ACCOUNT NO. 140

DATE		ITEM	POST. REF.	DEBIT	CREDIT	BALANCE	
						DEBIT	CREDIT
Oct.	31	Balance	✓			2 1 8 0 00	

ACCOUNT Prepaid Insurance   ACCOUNT NO. 150

DATE		ITEM	POST. REF.	DEBIT	CREDIT	BALANCE	
						DEBIT	CREDIT
Oct.	31	Balance	✓			9 5 7 00	

1., 2. GENERAL LEDGER

ACCOUNT Accounts Payable—Tampa Supply   ACCOUNT NO. 210

DATE		ITEM	POST. REF.	DEBIT	CREDIT	BALANCE DEBIT	BALANCE CREDIT
Oct. 20--	31	Balance	✔				6 1 2 00

ACCOUNT Ron Rolstad, Capital   ACCOUNT NO. 310

DATE		ITEM	POST. REF.	DEBIT	CREDIT	BALANCE DEBIT	BALANCE CREDIT
Oct. 20--	31	Balance	✔				9 3 3 7 00

ACCOUNT Ron Rolstad, Drawing   ACCOUNT NO. 320

DATE		ITEM	POST. REF.	DEBIT	CREDIT	BALANCE DEBIT	BALANCE CREDIT
Oct. 20--	31	Balance	✔			6 0 0 00	

ACCOUNT Income Summary   ACCOUNT NO. 330

DATE		ITEM	POST. REF.	DEBIT	CREDIT	BALANCE DEBIT	BALANCE CREDIT

ACCOUNT Sales   ACCOUNT NO. 410

DATE		ITEM	POST. REF.	DEBIT	CREDIT	BALANCE DEBIT	BALANCE CREDIT
Oct. 20--	31	Balance	✔				3 2 6 9 00

8-4 MASTERY PROBLEM (continued)

1., 2. <center>**GENERAL LEDGER**</center>

ACCOUNT Advertising Expense   ACCOUNT NO. 510

DATE		ITEM	POST. REF.	DEBIT	CREDIT	BALANCE DEBIT	BALANCE CREDIT
Oct.	31	Balance	✔			4 5 0 00	

ACCOUNT Insurance Expense   ACCOUNT NO. 520

DATE		ITEM	POST. REF.	DEBIT	CREDIT	BALANCE DEBIT	BALANCE CREDIT

ACCOUNT Miscellaneous Expense   ACCOUNT NO. 530

DATE		ITEM	POST. REF.	DEBIT	CREDIT	BALANCE DEBIT	BALANCE CREDIT
Oct.	31	Balance	✔			8 5 00	

ACCOUNT Supplies Expense   ACCOUNT NO. 540

DATE		ITEM	POST. REF.	DEBIT	CREDIT	BALANCE DEBIT	BALANCE CREDIT

ACCOUNT Utilities Expense   ACCOUNT NO. 550

DATE		ITEM	POST. REF.	DEBIT	CREDIT	BALANCE DEBIT	BALANCE CREDIT
Oct.	31	Balance	✔			1 6 4 1 00	

ACCOUNT   ACCOUNT NO.

DATE		ITEM	POST. REF.	DEBIT	CREDIT	BALANCE DEBIT	BALANCE CREDIT

3.

ACCOUNT TITLE	DEBIT	CREDIT

8-5 CHALLENGE PROBLEM, p. 223

Journalizing and posting adjusting and closing entries with two revenue accounts and a net loss; preparing a post-closing trial balance

1., 2.

JOURNAL

PAGE

	DATE	ACCOUNT TITLE	DOC. NO.	POST. REF.	GENERAL DEBIT	GENERAL CREDIT	SALES CREDIT	CASH DEBIT	CASH CREDIT	
1										1
2										2
3										3
4										4
5										5
6										6
7										7
8										8
9										9
10										10
11										11
12										12
13										13
14										14
15										15
16										16
17										17
18										18
19										19
20										20
21										21
22										22

1., 2. **GENERAL LEDGER**

ACCOUNT Cash   ACCOUNT NO. 110

DATE	ITEM	POST. REF.	DEBIT	CREDIT	BALANCE DEBIT	BALANCE CREDIT
Sept. 30	Balance	✔			1 8 9 8 00	

ACCOUNT Accounts Receivable—Sandra Rohe   ACCOUNT NO. 120

DATE	ITEM	POST. REF.	DEBIT	CREDIT	BALANCE DEBIT	BALANCE CREDIT
Sept. 30	Balance	✔			9 5 00	

ACCOUNT Supplies   ACCOUNT NO. 130

DATE	ITEM	POST. REF.	DEBIT	CREDIT	BALANCE DEBIT	BALANCE CREDIT
Sept. 30	Balance	✔			3 8 5 0 00	

ACCOUNT Prepaid Insurance   ACCOUNT NO. 140

DATE	ITEM	POST. REF.	DEBIT	CREDIT	BALANCE DEBIT	BALANCE CREDIT
Sept. 30	Balance	✔			1 6 0 0 00	

ACCOUNT Accounts Payable—Corner Garage   ACCOUNT NO. 210

DATE	ITEM	POST. REF.	DEBIT	CREDIT	BALANCE DEBIT	BALANCE CREDIT
Sept. 30	Balance	✔				5 8 00

8-5   **CHALLENGE PROBLEM (continued)**

1., 2.   **GENERAL LEDGER**

ACCOUNT Accounts Payable—Broadway Gas   ACCOUNT NO. 220

DATE	ITEM	POST. REF.	DEBIT	CREDIT	BALANCE DEBIT	BALANCE CREDIT
Sept. 30	Balance	✔				1 1 0 00

ACCOUNT Accounts Payable—Esko Repair   ACCOUNT NO. 230

DATE	ITEM	POST. REF.	DEBIT	CREDIT	BALANCE DEBIT	BALANCE CREDIT
Sept. 30	Balance	✔				2 1 5 00

ACCOUNT Ryo Morrison, Capital   ACCOUNT NO. 310

DATE	ITEM	POST. REF.	DEBIT	CREDIT	BALANCE DEBIT	BALANCE CREDIT
Sept. 30	Balance	✔				4 0 0 0 00

ACCOUNT Ryo Morrison, Drawing   ACCOUNT NO. 320

DATE	ITEM	POST. REF.	DEBIT	CREDIT	BALANCE DEBIT	BALANCE CREDIT
Sept. 30	Balance	✔			1 0 0 00	

ACCOUNT Income Summary   ACCOUNT NO. 330

DATE	ITEM	POST. REF.	DEBIT	CREDIT	BALANCE DEBIT	BALANCE CREDIT

ACCOUNT Sales—Lawn Care   ACCOUNT NO. 410

DATE	ITEM	POST. REF.	DEBIT	CREDIT	BALANCE DEBIT	BALANCE CREDIT
Sept. 30	Balance	✔				4 9 0 0 00

1., 2. **GENERAL LEDGER**

ACCOUNT Sales—Shrub Care   ACCOUNT NO. 420

DATE		ITEM	POST. REF.	DEBIT	CREDIT	BALANCE DEBIT	BALANCE CREDIT
Sept. 20--	30	Balance	✔				2 5 0 0 00

ACCOUNT Advertising Expense   ACCOUNT NO. 510

DATE		ITEM	POST. REF.	DEBIT	CREDIT	BALANCE DEBIT	BALANCE CREDIT
Sept. 20--	30	Balance	✔			3 9 0 00	

ACCOUNT Insurance Expense   ACCOUNT NO. 520

DATE		ITEM	POST. REF.	DEBIT	CREDIT	BALANCE DEBIT	BALANCE CREDIT

ACCOUNT Miscellaneous Expense   ACCOUNT NO. 530

DATE		ITEM	POST. REF.	DEBIT	CREDIT	BALANCE DEBIT	BALANCE CREDIT
Sept. 20--	30	Balance	✔			5 5 0 00	

ACCOUNT Rent Expense   ACCOUNT NO. 540

DATE		ITEM	POST. REF.	DEBIT	CREDIT	BALANCE DEBIT	BALANCE CREDIT
Sept. 20--	30	Balance	✔			3 3 0 0 00	

ACCOUNT Supplies Expense   ACCOUNT NO. 550

DATE		ITEM	POST. REF.	DEBIT	CREDIT	BALANCE DEBIT	BALANCE CREDIT

8-5 **CHALLENGE PROBLEM (continued)**

3.

ACCOUNT TITLE	DEBIT	CREDIT

4.

_____
_____
_____
_____
_____
_____
_____
_____
_____
_____
_____
_____
_____
_____
_____
_____
_____
_____
_____
_____
_____
_____
_____
_____
_____
_____
_____
_____
_____
_____
_____
_____

REINFORCEMENT ACTIVITY 1

PART B, p. 228

An Accounting Cycle for a Proprietorship: End-of-Fiscal-Period Work

The general ledger prepared in Reinforcement Activity 1, Part A, is needed to complete Reinforcement Activity 1, Part B.

12., 13., 14., 15., 16.

ACCOUNT TITLE	TRIAL BALANCE		ADJUSTMENTS		INCOME STATEMENT		BALANCE SHEET	
	DEBIT 1	CREDIT 2	DEBIT 3	CREDIT 4	DEBIT 5	CREDIT 6	DEBIT 7	CREDIT 8
1								
2								
3								
4								
5								
6								
7								
8								
9								
10								
11								
12								
13								
14								
15								
16								
17								
18								
19								
20								
21								
22								
23								

REINFORCEMENT ACTIVITY 1

PART B (continued)

17. Income Statement

			% OF SALES

18. Balance Sheet

REINFORCEMENT ACTIVITY 1

PART B (continued)

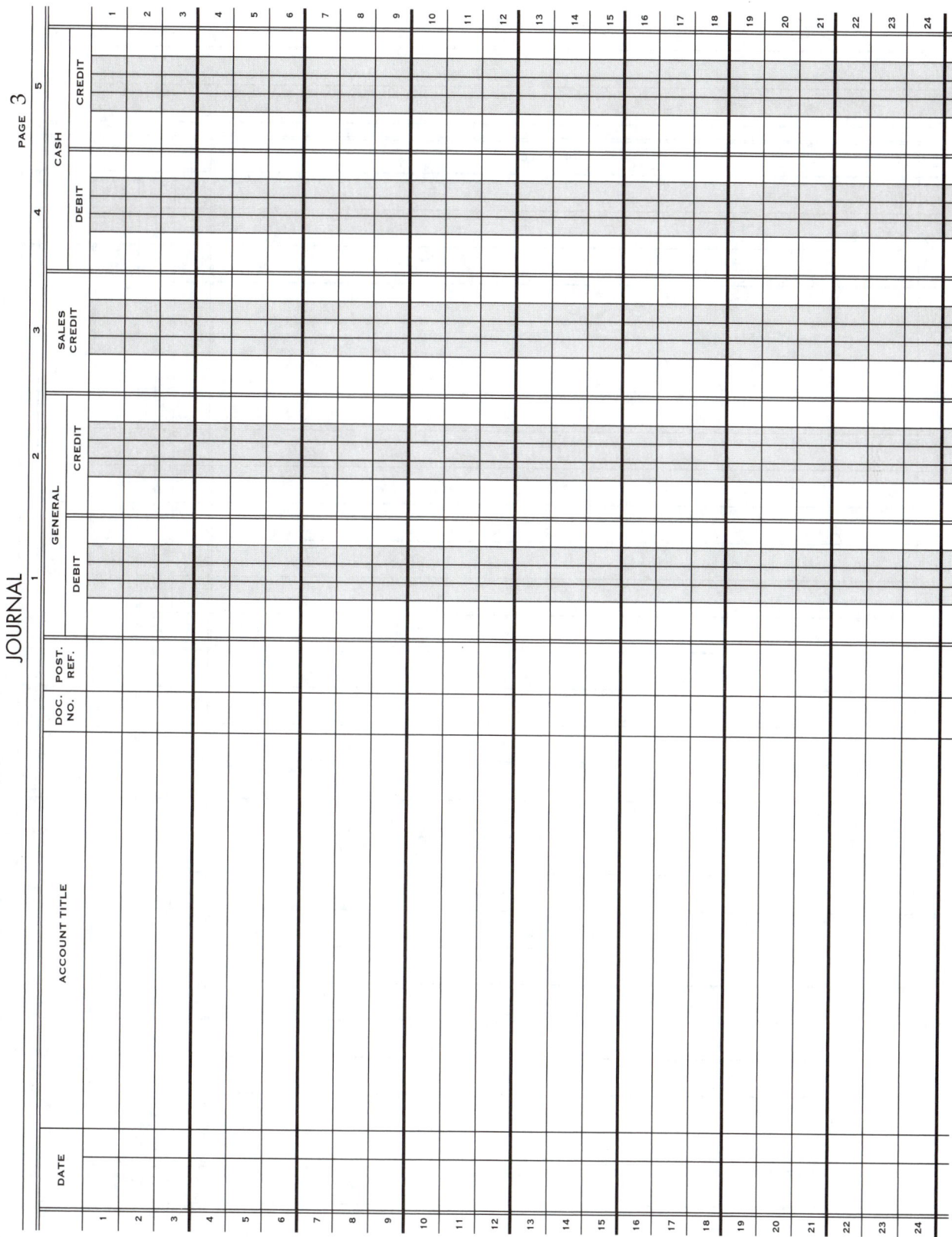

JOURNAL

PAGE 3

19.., 20.

DATE	ACCOUNT TITLE	DOC. NO.	POST. REF.	GENERAL DEBIT 1	GENERAL CREDIT 2	SALES CREDIT 3	CASH DEBIT 4	CASH CREDIT 5

REINFORCEMENT ACTIVITY 1

PART B (concluded)

21. Post-Closing Trial Balance

ACCOUNT TITLE	DEBIT	CREDIT

Study Guide 9

Name	Perfect Score	Your Score
Identifying Accounting Terms	29 Pts.	
Analyzing Accounting Concepts and Practices	27 Pts.	
Analyzing Transactions Recorded in Special Journals	24 Pts.	
Total	80 Pts.	

Part One—Identifying Accounting Terms

Directions: Select the one term in Column I that best fits each definition in Column II. Print the letter identifying your choice in the Answers column.

Column I	Column II	Answers
A. capital stock	**1.** Goods that a business purchases to sell. (p. 234)	1._____
B. cash discount	**2.** A business that purchases and sells goods. (p. 234)	2._____
C. cash over	**3.** A merchandising business that sells to those who use or consume the goods. (p. 234)	3._____
D. cash payments journal	**4.** A business that buys and resells merchandise to retail merchandising businesses. (p. 234)	4._____
E. cash short	**5.** An organization with the legal rights of a person and which many persons may own. (p. 234)	5._____
F. contra account	**6.** Each unit of ownership in a corporation. (p. 234)	6._____
G. corporation	**7.** Total shares of ownership in a corporation. (p. 234)	7._____
H. cost of merchandise	**8.** An owner of one or more shares of a corporation. (p. 234)	8._____
I. debit memorandum	**9.** A journal used to record only one kind of transaction. (p. 235)	9._____
J. general amount column	**10.** The price a business pays for goods it purchases to sell. (p. 236)	10._____
K. list price	**11.** The amount added to the cost of merchandise to establish the selling price. (p. 236)	11._____
L. markup	**12.** A business from which merchandise is purchased or supplies or other assets are bought. (p. 236)	12._____
M. merchandise	**13.** A transaction in which the merchandise purchased is to be paid for later. (p. 236)	13._____
N. merchandising business	**14.** A special journal used to record only purchases of merchandise on account. (p. 237)	14._____
O. purchase invoice	**15.** A journal amount column headed with an account title. (p. 237)	15._____
P. purchase on account	**16.** An invoice used as a source document for recording a purchase on account transaction. (p. 238)	16._____

COPYRIGHT © SOUTH-WESTERN CENGAGE LEARNING

Q. purchases allowance	17. An agreement between a buyer and a seller about payment for merchandise. (p. 238)	17. _____
R. purchases discount	18. A special journal used to record only cash payment transactions. (p. 242)	18. _____
S. purchases journal	19. A deduction that a vendor allows on the invoice amount to encourage prompt payment. (p. 242)	19. _____
T. purchases return	20. A cash discount on purchases taken by a customer. (p. 242)	20. _____
U. retail merchandising business	21. A journal amount column that is not headed with an account title. (p. 242)	21. _____
V. share of stock	22. The retail price listed in a catalog or on an Internet site. (p. 244)	22. _____
W. special amount column	23. A reduction in the list price granted to customers. (p. 244)	23. _____
X. special journal	24. An account that reduces a related account on a financial statement. (p. 245)	24. _____
Y. stockholder	25. A petty cash on hand amount that is less than a recorded amount. (p. 248)	25. _____
Z. terms of sale	26. A petty cash on hand amount that is more than a recorded amount. (p. 248)	26. _____
AA. trade discount	27. Credit allowed for the purchase price of returned merchandise, resulting in a decrease in the customer's accounts payable. (p. 256)	27. _____
BB. vendor	28. Credit allowed for part of the purchase price of merchandise that is not returned, resulting in a decrease in the customer's accounts payable. (p. 256)	28. _____
CC. wholesale merchandising business	29. A form prepared by the customer showing the price deduction taken by the customer for returns and allowances. (p. 256)	29. _____

Part Two—Analyzing Accounting Concepts and Practices

Directions: Place a *T* for True or an *F* for False in the Answers column to show whether each of the following statements is true or false.

Answers

1. Unlike a proprietorship, a corporation exists independent of its owners. (p. 234) 1. _____

2. A corporation can incur liabilities but cannot own property. (p. 234) 2. _____

3. As in proprietorships, information in a corporation's accounting system is kept separate from the personal records of the owners, and this accounting concept application is called a Business Entity. (p. 234) 3. _____

4. The selling price of merchandise must be greater than the cost of merchandise for a business to make a profit. (p. 236) 4. _____

5. The cost account Purchases is used only to record the value of merchandise purchased. (p. 236) 5. _____

6. When purchases are recorded at their cost, including any related shipping costs and taxes, the Historical Cost accounting concept is being applied. (p. 236) 6. _____

7. Recording entries in a journal with special amount columns saves time. (p. 237) 7. _____

8. All purchase transactions, including purchases made on account and purchases made for cash, are recorded in the purchases journal. (p. 237) 8. _____

9. The source document for recording a purchase on account transaction is a memorandum describing the merchandise purchased. (p. 238) 9. _____

10. By listing the quantity, the description, the price of each item, and the total amount purchased, the Objective Evidence concept is applied. (p. 238) 10. _____

11. A purchase invoice usually lists only the total cost of the merchandise. (p. 238) 11. _____

12. A purchase on account transaction increases the amount owed to a vendor. (p. 239) 12. _____

13. A cash payments journal includes a special amount column for the cash account and the accounts payable account. (p. 242) 13. _____

14. The source document for most cash payments is the check issued. (p. 242) 14. _____

15. When supplies are purchased for use in the business, the amount is recorded in the purchases account. (p. 243) 15. _____

16. A special journal entry is made to show the amount of a trade discount. (p. 244) 16. _____

17. The terms of sale 2/15, n/30 mean that 2% of the invoice amount may be deducted if paid within 15 days of the invoice date or the total invoice amount must be paid within 30 days. (p. 245) 17. _____

18. Purchase discounts are recorded in the general journal. (p. 245) 18. _____

19. The contra account Purchases Discount has a normal credit balance. (p. 245) 19. _____

20. The custodian prepares a petty cash report when the petty cash fund is to be replenished. (p. 248) 20. _____

21. The petty cash account Cash Short and Over is a permanent account. (p. 249) 21. _____

22. A journal is proved and ruled only at the end of a fiscal period. (p. 250) 22. _____

23. To begin a new journal page, the totals from the previous journal page are carried forward to the next journal page. (p. 251) 23. _____

24. Buying supplies on account is recorded in the general journal. (p. 254) 24. _____

25. When supplies are purchased on account, the Store Supplies account balance increases and the Accounts Payable account balance increases. (p. 255) 25. _____

26. The source document for a purchases return is a check. (p. 256) 26. _____

27. The normal account balance of Purchases Returns and Allowances is a credit. (p. 257) 27. _____

Part Three—Analyzing Transactions Recorded in Special Journals

Directions: In Answers Column l, print the abbreviation for the journal in which each transaction is to be recorded. In Answers Columns 2 and 3, print the letters identifying the accounts to be debited and credited for each transaction.

PJ—Purchases journal; **GJ**—General journal; **CPJ**—Cash payments journal

Account Titles	Transactions	Answers Journal	Debit	Credit
A. Accounts Payable	**1–2–3.** Purchased merchandise on account from Wixom Sports. (p. 239)	1. ____	2. ____	3. ____
B. Cash	**4–5–6.** Paid cash for rent. (p. 243)	4. ____	5. ____	6. ____
C. Cash Short and Over	**7–8–9.** Purchased merchandise for cash. (p. 244)	7. ____	8. ____	9. ____
D. Miscellaneous Expense	**10–11–12.** Paid cash on account to Wixom Sports, less purchases discount. (p. 245)	10. ____	11. ____	12. ____
E. Petty Cash				
F. Purchases	**13–14–15.** Paid cash on account to Tri-County Suppliers. (p. 246)	13. ____	14. ____	15. ____
G. Purchases Discount	**16–17–18.** Paid cash to replenish the petty cash fund: supplies, miscellaneous, cash over. (p. 249)	16. ____	17. ____	18. ____
H. Purchases Returns and Allowances	**19–20–21.** Bought supplies on account from Yukon Outfitters. (p. 255)	19. ____	20. ____	21. ____
I. Rent Expense	**22–23–24.** Returned merchandise to Tri-County Suppliers. (p. 257)	22. ____	23. ____	24. ____
J. Supplies				
K. Tri-County Suppliers				
L. Wixom Sports				
M. Yukon Outfitters				

9-1 **WORK TOGETHER, p. 241**

Journalizing purchases using a purchases journal

PURCHASES JOURNAL   PAGE

	DATE		ACCOUNT CREDITED	PURCH. NO.	POST. REF.	PURCHASES DR. ACCTS. PAY. CR.	
1							1
2							2
3							3
4							4
5							5
6							6
7							7
8							8
9							9
10							10
11							11
12							12
13							13
14							14
15							15
16							16
17							17
18							18
19							19
20							20
21							21
22							22
23							23
24							24
25							25
26							26
27							27
28							28
29							29
30							30
31							31
32							32
33							33

Journalizing purchases using a purchases journal

PURCHASES JOURNAL   PAGE

	DATE	ACCOUNT CREDITED	PURCH. NO.	POST. REF.	PURCHASES DR. ACCTS. PAY. CR.	
1						1
2						2
3						3
4						4
5						5
6						6
7						7
8						8
9						9
10						10
11						11
12						12
13						13
14						14
15						15
16						16
17						17
18						18
19						19
20						20
21						21
22						22
23						23
24						24
25						25
26						26
27						27
28						28
29						29
30						30
31						31
32						32
33						33

9-2 **WORK TOGETHER, p. 247**

Journalizing cash payments using a cash payments journal

CASH PAYMENTS JOURNAL

PAGE

				GENERAL		ACCOUNTS PAYABLE DEBIT	PURCHASES DISCOUNT CREDIT	CASH CREDIT	
DATE	ACCOUNT TITLE	CK. NO.	POST. REF.	DEBIT	CREDIT				
				1	2	3	4	5	
1									1
2									2
3									3
4									4
5									5
6									6
7									7
8									8
9									9
10									10
11									11
12									12
13									13
14									14
15									15
16									16
17									17
18									18
19									19
20									20
21									21
22									22
23									23
24									24

Journalizing cash payments using a cash payments journal

CASH PAYMENTS JOURNAL

PAGE 5

				1 GENERAL		2	3 ACCOUNTS	4 PURCHASES	5 CASH
DATE	ACCOUNT TITLE	CK. NO.	POST. REF.	DEBIT		CREDIT	PAYABLE DEBIT	DISCOUNT CREDIT	CREDIT

9-3 WORK TOGETHER, p. 253

Performing other cash payments journal operations

CASH PAYMENTS JOURNAL   PAGE 5

	DATE	ACCOUNT TITLE	CK. NO.	POST. REF.	GENERAL DEBIT	GENERAL CREDIT	ACCOUNTS PAYABLE DEBIT	PURCHASES DISCOUNT CREDIT	CASH CREDIT	
23	27	Supplies	534		2 3 4 30				2 3 4 30	23
24	27	Ace Manufacturing	535				1 8 9 60	3 79	1 8 5 81	24
25					18 4 8 6 85	4 5 8 56	16 4 8 3 50	2 5 1 34	34 2 6 0 45	25

CASH PAYMENTS JOURNAL   PAGE 6

	DATE	ACCOUNT TITLE	CK. NO.	POST. REF.	GENERAL DEBIT	GENERAL CREDIT	ACCOUNTS PAYABLE DEBIT	PURCHASES DISCOUNT CREDIT	CASH CREDIT	
1	Mar. 27	Brought Forward		✔	18 4 8 6 85	4 5 8 56	16 4 8 3 50	2 5 1 34	34 2 6 0 45	1
2	31	Supplies—Office	536		4 5 23				1 5 9 41	2
3		Supplies—Store			6 6 18					3
4		Miscellaneous Expense			4 9 25					4
5		Cash Short and Over				1 25				5
6										6

PETTY CASH REPORT

Date: _____   Custodian: _____

Explanation		Reconciliation	Replenish Amount
Fund Total Payments: _____			
_____			
_____			
_____			
Less: Total payments			→
Equals: Recorded amount on hand			
Less: Actual amount on hand			
Equals: Cash short (over)			→
Amount to Replenish			

Column Title	Debit Column Totals	Credit Column Totals
General Debit	_____	
General Credit		_____
Accounts Payable Debit	_____	
Purchases Discount Credit		_____
Cash Credit		_____
Totals	_____	_____

Performing other cash payments journal operations

CASH PAYMENTS JOURNAL   PAGE 11

	DATE	ACCOUNT TITLE	CK. NO.	POST. REF.	GENERAL DEBIT	GENERAL CREDIT	ACCOUNTS PAYABLE DEBIT	PURCHASES DISCOUNT CREDIT	CASH CREDIT	
23	28	Advertising Expense	625		1 5 0 0 00				1 5 0 0 00	23
24	28	GRF Manufacturing, Inc.	626				2 5 1 8 00	5 0 36	2 4 6 7 64	24
25					25 6 2 4 85	9 5 8 48	35 1 4 2 50	4 9 2 15	59 3 1 6 72	25

CASH PAYMENTS JOURNAL   PAGE 12

	DATE	ACCOUNT TITLE	CK. NO.	POST. REF.	GENERAL DEBIT	GENERAL CREDIT	ACCOUNTS PAYABLE DEBIT	PURCHASES DISCOUNT CREDIT	CASH CREDIT	
1	20-- Jun. 28	Brought Forward		✔	25 6 2 4 85	9 5 8 48	35 1 4 2 50	4 9 2 15	59 3 1 6 72	1
2	30	Supplies—Office	627		5 6 21				2 2 3 52	2
3		Supplies—Store			4 8 27					3
4		Repair Expense			8 2 25					4
5		Miscellaneous Expense			3 6 17					5
6		Cash Short and Over			0 62					6
7										7

PETTY CASH REPORT

Date: _____   Custodian: _____

	Explanation	Reconciliation	Replenish Amount
Fund Total Payments:	_____		
	_____		
	_____		
	_____		
Less:	Total payments	→	
Equals:	Recorded amount on hand		
Less:	Actual amount on hand		
Equals:	Cash short (over)	→	
Amount to Replenish			

Column Title	Debit Column Totals	Credit Column Totals
General Debit	_____	
General Credit		_____
Accounts Payable Debit	_____	
Purchases Discount Credit		_____
Cash Credit		_____
Totals	_____	_____

9-4 **WORK TOGETHER and ON YOUR OWN, p. 258**

Journalizing other transactions using a general journal

GENERAL JOURNAL

PAGE _____

DATE	ACCOUNT TITLE	DOC. NO.	POST. REF.	DEBIT	CREDIT	
						1
						2
						3
						4
						5
						6
						7
						8
						9
						10
						11
						12
						13
						14
						15
						16
						17
						18
						19
						20
						21
						22
						23
						24

Journalizing purchases using a purchases journal

PURCHASES JOURNAL

PAGE

	DATE	ACCOUNT CREDITED	PURCH. NO.	POST. REF.	PURCHASES DR. ACCTS. PAY. CR.	
1						1
2						2
3						3
4						4
5						5
6						6
7						7
8						8
9						9
10						10
11						11
12						12
13						13
14						14
15						15
16						16
17						17
18						18
19						19
20						20
21						21
22						22
23						23
24						24
25						25
26						26
27						27
28						28
29						29
30						30
31						31
32						32
33						33

9-2 APPLICATION PROBLEM, p. 260

Journalizing cash payments using a cash payments journal

CASH PAYMENTS JOURNAL

PAGE 5

	DATE	ACCOUNT TITLE	CK. NO.	POST. REF.	GENERAL DEBIT	GENERAL CREDIT	ACCOUNTS PAYABLE DEBIT	PURCHASES DISCOUNT CREDIT	CASH CREDIT	
1										1
2										2
3										3
4										4
5										5
6										6
7										7
8										8
9										9
10										10
11										11
12										12
13										13
14										14

	Debit	Credit
Column Title	**Column Totals**	**Column Totals**
General Debit	_____	
General Credit		_____
Accounts Payable Debit	_____	
Purchases Discount Credit		_____
Cash Credit		_____
Totals	_____	_____

Note: Line 12 of the journal and the journal proof above are completed in Application Problem 9-4.

9-3 **APPLICATION PROBLEM, p. 261**

Preparing a petty cash report

PETTY CASH REPORT

Date: _____   Custodian: _____

	Explanation		Reconciliation	Replenish Amount
Fund Total Payments:	_____			
	_____			
	_____			
	_____			
Less:	Total payments		_____ →	
Equals:	Recorded amount on hand		_____	
Less:	Actual amount on hand		_____	
Equals:	Cash short (over)		_____ →	
Amount to Replenish				

9-4 **APPLICATION PROBLEM, p. 261**

Performing additional cash payments journal operations

PETTY CASH REPORT

Date: _____   Custodian: _____

	Explanation		Reconciliation	Replenish Amount
Fund Total Payments:	_____			
	_____			
	_____			
	_____			
Less:	Total payments		_____ →	
Equals:	Recorded amount on hand		_____	
Less:	Actual amount on hand		_____	
Equals:	Cash short (over)		_____ →	
Amount to Replenish				

9-4 APPLICATION PROBLEM (concluded)

CASH PAYMENTS JOURNAL

PAGE 5

| | | | | GENERAL | | ACCOUNTS PAYABLE DEBIT | PURCHASES DISCOUNT CREDIT | CASH CREDIT | |
DATE	ACCOUNT TITLE	CK. NO.	POST. REF.	DEBIT	CREDIT				
									1
									2
									3
									4
									5
									6
									7
									8
									9
									10

Column Title	Debit Column Totals	Credit Column Totals
General Debit		
General Credit		
Accounts Payable Debit		
Purchases Discount Credit		
Cash Credit		
Totals		

APPLICATION PROBLEM, p. 262

Journalizing other transactions using a general journal

GENERAL JOURNAL   PAGE

	DATE	ACCOUNT TITLE	DOC. NO.	POST. REF.	DEBIT	CREDIT	
1							1
2							2
3							3
4							4
5							5
6							6
7							7
8							8
9							9
10							10
11							11
12							12
13							13
14							14
15							15
16							16
17							17
18							18
19							19
20							20
21							21
22							22
23							23
24							24
25							25
26							26
27							27
28							28
29							29
30							30
31							31
32							32
33							33

9-6 **MASTERY PROBLEM, p. 262**

Journalizing purchases, cash payments, and other transactions

1., 2.

CASH PAYMENTS JOURNAL

PAGE 5

				1	2	3	4	5
				GENERAL		ACCOUNTS PAYABLE DEBIT	PURCHASES DISCOUNT CREDIT	CASH CREDIT
DATE	ACCOUNT TITLE	CK. NO.	POST. REF.	DEBIT	CREDIT			
1								
2								
3								
4								
5								
6								
7								
8								
9								
10								
11								
12								
13								
14								
15								

2.

Column Title	Debit Column Totals	Credit Column Totals
General Debit		
General Credit		
Accounts Payable Debit		
Purchases Discount Credit		
Cash Credit		
Totals		

1., 5.

PURCHASES JOURNAL   PAGE

	DATE	ACCOUNT CREDITED	PURCH. NO.	POST. REF.	PURCHASES DR. ACCTS. PAY. CR.	
1						1
2						2
3						3
4						4
5						5
6						6
7						7
8						8
9						9
10						10
11						11
12						12
13						13
14						14

1.

GENERAL JOURNAL   PAGE

	DATE	ACCOUNT TITLE	DOC. NO.	POST. REF.	DEBIT	CREDIT	
1							1
2							2
3							3
4							4
5							5
6							6
7							7
8							8
9							9
10							10
11							11
12							12
13							13
14							14

9-6 **MASTERY PROBLEM (concluded)**

3., 4., 6., 7.

CASH PAYMENTS JOURNAL   PAGE

DATE	ACCOUNT TITLE	CK. NO.	POST. REF.	GENERAL DEBIT	GENERAL CREDIT	ACCOUNTS PAYABLE DEBIT	PURCHASES DISCOUNT CREDIT	CASH CREDIT

6.

Column Title	Debit Column Totals	Credit Column Totals
General Debit		
General Credit		
Accounts Payable Debit		
Purchases Discount Credit		
Cash Credit		
Totals		

CHALLENGE PROBLEM, p. 263

Journalizing purchases, cash payments, and other transactions

1.

PURCHASES JOURNAL

PAGE

	DATE	ACCOUNT CREDITED	PURCH. NO.	POST. REF.	PURCHASES DR. ACCTS. PAY. CR.	
1						1
2						2
3						3
4						4
5						5
6						6
7						7
8						8
9						9
10						10
11						11
12						12
13						13
14						14
15						15
16						16
17						17
18						18
19						19
20						20
21						21
22						22
23						23
24						24
25						25

1.

CASH PAYMENTS JOURNAL

			GENERAL		ACCOUNTS	PURCHASES	CASH
					PAYABLE	DISCOUNT	CREDIT
DATE	ACCOUNT TITLE	CK. NO.	POST. REF.	DEBIT	CREDIT	DEBIT	CREDIT

PAGE

1.

GENERAL JOURNAL   PAGE

	DATE		ACCOUNT TITLE	DOC. NO.	POST. REF.	DEBIT	CREDIT	
1								1
2								2
3								3
4								4
5								5
6								6
7								7
8								8
9								9
10								10
11								11
12								12
13								13
14								14
15								15
16								16
17								17
18								18
19								19
20								20
21								21
22								22
23								23
24								24
25								25
26								26
27								27
28								28
29								29
30								30
31								31

9-7 **CHALLENGE PROBLEM (concluded)**

2.

Journalizing purchases, cash payments, and other transactions from source documents

Suddard Industries 1423 Commercial Road Bell City, LA 70630-6213	INVOICE	REC'D 10/03/- - P324 Form _1_

TO: Messler Sailing
142 River Street
Naperville, IL 60540-3172

DATE: *9/30/- -*
INV. NO. *6234*
TERMS: *30 days*
ACCT. NO. *2450*

QUANTITY	CAT. NO.	DESCRIPTION	UNIT PRICE	TOTAL
25	4323	jib sheet	$ 45.00	$ 1,125.00
20	4233	jib halyard	$ 55.00	$ 1,100.00
		TOTAL		$ 2,225.00

NO. **458**	$ *1,520.00*	Form *2*

Date: *October 4*   20 - -
To: *Seaside Manufacturing*

For: *On account*

BAL. BRO'T. FOR'D. . . .	12,485	25
AMT. DEPOSITED . . . . Date		
SUBTOTAL	12,485	25
OTHER:		
SUBTOTAL	12,485	25
AMT. THIS CHECK	1,520	00
BAL. CAR'D. FOR'D.	10,965	25

USING SOURCE DOCUMENTS (continued)

Messler Sailing	MEMORANDUM Form _3_
	NO. 39
	DATE October 4, 20--
	Attached invoice from Sullivan Supply Co. is for store supplies, bought on account, $105.00

DEBIT MEMORANDUM NO. 25   Form _4_

DATE
October 8, 20--

Messler Sailing
142 River Street
Naperville, IL 60540-3172

TO
Seaside Manufacturing
1430 Industrial Road
Ocean City, WA 98569-2198

ACCOUNT NO.
2040

QUANTITY	CAT. NO.	DESCRIPTION	UNIT PRICE	TOTAL
11	JS-342	Life preservers damaged in transit	$ 25.00	$ 275.00

NO. **459** $ *625.00*   Form *5*
Date: *October 10*   20 - -
To: *Willcutt & Bishop*

For: *Office Supplies*

BAL. BRO'T. FOR'D. . .		10,965	25
AMT. DEPOSITED	10 09 20 - Date	1,264	00
SUBTOTAL		12,229	25
OTHER:			
SUBTOTAL		12,229	25
AMT. THIS CHECK		625	00
BAL. CAR'D. FOR'D.		11,604	25

		INVOICE		REC'D 10/11/-- P325

Aquatic Manufacturing
42 Industrial Road
Stratford, CA 93266-4762

Form _6_

TO: Messler Sailing
142 River Street
Naperville, IL 60540-3172

DATE: _10/8/--_
INV. NO. _15484_
TERMS: _2/10, n/30_
ACCT. NO. _1420_

QUANTITY	CAT. NO.	DESCRIPTION	UNIT PRICE	TOTAL
5	532	Fiberglass repair kit	$ 60.00	$ 300.00
10	6346	U-bolts, 1"	$ 16.00	$ 160.00
20	6347	U-bolts, 2"	$ 23.00	$ 460.00
		TOTAL		$ 920.00

Messler Sailing

MEMORANDUM   Form _7_

NO.   40

DATE   October 12, 20--

Attached invoice from Office
Zone is for office supplies,
bought on account, $95.00

NO. **460**	$ _425.00_	Form _8_

Date: _October 15_ 20 - -
To: _Northern Electric_

For: _Utilities_

BAL. BRO'T. FOR'D. . . .	11,604	25
AMT. DEPOSITED		
SUBTOTAL	11,604	25
OTHER:		
SUBTOTAL	11,604	25
AMT. THIS CHECK	425	00
BAL. CAR'D. FOR'D.	11,179	25

USING SOURCE DOCUMENTS (continued)

NO. **461**	$ *901.60*	Form *9*

Date: *October 19*   20 - -

To: *Aquatic Manufacturing*

For: *On account; $920.00 less*
    2% cash discount

BAL. BRO'T. FOR'D. . . .	11,179	25
AMT. DEPOSITED . . . . 10 18 20 - Date	546	50
SUBTOTAL	11,725	75
OTHER:		
_____		
_____		
SUBTOTAL	11,725	75
AMT. THIS CHECK	901	60
BAL. CAR'D. FOR'D.	10,824	15

REC'D 10/20/-- P326

NORTHERN SAIL COMPANY
253 Beach Blvd.
Boston, MA 02169-5029

INVOICE

Form *10*

TO: Messler Sailing
142 River Street
Naperville, IL 60540-3172

DATE:	*10/18/--*
INV. NO.	*895*
TERMS:	*30 days*
ACCT. NO.	*1820*

QUANTITY	CAT. NO.	DESCRIPTION	UNIT PRICE	TOTAL
2	*B-23*	*Viking-16 mainsail*	$ *1,599.00*	$ *3,198.00*
3	*B-44*	*Sunset-13 mainsail*	$ *459.00*	$ *1,377.00*
		TOTAL		$ *4,575.00*

NO. **462**	$ _2,560.00_	Form _11_
Date: _October 20_		20 _--_
To: _WRRX Radio_		
For: _Advertising_		

BAL. BRO'T. FOR'D. . . .	10,824	15
AMT. DEPOSITED		
SUBTOTAL	10,824	15
OTHER:		
SUBTOTAL	10,824	15
AMT. THIS CHECK	2,560	00
BAL. CAR'D. FOR'D.	8,264	15

DEBIT MEMORANDUM NO. 26   Form _12_

DATE
October 22, 20--

TO
Aquatic Manufacturing
42 Industrial Road
Stratford, CA 93266-4762

ACCOUNT NO.
1420

Messler Sailing
142 River Street
Naperville, IL 60540-3172

QUANTITY	CAT. NO.	DESCRIPTION	UNIT PRICE	TOTAL
2	532	_Fiberglass repair kit missing components_	$ 60.00	$ 120.00

USING SOURCE DOCUMENTS (continued)

NO. **463**	$ 224.00	Form 13
Date: October 22		20 - -
To: Michigan Sail Co.		
For: Purchases		

BAL. BRO'T. FOR'D. . .	8,264	15
AMT. DEPOSITED . . . . ☐☐☐ Date	1,421	08
SUBTOTAL	9,685	23
OTHER:		
SUBTOTAL	9,685	23
AMT. THIS CHECK	224	00
BAL. CAR'D. FOR'D.	9,461	23

NO. **464**	$ 2,225.00	Form 14
Date: October 29		20 - -
To: Suddard Industries		
For: On account		

BAL. BRO'T. FOR'D. . .	9,461	23
AMT. DEPOSITED . . . . ☐☐☐ Date		
SUBTOTAL	9,461	23
OTHER:		
SUBTOTAL	9,461	23
AMT. THIS CHECK	2,225	00
BAL. CAR'D. FOR'D.	7,236	23

NO. **465**	$ 112.94	Form 15
Date: October 31		20 - -
To: Mary Donovan, Petty Cash		
For: Petty cash; office supplies, $23.45; store supplies, $65.25; misc. expense, $25.11; cash over, $0.87		

BAL. BRO'T. FOR'D. . .	7,236	23
AMT. DEPOSITED . . . . 10 30 20 - Date	648	22
SUBTOTAL	7,884	45
OTHER:		
SUBTOTAL	7,884	45
AMT. THIS CHECK	112	94
BAL. CAR'D. FOR'D.	7,771	51

CASH PAYMENTS JOURNAL

PAGE

		DATE	ACCOUNT TITLE	CK. NO.	POST. REF.	GENERAL DEBIT	GENERAL CREDIT	ACCOUNTS PAYABLE DEBIT	PURCHASES DISCOUNT CREDIT	CASH CREDIT		
						1	2	3	4	5		
1												1
2												2
3												3
4												4
5												5
6												6
7												7
8												8
9												9
10												10
11												11
12												12
13												13

USING SOURCE DOCUMENTS (concluded)

PURCHASES JOURNAL

PAGE

	DATE	ACCOUNT CREDITED	PURCH. NO.	POST. REF.	PURCHASES DR. ACCTS. PAY. CR.	
1						1
2						2
3						3
4						4
5						5
6						6
7						7
8						8
9						9

GENERAL JOURNAL

PAGE

	DATE	ACCOUNT TITLE	DOC. NO.	POST. REF.	DEBIT	CREDIT	
1							1
2							2
3							3
4							4
5							5
6							6
7							7
8							8
9							9
10							10
11							11
12							12

Study Guide 10

Name	Perfect Score	Your Score
Identifying Accounting Terms	14 Pts.	
Analyzing Sales and Cash Receipts	24 Pts.	
Analyzing Transactions Recorded in Special Journals	15 Pts.	
Total	53 Pts.	

Part One—Identifying Accounting Terms

Directions: Select the term in Column I that best fits each definition in Column II. Print the letter identifying your choice in the Answers column.

Column I	Column II	Answers
A. batch report	**1.** A person or business to whom merchandise or services are sold. (p. 270)	1. _____
B. batching out	**2.** A tax on a sale of merchandise or services. (p. 270)	2. _____
C. cash receipts journal	**3.** A special journal used to record only sales of merchandise on account. (p. 272)	3. _____
D. cash sale	**4.** A sale in which cash is received for the total amount of the sale at the time of the transaction. (p. 276)	4. _____
E. credit card sale	**5.** A sale in which a credit card is used for the total amount of the sale at the time of the transaction. (p. 276)	5. _____
F. credit memorandum	**6.** A computer used to collect, store, and report all the information of a sales transaction. (p. 276)	6. _____
G. customer	**7.** The report that summarizes the cash and credit card sales of a point-of-sale terminal. (p. 276)	7. _____
H. point-of-sale (POS) terminal	**8.** A report of credit card sales produced by a point-of-sale terminal. (p. 278)	8. _____
I. sales allowance	**9.** The process of preparing a batch report of credit card sales from a point-of-sale terminal. (p. 278)	9. _____
J. sales discount	**10.** A special journal used to record only cash receipt transactions. (p. 278)	10. _____
K. sales journal	**11.** A cash discount on sales taken by a customer. (p. 278)	11. _____
L. sales return	**12.** Credit allowed a customer for the sales price of returned merchandise, resulting in a decrease in the vendor's accounts receivable. (p. 285)	12. _____
M. sales tax	**13.** Credit allowed a customer for part of the sales price of merchandise that is not returned, resulting in a decrease in the vendor's accounts receivable. (p. 285)	13. _____
N. terminal summary	**14.** A form prepared by the vendor showing the amount deducted for returns and allowances. (p. 285)	14. _____

Part Two—Analyzing Sales and Cash Receipts

Directions: Place a *T* for True or an *F* for False in the Answers column to show whether each of the following statements is true or false.

1. Most states do not require a business to collect sales tax from customers. (p. 270)   1. _____

2. Sales tax rates are usually stated as a percentage of sales. (p. 270)   2. _____

3. A sale of merchandise increases the revenue of a business. (p. 271)   3. _____

4. The Realization of Revenue accounting concept is applied when a sale is recorded at the time the sale is made. (p. 271)   4. _____

5. A sale on account is not the same as a charge sale. (p. 271)   5. _____

6. A credit card sale is a sale in which cash is received for the total amount of the sale at the time of the transaction. (p. 276)   6. _____

7. A cash sale is a sale in which a credit card is used for the total amount of the sale at the time of the transaction. (p. 276)   7. _____

8. At the end of the week, all credit card slips are gathered together, sorted by issuing bank, and mailed individually to each of the banks to collect payment. (p. 278)   8. _____

9. All cash receipts, including cash sales and credit card sales, are recorded in the cash receipts journal. (p. 278)   9. _____

10. The total of a terminal summary can be recorded as a single cash sales transaction. (p. 279)   10. _____

11. For cash and credit card sales, the asset account Cash is debited for the total of sales and sales tax, but the revenue account Sales is credited only for the total of sales. (p. 279)   11. _____

12. The revenue account Sales has a normal credit balance. (p. 279)   12. _____

13. The liability account Sales Tax Payable has a normal debit balance. (p. 279)   13. _____

14. The source document for cash received on account from a customer is a receipt. (p. 280)   14. _____

15. When cash is received on account, the cash account balance increases and the accounts receivable account balance increases. (p. 280)   15. _____

16. When a sales discount is taken, a customer pays less cash than the invoice amount previously recorded in the sales account. (p. 281)   16. _____

17. The account Sales Discount increases sales. (p. 282)   17. _____

18. Maintaining a separate account for sales discounts provides business managers with information to evaluate whether a sales discount is a cost-effective method. (p. 282)   18. _____

19. If a customer does not pay the amount owed within the sales discount period, the full invoice amount is due. (p. 282)   19. _____

20. After the cash receipts journal is proved at the end of the month, cash is proved. (p. 283)   20. _____

21. All transactions can be recorded in a special journal. (p. 285)   21. _____

22. Credit may be granted to a customer only when merchandise is returned. (p. 285)   22. _____

23. Sales returns and sales allowances increase the amount of sales. (p. 285)   23. _____

24. The account Sales Returns and Allowances is a contra account. (p. 285)   24. _____

Part Three—Analyzing Transactions Recorded in Special Journals

Directions: In Answers Column l, print the abbreviation for the journal in which each transaction is to be recorded. In Answers Columns 2 and 3, print the letters identifying the accounts to be debited and credited for each transaction.

SJ—Sales journal; **GJ**—General journal; **CRJ**—Cash receipts journal

Account Titles	Transactions	Answers Journal	Debit	Credit
A. Accounts Receivable	**1–2–3.** Sold merchandise on account to Penny Kellar, plus sales tax. (p. 273)	1._____	2._____	3._____
B. Cash	**4–5–6.** Recorded cash and credit card sales, plus sales tax. (p. 279)	4._____	5._____	6._____
C. Penny Kellar				
D. Jim Tauras	**7–8–9.** Received cash on account from Jim Tauras. (p. 280)	7._____	8._____	9._____
E. Sales				
F. Sales Discount	**10–11–12.** Received cash on account from Penny Kellar, less sales discount. (p. 282)	10._____	11._____	12._____
G. Sales Returns and Allowances	**13–14–15.** Granted credit to Jim Tauras for merchandise returned, plus sales tax. (p. 286)	13._____	14._____	15._____
H. Sales Tax Payable				

10-1 WORK TOGETHER, p. 275

Journalizing sales on account; proving and ruling a sales journal

1., 2.

SALES JOURNAL   PAGE _____

	DATE		ACCOUNT DEBITED	SALE NO.	POST. REF.	ACCOUNTS RECEIVABLE DEBIT (1)	SALES CREDIT (2)	SALES TAX PAYABLE CREDIT (3)	
1									1
2									2
3									3
4									4
5									5
6									6
7									7
8									8
9									9
10									10
11									11
12									12
13									13
14									14
15									15

2.

Col. No.	Column Title	Debit Totals	Credit Totals
1	Accounts Receivable Debit	_____	
2	Sales Credit		_____
3	Sales Tax Payable Credit		_____
	Totals	_____	_____

Journalizing sales on account; proving and ruling a sales journal

1., 2.

SALES JOURNAL

	DATE		ACCOUNT DEBITED	SALE NO.	POST. REF.	ACCOUNTS RECEIVABLE DEBIT 1	SALES CREDIT 2	SALES TAX PAYABLE CREDIT 3	
1									1
2									2
3									3
4									4
5									5
6									6
7									7
8									8
9									9
10									10
11									11
12									12
13									13
14									14
15									15

2.

Col. No.	Column Title	Debit Totals	Credit Totals
1	Accounts Receivable Debit	_____	
2	Sales Credit		_____
3	Sales Tax Payable Credit		_____
	Totals	=========	=========

10-2 WORK TOGETHER, p. 284

Journalizing cash receipts; proving and ruling a cash receipts journal

1., 2., 4.

CASH RECEIPTS JOURNAL

PAGE 7

	DATE	ACCOUNT TITLE	DOC. NO.	POST. REF.	GENERAL DEBIT	GENERAL CREDIT	ACCOUNTS RECEIVABLE CREDIT	SALES CREDIT	SALES TAX PAYABLE CREDIT	SALES DISCOUNT DEBIT	CASH DEBIT	
					1	2	3	4	5	6	7	
1												1
2												2
3												3
4												4
5												5
6												6
7												7
8												8
9												9
10												10
11												11
12												12
13												13

2.

Col. No.	Column Title	Debit Totals	Credit Totals
1	General Debit		
2	General Credit		
3	Accounts Receivable Credit		
4	Sales Credit		
5	Sales Tax Payable Credit		
6	Sales Discount Debit		
7	Cash Debit		
	Totals		

3.

CASH PROOF

Cash on hand at the beginning of the month ....
Plus total cash received during the month ....
Equals total ....
Less total cash paid during the month ....
Equals cash balance on hand at end of the month ....
Checkbook balance on the next unused check stub ....

Journalizing cash receipts; proving and ruling a cash receipts journal

1., 2., 4.

CASH RECEIPTS JOURNAL

PAGE _____

				1	2	3	4	5	6	7	
				GENERAL		ACCOUNTS RECEIVABLE CREDIT	SALES CREDIT	SALES TAX PAYABLE CREDIT	SALES DISCOUNT DEBIT	CASH DEBIT	
DATE	ACCOUNT TITLE	DOC. NO.	POST. REF.	DEBIT	CREDIT						
											1
											2
											3
											4
											5
											6
											7
											8
											9
											10
											11
											12
											13

2.

Col. No.	Column Title	Debit Totals	Credit Totals
1	General Debit		
2	General Credit		
3	Accounts Receivable Credit		
4	Sales Credit		
5	Sales Tax Payable Credit		
6	Sales Discount Debit		
7	Cash Debit		
	Totals		

3.

CASH PROOF

Cash on hand at the beginning of the month . . . . _____

Plus total cash received during the month . . . . _____

Equals total . . . . _____

Less total cash paid during the month . . . . _____

Equals cash balance on hand at end of the month . . . . _____

Checkbook balance on the next unused check stub . . . . _____

Name _____ Date _____ Class _____

Journalizing sales returns and allowances using a general journal

1.

GENERAL JOURNAL   PAGE

	DATE	ACCOUNT TITLE	DOC. NO.	POST. REF.	DEBIT	CREDIT	
1							1
2							2
3							3
4							4
5							5
6							6
7							7
8							8
9							9
10							10
11							11
12							12
13							13
14							14
15							15
16							16
17							17
18							18
19							19
20							20
21							21
22							22
23							23
24							24
25							25

Journalizing sales returns and allowances using a general journal

1.

GENERAL JOURNAL

PAGE

	DATE		ACCOUNT TITLE	DOC. NO.	POST. REF.	DEBIT	CREDIT	
1								1
2								2
3								3
4								4
5								5
6								6
7								7
8								8
9								9
10								10
11								11
12								12
13								13
14								14
15								15
16								16
17								17
18								18
19								19
20								20
21								21
22								22
23								23
24								24
25								25

10-1 APPLICATION PROBLEM, p. 289

Journalizing sales on account; proving and ruling a sales journal

1., 2.

SALES JOURNAL PAGE

	DATE		ACCOUNT DEBITED	SALE NO.	POST. REF.	1 ACCOUNTS RECEIVABLE DEBIT	2 SALES CREDIT	3 SALES TAX PAYABLE CREDIT	
1									1
2									2
3									3
4									4
5									5
6									6
7									7
8									8
9									9
10									10
11									11
12									12
13									13
14									14
15									15
16									16
17									17
18									18
19									19

2.

Col. No.	Column Title	Debit Totals	Credit Totals
1	Accounts Receivable Debit	_____	
2	Sales Credit		_____
3	Sales Tax Payable Credit		_____
		==========	==========

Journalizing cash receipts; proving and ruling a cash receipts journal

1., 2., 4.

CASH RECEIPTS JOURNAL

PAGE _____

				GENERAL		ACCOUNTS RECEIVABLE CREDIT	SALES CREDIT	SALES TAX PAYABLE CREDIT	SALES DISCOUNT DEBIT	CASH DEBIT	
DATE	ACCOUNT TITLE	DOC. NO.	POST. REF.	DEBIT	CREDIT						
											1
											2
											3
											4
											5
											6
											7
											8
											9
											10
											11
											12
											13
											14

2.

Col. No.	Column Title	Debit Totals	Credit Totals
1	General Debit		
2	General Credit		
3	Accounts Receivable Credit		
4	Sales Credit		
5	Sales Tax Payable Credit		
6	Sales Discount Debit		
7	Cash Debit		
	Totals		

3.

CASH PROOF

Cash on hand at the beginning of the month . . . .
Plus total cash received during the month . . . .
Equals total . . . .
Less total cash paid during the month . . . .
Equals cash balance on hand at end of the month . . . .
Checkbook balance on the next unused check stub . . . .

10-3 APPLICATION PROBLEM, p. 290

Journalizing sales returns and allowances using a general journal

1.

GENERAL JOURNAL   PAGE _____

	DATE		ACCOUNT TITLE	DOC. NO.	POST. REF.	DEBIT	CREDIT	
1								1
2								2
3								3
4								4
5								5
6								6
7								7
8								8
9								9
10								10
11								11
12								12
13								13
14								14
15								15
16								16
17								17
18								18
19								19
20								20
21								21
22								22
23								23
24								24
25								25

Journalizing sales and cash receipts transactions; proving and ruling journals

1., 2., 3.

SALES JOURNAL

	DATE	ACCOUNT DEBITED	SALE NO.	POST. REF.	ACCOUNTS RECEIVABLE DEBIT (1)	SALES CREDIT (2)	SALES TAX PAYABLE CREDIT (3)	
1	Oct. 24	Brought Forward		✔	1 4 9 6 6 70	1 4 5 2 1 55	4 4 5 15	1
2								2
3								3
4								4
5								5
6								6
7								7
8								8
9								9
10								10
11								11
12								12
13								13
14								14
15								15
16								16
17								17
18								18

8.

Col. No.	Column Title	Debit Totals	Credit Totals
1	Accounts Receivable Debit	_____	
2	Sales Credit		_____
3	Sales Tax Payable Credit		_____
	Totals	_____	_____

10-4 **MASTERY PROBLEM (continued)**

1., 4., 5., 6.

CASH RECEIPTS JOURNAL

PAGE 20

DATE	ACCOUNT TITLE	DOC. NO.	POST. REF.	GENERAL DEBIT	GENERAL CREDIT	ACCOUNTS RECEIVABLE CREDIT	SALES CREDIT	SALES TAX PAYABLE CREDIT	SALES DISCOUNT DEBIT	CASH DEBIT	
20-- Oct. 24	Brought Forward		✔			12158 25	23154 12	926 16		36238 53	1
											2
											3
											4
											5
											6
											7
											8
											9
											10
											11
											12
											13
											14

2.

Col. No.	Column Title	Debit Totals	Credit Totals
1	General Debit........................		
2	General Credit.......................		
3	Accounts Receivable Credit........		
4	Sales Credit.........................		
5	Sales Tax Payable Credit...........		
6	Sales Discount Debit................		
7	Cash Debit..........................		
	Totals..............................		

3.

CASH PROOF

Cash on hand at the beginning of the month . . . .

Plus total cash received during the month . . . .

Equals total . . . .

Less total cash paid during the month . . . .

Equals cash balance on hand at end of the month . . . . .

Checkbook balance on the next unused check stub . . .

1.

GENERAL JOURNAL   PAGE

	DATE	ACCOUNT TITLE	DOC. NO.	POST. REF.	DEBIT	CREDIT	
1							1
2							2
3							3
4							4
5							5
6							6
7							7
8							8
9							9
10							10
11							11
12							12
13							13
14							14
15							15
16							16
17							17
18							18
19							19
20							20
21							21
22							22
23							23
24							24
25							25

10-5 CHALLENGE PROBLEM, p. 291

Journalizing transactions; proving and ruling special journals

1., 2., 5.

SALES JOURNAL   PAGE

	DATE	ACCOUNT DEBITED	SALE NO.	POST. REF.	1 ACCOUNTS RECEIVABLE DEBIT	2 SALES CREDIT	3 SALES TAX PAYABLE CREDIT	
1								1
2								2
3								3
4								4
5								5
6								6
7								7
8								8
9								9
10								10
11								11
12								12
13								13
14								14
15								15
16								16
17								17
18								18

3.

Col. No.	Column Title	Debit Totals	Credit Totals
1	Accounts Receivable Debit	_____	
2	Sales Credit		_____
3	Sales Tax Payable Credit		_____
	Totals	_____	_____

1., 2., 5.

PURCHASES JOURNAL   PAGE

	DATE		ACCOUNT CREDITED	PURCH. NO.	POST. REF.	PURCHASES DR. ACCTS. PAY. CR.	
1							1
2							2
3							3
4							4
5							5
6							6
7							7
8							8
9							9
10							10
11							11
12							12
13							13
14							14
15							15
16							16
17							17
18							18
19							19
20							20
21							21
22							22
23							23
24							24
25							25

10-5 CHALLENGE PROBLEM (continued)

1., 2., 5.

CASH PAYMENTS JOURNAL

PAGE _____

DATE	ACCOUNT TITLE	CK. NO.	POST. REF.	GENERAL DEBIT	GENERAL CREDIT	ACCOUNTS PAYABLE DEBIT	PURCHASES DISCOUNT CREDIT	CASH CREDIT	
									1
									2
									3
									4
									5
									6
									7
									8
									9
									10
									11
									12
									13
									14
									15
									16

3.

Column Title	Debit Column Totals	Credit Column Totals
General Debit	_____	
General Credit		_____
Accounts Payable Debit	_____	
Purchases Discount Credit		_____
Cash Credit		_____
Totals	_____	_____

1., 2., 5.

CASH RECEIPTS JOURNAL

PAGE

| | | | | GENERAL | | ACCOUNTS RECEIVABLE CREDIT | SALES CREDIT | SALES TAX PAYABLE CREDIT | SALES DISCOUNT DEBIT | CASH DEBIT | |
DATE	ACCOUNT TITLE	DOC. NO.	POST. REF.	DEBIT	CREDIT						
											1
											2
											3
											4
											5
											6
											7
											8
											9
											10
											11
											12
											13
											14

3.

Col. No.	Column Title	Debit Totals	Credit Totals
1	General Debit.		
2	General Credit.		
3	Accounts Receivable Credit.		
4	Sales Credit.		
5	Sales Tax Payable Credit		
6	Sales Discount Debit		
7	Cash Debit.		
	Totals		

4.

CASH PROOF

Cash on hand at the beginning of the month . . . .

Plus total cash received during the month . . . .

Equals total . . . .

Less total cash paid during the month . . . .

Equals cash balance on hand at end of the month . . . .

Checkbook balance on the next unused check stub . . . .

10-5   CHALLENGE PROBLEM (concluded)

1.

GENERAL JOURNAL   PAGE _____

	DATE		ACCOUNT TITLE	DOC. NO.	POST. REF.	DEBIT	CREDIT	
1								1
2								2
3								3
4								4
5								5
6								6
7								7
8								8
9								9
10								10
11								11
12								12
13								13
14								14
15								15
16								16
17								17
18								18
19								19
20								20
21								21
22								22
23								23
24								24
25								25

Journalizing sales and cash receipts transactions; proving and ruling journals

NO. **658**			Form _1_
DATE:	*November 25*		20--
FROM:	*Putt-A-Round*		
FOR:	*On Account*		

On account		$ 150.00
Sales discount		$ 3.00
Cash received		$ 147.00

GOLFER'S PARADISE
142 Glade Road
Crossville, TN 38555-8102

Form _2_

NO. **443**

Sold to: Daniel Pearson
2345 Lakeview Drive
Crossville, TN 38555-5819

DATE: *11/27/--*
TERMS: *30 days*
CUST. NO. *480*

CAT. NO.	DESCRIPTION	QUANTITY	UNIT PRICE	TOTAL
2432	*9 degree titanium driver*	1	$ 439.50	$ 439.50
745	*practice golf balls, dz.*	5	10.00	50.00
			SUBTOTAL	$ 489.50
			TAX	39.16
			TOTAL	$ 528.66

Serving Crossville and Fairfield Glade With All Your Recreational Equipment

USING SOURCE DOCUMENTS (continued)

Form __3__

CODE:		54
DATE:		11/27/--
TIME:		18:24

Credit Card	034	
Sales		989.95
Sales Tax		79.20
Total		1,069.15

MasterCard	042	
Sales		806.09
Sales Tax		64.49
Total		870.58

Cash	152	
Sales		1,894.44
Sales Tax		151.56
Total		2,046.00

Totals		
Sales		3,690.48
Sales Tax		295.25
Total		3,985.73

NO. **659** Form __4__

DATE: *November 28* 20--

FROM: *Mary Ann Ingram*

FOR: *On Account*

On account	$ 420.48
Sales discount	
Cash received	$ 420.48

CREDIT MEMORANDUM NO. 63 Form __5__

DATE
November 29, 20--

TO
Nelson Lang
354 Lang Drive
Crossville, TN 38555-2615

GOLFER'S PARADISE
142 Glade Road
Crossville, TN 38555-8102

ACCOUNT NO.
340

QUANTITY	CAT. NO.	DESCRIPTION	UNIT PRICE	TOTAL
2	643	golf bag	$130.00	$260.00
		SUBTOTAL		$260.00
		SALES TAX		20.80
		TOTAL		$280.80

GOLFER'S PARADISE
142 Glade Road
Crossville, TN 38555-8102

Form __6__

NO. **444**

Sold to: Janice Adams
594 Eagles Nest Road
Crossville, TN 38555-7364

DATE: 11/29/--
TERMS: 30 days
CUST. NO. 140

CAT. NO.	DESCRIPTION	QUANTITY	UNIT PRICE	TOTAL
BG-34	oversized irons, graphite shafts	1	$ 405.50	$ 405.50
			SUBTOTAL	$ 405.50
			TAX	32.44
			TOTAL	$ 437.94

Serving Crossville and Fairfield Glade With All Your Recreational Equipment

---

Form __7__

CODE: 55
DATE: 11/30/--
TIME: 18:45

Credit Card 005
Sales 251.05
Sales Tax 20.08
Total 271.13

MasterCard 007
Sales 315.15
Sales Tax 25.21
Total 340.36

Cash 062
Sales 612.15
Sales Tax 48.97
Total 661.12

Totals
Sales 1,178.35
Sales Tax 94.26
Total 1,272.61

USING SOURCE DOCUMENTS (continued)

1., 2., 3.

SALES JOURNAL   PAGE 18

	DATE	ACCOUNT DEBITED	SALE NO.	POST. REF.	ACCOUNTS RECEIVABLE DEBIT (1)	SALES CREDIT (2)	SALES TAX PAYABLE CREDIT (3)	
1	Nov. 24	Brought Forward		✔	8 7 2 6 89	6 1 5 4 25	2 5 7 2 64	1
2								2
3								3
4								4
5								5
6								6

2.

Col. No.	Column Title	Debit Totals	Credit Totals
1	Accounts Receivable Debit	_____	
2	Sales Credit		_____
3	Sales Tax Payable Credit		_____
	Totals	══════	══════

1., 4., 6.

CASH RECEIPTS JOURNAL

PAGE 24

DATE	ACCOUNT TITLE	DOC. NO.	POST. REF.	1 GENERAL DEBIT	2 GENERAL CREDIT	3 ACCOUNTS RECEIVABLE CREDIT	4 SALES CREDIT	5 SALES TAX PAYABLE CREDIT	6 SALES DISCOUNT DEBIT	7 CASH DEBIT	
20-- Nov. 24	Brought Forward		✓			15 488 24	28 148 16	2 251 85		45 888 25	1
											2
											3
											4
											5
											6
											7
											8

4.

Col. No.	Column Title	Debit Totals	Credit Totals
1	General Debit..................		
2	General Credit.................		
3	Accounts Receivable Credit.........		
4	Sales Credit..................		
5	Sales Tax Payable Credit..........		
6	Sales Discount Debit.............		
7	Cash Debit...................		
	Totals.....................		

5.

CASH PROOF

Cash on hand at the beginning of the month	
Plus total cash received during the month	
Equals total	
Less total cash paid during the month	
Equals cash balance on hand at end of the month	
Checkbook balance on the next unused check stub	

USING SOURCE DOCUMENTS (concluded)

1.

GENERAL JOURNAL PAGE

	DATE		ACCOUNT TITLE	DOC. NO.	POST. REF.	DEBIT	CREDIT	
1								1
2								2
3								3
4								4
5								5
6								6

Study Guide 11

Name	Perfect Score	Your Score
Identifying Accounting Terms	6 Pts.	
Analyzing a Journal and Ledgers	21 Pts.	
Analyzing Posting and Subsidiary Ledgers	10 Pts.	
Total	37 Pts.	

Part One—Identifying Accounting Terms

Directions: Select the term in Column I that best fits each definition in Column II. Print the letter identifying your choice in the Answers column.

Column I	Column II	Answers
A. accounts payable ledger	**1.** A ledger that is summarized in a single general ledger account. (p. 298)	1. _____
B. accounts receivable ledger	**2.** A subsidiary ledger containing only accounts for vendors from whom items are purchased or bought on account. (p. 298)	2. _____
C. controlling account	**3.** A subsidiary ledger containing only accounts for charge customers. (p. 298)	3. _____
D. schedule of accounts payable	**4.** An account in a general ledger that summarizes all accounts in a subsidiary ledger. (p. 298)	4. _____
E. schedule of accounts receivable	**5.** A listing of vendor accounts, account balances, and total amounts due all vendors. (p. 305)	5. _____
F. subsidiary ledger	**6.** A listing of customer accounts, account balances, and total amount due from all customers. (p. 313)	6. _____

Part Two—Analyzing a Journal and Ledgers

Directions: Place a *T* for True or an *F* for False in the Answers column to show whether each of the following statements is true or false.

Answers

1. When using an accounts receivable ledger, the total amount due from all customers is summarized in a single general ledger account. (p. 298)

    1. _____

2. Accounts are arranged in alphabetical order within the subsidiary ledgers. (p. 299)

    2. _____

3. A change in the balance of a vendor account also changes the balance of the controlling account Accounts Payable. (p. 299)

    3. _____

4. The total amount owed to all vendors is summarized in a single general ledger account, Accounts Payable. (p. 299)

    4. _____

5. The number of entries that may be recorded on each ledger account form is limited to fifteen. (p. 300)

    5. _____

6. The amount on each line of a purchases journal is posted as a credit to a vendor account in the accounts payable ledger. (p. 301)

    6. _____

7. Posting frequently keeps each vendor account balance up to date. (p. 301)

    7. _____

8. Entries in a general journal may affect account balances in an accounts payable ledger. (p. 303)

    8. _____

9. A controlling account balance in a general ledger must equal the sum of all account balances in a subsidiary ledger. (p. 305)

    9. _____

10. A schedule of accounts payable is prepared before all entries in a journal are posted. (p. 305)

    10. _____

11. A change in the balance of a customer account does not affect the balance of the controlling account Accounts Receivable. (p. 307)

    11. _____

12. The form used in the accounts receivable ledger has a Debit Balance column. (p. 308)

    12. _____

13. Each amount in a sales journal's Accounts Receivable Debit column is posted as a credit to the customer account in the accounts receivable ledger. (p. 309)

    13. _____

14. Each entry in the Accounts Receivable Credit column of the cash receipts journal is posted to the proper customer account in the accounts receivable ledger. (p. 310)

    14. _____

15. The accounts receivable ledger is proved when the balance of Accounts Receivable in the general ledger is the same as the total of the schedule of accounts receivable. (p. 313)

    15. _____

16. Each amount in the General columns of a cash payments journal is posted as a total at the end of the month. (p. 316)

    16. _____

17. The monthly total of each special amount column in a cash payments journal is posted to a general ledger account. (p. 316)

    17. _____

18. Transactions recorded in a general journal can affect both subsidiary ledger and general ledger accounts. (p. 318)

    18. _____

19. A diagonal line in the Post. Ref. column allows the posting reference of two account numbers. (p. 318)

    19. _____

20. Errors made in recording amounts in subsidiary ledgers always affect the general ledger controlling account. (p. 327)

    20. _____

21. The steps for posting a journal entry to correct customer accounts are exactly the same as posting other transactions to subsidiary ledgers. (p. 328)

    21. _____

Part Three—Analyzing Posting and Subsidiary Ledgers

Directions: For each item below, select the choice that best completes the statement. Print the letter identifying your choice in the Answers column.

Answers

1. When a debit is posted to the accounts payable ledger, the (A) debit amount is written in the Debit column of the account (B) cash account increases (C) controlling account is increased by the entry (D) all of the above. (p. 302)

   1. _____

2. When a credit is posted to the accounts payable ledger, the (A) source document number and page number of the journal are written in the Post. Ref. column of the account (B) previous balance is added to the new amount posted in the Credit column (C) credit amount is written in the Debit column of the account (D) word *Balance* is written in the Item column. (p. 303)

   2. _____

3. The total of all customer account balances in the accounts receivable ledger equals (A) the balance in the accounts receivable controlling account (B) the balance in the accounts payable controlling account (C) the cash account (D) none of these. (p. 307)

   3. _____

4. A form in the accounts receivable ledger has (A) a Debit Balance column (B) a Credit Balance column (C) both Debit Balance and Credit Balance columns (D) none of these. (p. 308)

   4. _____

5. The separate amounts in the Accounts Receivable Debit column of a sales journal are (A) posted individually to the general ledger (B) posted individually to the accounts receivable ledger (C) not posted to the general ledger (D) none of these. (p. 309)

   5. _____

6. When all lines have been used in a ledger account form, a new page is prepared with the account name, account number, and (A) page number (B) account balance (C) company name (D) none of these. (p. 315)

   6. _____

7. Posting the special amount column totals in the cash payments journal is done (A) weekly (B) daily (C) after each transaction (D) none of these. (p. 316)

   7. _____

8. The total amount of the purchases journal is posted to the general ledger (A) daily (B) weekly (C) at the end of the month (D) none of these. (p. 321)

   8. _____

9. A check mark is placed in parentheses below the General Debit and General Credit column totals in the journal to indicate that the two column totals are (A) posted individually (B) posted only as part of the column total (C) not posted (D) none of these. (p. 324)

   9. _____

10. The journal that should be posted first is the (A) sales journal (B) purchases journal (C) general journal (D) cash payments journal. (p. 325)

    10. _____

11-1 WORK TOGETHER, p. 306

Posting to an accounts payable ledger

2., 3., 4.

PURCHASES JOURNAL   PAGE 10

DATE	ACCOUNT CREDITED	PURCH. NO.	POST. REF.	PURCHASES DR. ACCTS. PAY. CR.	
19	Regal Designs	89		1 4 0 3 20	7
31	Total			11 8 1 8 40	14
					15

3.

CASH PAYMENTS JOURNAL   PAGE 15

DATE	ACCOUNT TITLE	CK. NO.	POST. REF.	GENERAL DEBIT	GENERAL CREDIT	ACCOUNTS PAYABLE DEBIT	PURCHASES DISCOUNT CREDIT	CASH CREDIT	
19	Supplies—Office	290		6 9 60				6 9 60	14
20	Electro-Graphics Supply	291				7 7 6 00		7 7 6 00	15
31	Totals			1 1 6 7 1 38	1 4 9 4 74	8 6 5 6 00	1 2 8 48	1 8 7 0 4 16	24
									25

4.

GENERAL JOURNAL   PAGE 11

DATE	ACCOUNT TITLE	DOC. NO.	POST. REF.	DEBIT	CREDIT	
Oct. 12	Sales Returns and Allowances	CM29		5 2 00		1
	Sales Tax Payable			3 12		2
	Accounts Receivable/David Bishop				5 5 12	3
26	Supplies—Office	M32		2 5 4 4 00		4
	Accounts Payable/Electro-Graphics Supply				2 5 4 4 00	5
28	Accounts Payable/Art and Things	DM37		1 2 5 00		6
	Purchases Returns and Allowances				1 2 5 00	7

*(Note: The journals in this problem are needed to complete Work Together 11-3 and 11-4.
The general journal is also needed to complete Work Together 11-2.)*

1., 2., 3., 4.   **ACCOUNTS PAYABLE LEDGER**

VENDOR Art and Things   VENDOR NO. 210

DATE		ITEM	POST. REF.	DEBIT	CREDIT	CREDIT BALANCE
20-- Oct.	1	Balance	✔			8 7 3 00

VENDOR Can Do Graphics   VENDOR NO. 220

DATE		ITEM	POST. REF.	DEBIT	CREDIT	CREDIT BALANCE
20-- Oct.	1	Balance	✔			1 8 1 4 00
	13		CP15	8 2 8 00		9 8 6 00

VENDOR Electro-Graphics Supply   VENDOR NO. 230

DATE		ITEM	POST. REF.	DEBIT	CREDIT	CREDIT BALANCE
20-- Oct.	1	Balance	✔			7 7 6 00

VENDOR   VENDOR NO.

DATE		ITEM	POST. REF.	DEBIT	CREDIT	CREDIT BALANCE

5.

11-1 ON YOUR OWN, p. 306

Posting to an accounts payable ledger

2.

PURCHASES JOURNAL PAGE 9

	DATE	ACCOUNT CREDITED	PURCH. NO.	POST. REF.	PURCHASES DR. ACCTS. PAY. CR.	
11	14	Swann Industries	458		2 4 8 5 00	11
22	30	Total			4 8 5 7 5 25	22
23						23

3.

CASH PAYMENTS JOURNAL PAGE 20

	DATE	ACCOUNT TITLE	CK. NO.	POST. REF.	GENERAL DEBIT	GENERAL CREDIT	ACCOUNTS PAYABLE DEBIT	PURCHASES DISCOUNT CREDIT	CASH CREDIT	
18	21	Supplies—Store	647		1 2 4 20				1 2 4 20	18
19	22	Miller Supply	648				4 8 9 00		4 8 9 00	19
23	30	Totals			4 2 1 5 8 25	1 6 4 8 25	3 3 2 3 7 26	4 2 5 22	7 3 3 2 2 04	23
24										24

4.

GENERAL JOURNAL PAGE 16

	DATE	ACCOUNT TITLE	DOC. NO.	POST. REF.	DEBIT	CREDIT	
1	Sept. 15	Sales Returns and Allowances	CM91		6 0 00		1
2		Sales Tax Payable			4 20		2
3		Accounts Receivable/Mary Burgia				6 4 20	3
4	27	Supplies—Store	M125		7 8 9 00		4
5		Accounts Payable/Miller Supply				7 8 9 00	5
6	29	Accounts Payable/Franklin Mfg. Corp.			1 1 0 00		6
7		Purchases Returns and Allowances				1 1 0 00	7

(Note: The journals in this problem are needed to complete On Your Own 11-3 and 11-4. The general journal is also needed to complete On Your Own 11-2.)

1., 2., 3., 4.   **ACCOUNTS PAYABLE LEDGER**

VENDOR Best Supply Co.   VENDOR NO. 210

DATE		ITEM	POST. REF.	DEBIT	CREDIT	CREDIT BALANCE
Sept. 20--	1	Balance	✔			
	3		P9		3 4 8 2 00	3 4 8 2 00

VENDOR Franklin Mfg. Corp.   VENDOR NO. 220

DATE		ITEM	POST. REF.	DEBIT	CREDIT	CREDIT BALANCE
Sept. 20--	1	Balance	✔			1 2 4 8 25

VENDOR Miller Supply   VENDOR NO. 230

DATE		ITEM	POST. REF.	DEBIT	CREDIT	CREDIT BALANCE
Sept. 20--	1	Balance	✔			4 8 9 00

VENDOR   VENDOR NO.

DATE		ITEM	POST. REF.	DEBIT	CREDIT	CREDIT BALANCE

5.

11-2 WORK TOGETHER, p. 314

Posting to an accounts receivable ledger

3.

CASH RECEIPTS JOURNAL

PAGE 12

DATE	ACCOUNT TITLE	DOC. NO.	POST. REF.	GENERAL DEBIT	GENERAL CREDIT	ACCOUNTS RECEIVABLE CREDIT	SALES CREDIT	SALES TAX PAYABLE CREDIT	SALES DISCOUNT DEBIT	CASH DEBIT
				1	2	3	4	5	6	7
21	Alfredo Lopez	R104				254 40				254 40
31	Totals					6360 00	18320 00	1099 20	31 40	25747 80

2.

SALES JOURNAL

PAGE 10

DATE	ACCOUNT DEBITED	SALE NO.	POST. REF.	ACCOUNTS RECEIVABLE DEBIT	SALES CREDIT	SALES TAX PAYABLE CREDIT
				1	2	3
20	Brandee Sparks	84		576 64	544 00	32 64
31	Totals			7377 60	6960 00	417 60

(Note: The journals in this problem are also needed to complete Work Together 11-4.)

1., 2., 3., 4. ACCOUNTS RECEIVABLE LEDGER

CUSTOMER David Bishop   CUSTOMER NO. 110

DATE		ITEM	POST. REF.	DEBIT	CREDIT	DEBIT BALANCE
20-- Oct.	1	Balance	✔			5 8 7 25
	10		CR12		3 4 8 75	2 3 8 50

CUSTOMER Maria Farrell   CUSTOMER NO. 120

DATE		ITEM	POST. REF.	DEBIT	CREDIT	DEBIT BALANCE
20-- Oct.	1	Balance	✔			2 8 6 20

CUSTOMER Alfredo Lopez   CUSTOMER NO. 130

DATE		ITEM	POST. REF.	DEBIT	CREDIT	DEBIT BALANCE
20-- Oct.	1	Balance	✔			2 5 4 40
	12		S10	1 2 7 2 00		1 5 2 6 40

CUSTOMER   CUSTOMER NO.

DATE	ITEM	POST. REF.	DEBIT	CREDIT	DEBIT BALANCE

5.

11-2 ON YOUR OWN, p. 314

Posting to an accounts receivable ledger

2.

SALES JOURNAL
PAGE 9

DATE	ACCOUNT DEBITED	SALE NO.	POST. REF.	ACCOUNTS RECEIVABLE DEBIT (1)	SALES CREDIT (2)	SALES TAX PAYABLE CREDIT (3)
21	Davis Sullivan	354		1470 50	1374 30	96 20
30	Totals			30118 36	28148 00	1970 36

3.

CASH RECEIPTS JOURNAL
PAGE 18

DATE	ACCOUNT TITLE	DOC. NO.	POST. REF.	GENERAL DEBIT (1)	GENERAL CREDIT (2)	ACCOUNTS RECEIVABLE CREDIT (3)	SALES CREDIT (4)	SALES TAX PAYABLE CREDIT (5)	SALES DISCOUNT DEBIT (6)	CASH DEBIT (7)
19	Harris Evans	R302				2158 00				2158 00
30	Totals					2948 25	48158 25	3248 25	223 00	80667 75

(*Note: The journals used in this problem are also used to complete On Your Own 11-4.*)

1., 2., 3., 4.   **ACCOUNTS RECEIVABLE LEDGER**

CUSTOMER Mary Burgin   CUSTOMER NO. 110

DATE		ITEM	POST. REF.	DEBIT	CREDIT	DEBIT BALANCE
20-- Sept.	1	Balance	✔			1 5 4 8 00
	6		CR18		2 5 2 00	1 2 9 6 00

CUSTOMER Harris Evans   CUSTOMER NO. 120

DATE		ITEM	POST. REF.	DEBIT	CREDIT	DEBIT BALANCE
20-- Sept.	1	Balance	✔			2 1 5 8 00
	13		S9	1 5 7 8 50		3 7 3 6 50

CUSTOMER Patrick Mussina   CUSTOMER NO. 130

DATE		ITEM	POST. REF.	DEBIT	CREDIT	DEBIT BALANCE
20-- Sept.	1	Balance	✔			1 1 4 2 00

CUSTOMER   CUSTOMER NO.

DATE		ITEM	POST. REF.	DEBIT	CREDIT	DEBIT BALANCE

5.

11-3 and 11-4   WORK TOGETHER, pp. 319, 326

Posting to a general ledger

1., 2., 3., 4., 5.

ACCOUNT Cash   ACCOUNT NO. 1110

DATE		ITEM	POST. REF.	DEBIT	CREDIT	BALANCE	
						DEBIT	CREDIT
20-- Oct.	1	Balance	✔			13 2 3 5 58	

ACCOUNT Accounts Receivable   ACCOUNT NO. 1130

DATE		ITEM	POST. REF.	DEBIT	CREDIT	BALANCE	
						DEBIT	CREDIT
20-- Oct.	1	Balance	✔			1 3 3 9 85	

ACCOUNT   ACCOUNT NO.

DATE		ITEM	POST. REF.	DEBIT	CREDIT	BALANCE	
						DEBIT	CREDIT

ACCOUNT Accounts Payable   ACCOUNT NO. 2110

DATE		ITEM	POST. REF.	DEBIT	CREDIT	BALANCE	
						DEBIT	CREDIT
20-- Oct.	1	Balance	✔				2 5 1 7 80

(Note: The general ledger accounts used in this problem are needed to complete Work Together 11-4.)

ACCOUNT Sales Tax Payable   ACCOUNT NO. 2140

DATE		ITEM	POST. REF.	DEBIT	CREDIT	BALANCE	
						DEBIT	CREDIT
20-- Oct.	1	Balance	✔				1 4 1 0 00

ACCOUNT Sales   ACCOUNT NO. 4110

DATE		ITEM	POST. REF.	DEBIT	CREDIT	BALANCE	
						DEBIT	CREDIT
20-- Oct.	1	Balance	✔				233 3 3 5 00

ACCOUNT Sales Discount   ACCOUNT NO. 4120

DATE		ITEM	POST. REF.	DEBIT	CREDIT	BALANCE	
						DEBIT	CREDIT
20-- Oct.	1	Balance	✔			2 1 9 8 00	

ACCOUNT Sales Returns and Allowances   ACCOUNT NO. 4130

DATE		ITEM	POST. REF.	DEBIT	CREDIT	BALANCE	
						DEBIT	CREDIT
20-- Oct.	1	Balance	✔			9 0 3 00	

11-3 WORK TOGETHER (concluded)

ACCOUNT Purchases   ACCOUNT NO. 5110

| DATE | | ITEM | POST. REF. | DEBIT | CREDIT | BALANCE | |
						DEBIT	CREDIT
20-- Oct.	1	Balance	✔			106 5 5 9 60	

ACCOUNT Purchases Discount   ACCOUNT NO. 5120

| DATE | | ITEM | POST. REF. | DEBIT | CREDIT | BALANCE | |
						DEBIT	CREDIT
20-- Oct.	1	Balance	✔				1 2 5 8 85

ACCOUNT Purchases Returns and Allowances   ACCOUNT NO. 5130

| DATE | | ITEM | POST. REF. | DEBIT | CREDIT | BALANCE | |
						DEBIT	CREDIT
20-- Oct.	1	Balance	✔				1 9 0 1 35

Posting to a general ledger

1., 2., 3., 4., 5.   **GENERAL LEDGER**

ACCOUNT Cash   ACCOUNT NO. 1110

DATE	ITEM	POST. REF.	DEBIT	CREDIT	BALANCE DEBIT	BALANCE CREDIT
20-- Sept. 1	Balance	✔			12 4 8 8 10	

ACCOUNT Accounts Receivable   ACCOUNT NO. 1130

DATE	ITEM	POST. REF.	DEBIT	CREDIT	BALANCE DEBIT	BALANCE CREDIT
20-- Sept. 1	Balance	✔			11 1 1 1 00	

ACCOUNT   ACCOUNT NO.

DATE	ITEM	POST. REF.	DEBIT	CREDIT	BALANCE DEBIT	BALANCE CREDIT

ACCOUNT Accounts Payable   ACCOUNT NO. 2110

DATE	ITEM	POST. REF.	DEBIT	CREDIT	BALANCE DEBIT	BALANCE CREDIT
20-- Sept. 1	Balance	✔				21 4 8 2 20

(Note: The general ledger accounts used in this problem are needed to complete On Your Own 11-4.)

11-3 ON YOUR OWN (continued)

ACCOUNT Sales Tax Payable   ACCOUNT NO. 2140

DATE		ITEM	POST. REF.	DEBIT	CREDIT	BALANCE	
						DEBIT	CREDIT
20-- Sept.	1	Balance	✔				5 2 1 8 61

ACCOUNT Sales   ACCOUNT NO. 4110

DATE		ITEM	POST. REF.	DEBIT	CREDIT	BALANCE	
						DEBIT	CREDIT
20-- Sept.	1	Balance	✔				408 7 4 2 25

ACCOUNT Sales Discount   ACCOUNT NO. 4120

DATE		ITEM	POST. REF.	DEBIT	CREDIT	BALANCE	
						DEBIT	CREDIT
20-- Sept.	1	Balance	✔			2 1 9 8 00	

ACCOUNT Sales Returns and Allowances   ACCOUNT NO. 4130

DATE		ITEM	POST. REF.	DEBIT	CREDIT	BALANCE	
						DEBIT	CREDIT
20-- Sept.	1	Balance	✔			5 1 2 3 00	

ACCOUNT Purchases   ACCOUNT NO. 5110

DATE		ITEM	POST. REF.	DEBIT	CREDIT	BALANCE	
						DEBIT	CREDIT
Sept. 20--	1	Balance	✔			212 1 8 4 66	

ACCOUNT Purchases Discount   ACCOUNT NO. 5120

DATE		ITEM	POST. REF.	DEBIT	CREDIT	BALANCE	
						DEBIT	CREDIT
Sept. 20--	1	Balance	✔				3 4 7 8 25

ACCOUNT Purchases Returns and Allowances   ACCOUNT NO. 5130

DATE		ITEM	POST. REF.	DEBIT	CREDIT	BALANCE	
						DEBIT	CREDIT
Sept. 20--	1	Balance	✔				3 2 7 6 00

11-5 WORK TOGETHER, p. 329

Journalizing and posting correcting entries affecting customer accounts

1.

GENERAL JOURNAL

PAGE 6

	DATE	ACCOUNT TITLE	DOC. NO.	POST. REF.	DEBIT	CREDIT	
6							6
7							7
8							8
9							9

2.

ACCOUNTS RECEIVABLE LEDGER

CUSTOMER Howell Clinic   CUSTOMER NO. 160

DATE	ITEM	POST. REF.	DEBIT	CREDIT	DEBIT BALANCE

CUSTOMER Howsley Dance Studio   CUSTOMER NO. 170

DATE		ITEM	POST. REF.	DEBIT	CREDIT	DEBIT BALANCE
20-- June	1	Balance	✔			4 1 4 99

Journalizing and posting correcting entries affecting customer accounts

1.

GENERAL JOURNAL   PAGE 7

	DATE	ACCOUNT TITLE	DOC. NO.	POST. REF.	DEBIT	CREDIT	
5							5
6							6
7							7
8							8
9							9
10							10

2.   **ACCOUNTS RECEIVABLE LEDGER**

CUSTOMER Keller Corp.   CUSTOMER NO. 140

DATE		ITEM	POST. REF.	DEBIT	CREDIT	DEBIT BALANCE
20-- July	1	Balance	✔			7 1 5 98

CUSTOMER Kellogg Co.   CUSTOMER NO. 150

DATE	ITEM	POST. REF.	DEBIT	CREDIT	DEBIT BALANCE

11-1 APPLICATION PROBLEM, p. 331

Posting to an accounts payable ledger

2.

PURCHASES JOURNAL PAGE 10

	DATE		ACCOUNT CREDITED	PURCH. NO.	POST. REF.	PURCHASES DR. ACCTS. PAY. CR.	
1	20-- Oct.	4	Nutrition Center	78		2 0 1 6 00	1
2		20	Cornucopia, Inc.	79		4 5 8 4 00	2
3		25	Sports Nutrition	80		5 4 0 0 00	3
4		30	Healthy Foods	81		3 3 9 6 00	4

1., 2.   **ACCOUNTS PAYABLE LEDGER**

VENDOR _____ VENDOR NO. _____

DATE	ITEM	POST. REF.	DEBIT	CREDIT	CREDIT BALANCE

VENDOR _____ VENDOR NO. _____

DATE	ITEM	POST. REF.	DEBIT	CREDIT	CREDIT BALANCE

VENDOR _____   VENDOR NO. _____

DATE	ITEM	POST. REF.	DEBIT	CREDIT	CREDIT BALANCE

VENDOR _____   VENDOR NO. _____

DATE	ITEM	POST. REF.	DEBIT	CREDIT	CREDIT BALANCE

VENDOR _____   VENDOR NO. _____

DATE	ITEM	POST. REF.	DEBIT	CREDIT	CREDIT BALANCE

11-1 APPLICATION PROBLEM (continued)

Posting to an accounts payable ledger

2.

CASH PAYMENTS JOURNAL
PAGE 10

DATE	ACCOUNT TITLE	CK. NO.	POST. REF.	GENERAL DEBIT	GENERAL CREDIT	ACCOUNTS PAYABLE DEBIT	PURCHASES DISCOUNT CREDIT	CASH CREDIT	
20-- Oct. 3	Cornucopia, Inc.	184				3 0 9 0 00	6 1 80	3 0 2 8 20	1
6	Healthy Foods	185				5 0 6 4 00	1 0 1 28	4 9 6 2 72	2
15	Sports Nutrition	186				4 5 1 2 00		4 5 1 2 00	3
28	Nutrition Center	187				2 0 1 6 00		2 0 1 6 00	4
									5
									6
									7
									8

GENERAL JOURNAL
PAGE 10

DATE	ACCOUNT TITLE	DOC. NO.	POST. REF.	DEBIT	CREDIT	
20-- Oct. 9	Supplies—Office	M26		9 6 00		1
	Accounts Payable/Office Center				9 6 00	2
25	Accounts Payable/Cornucopia, Inc.			1 2 4 00		3
	Purchases Returns and Allowances				1 2 4 00	4
						5
						6

3.

11-2 APPLICATION PROBLEM, p. 331

Posting to an accounts receivable ledger

2.

SALES JOURNAL   PAGE 10

	DATE	ACCOUNT DEBITED	SALE NO.	POST. REF.	1 ACCOUNTS RECEIVABLE DEBIT	2 SALES CREDIT	3 SALES TAX PAYABLE CREDIT	
1	20-- Oct. 6	Southwest Community Club	69		3 0 0 1 92	2 8 3 2 00	1 6 9 92	1
2	9	Children's Center	70		1 7 5 5 36	1 6 5 6 00	9 9 36	2
3	12	Eastman Sports Arena	71		1 1 1 9 36	1 0 5 6 00	6 3 36	3
4	25	Maple Tree Club	72		2 5 4 4 00	2 4 0 0 00	1 4 4 00	4

1., 2.   **ACCOUNTS RECEIVABLE LEDGER**

CUSTOMER   CUSTOMER NO.

DATE	ITEM	POST. REF.	DEBIT	CREDIT	DEBIT BALANCE

CUSTOMER   CUSTOMER NO.

DATE	ITEM	POST. REF.	DEBIT	CREDIT	DEBIT BALANCE

CUSTOMER   CUSTOMER NO.

DATE	ITEM	POST. REF.	DEBIT	CREDIT	DEBIT BALANCE

CUSTOMER   CUSTOMER NO.

DATE	ITEM	POST. REF.	DEBIT	CREDIT	DEBIT BALANCE

2.

GENERAL JOURNAL PAGE 10

	DATE		ACCOUNT TITLE	DOC. NO.	POST. REF.	DEBIT	CREDIT	
1	20-- Oct.	29	Sales Returns and Allowances			1 2 0 00		1
2			Sales Tax Payable			7 20		2
3			Accounts Receivable/Maple Tree Club				1 2 7 20	3
4								4
5								5
6								6
7								7
8								8
9								9
10								10
11								11
12								12
13								13
14								14
15								15
16								16
17								17
18								18
19								19
20								20
21								21
22								22
23								23
24								24
25								25
26								26
27								27
28								28
29								29
30								30
31								31
32								32
33								33

11-2 APPLICATION PROBLEM (continued)

Posting to an accounts receivable ledger

2.

CASH RECEIPTS JOURNAL   PAGE 10

	DATE	ACCOUNT TITLE	DOC. NO.	POST. REF.	GENERAL DEBIT	GENERAL CREDIT	ACCOUNTS RECEIVABLE CREDIT	SALES CREDIT	SALES TAX PAYABLE CREDIT	SALES DISCOUNT DEBIT	CASH DEBIT	
1	Oct. 5	Children's Center	R170				4 4 1 6 00				4 4 1 6 00	1
2	14	Eastman Sports Arena	R171				2 2 2 0 00				2 2 2 0 00	2
3	24	Maple Tree Club	R172				3 5 2 8 00				3 5 2 8 00	3
4												4
5												5
6												6
7												7
8												8
9												9
10												10
11												11
12												12
13												13
14												14
15												15
16												16
17												17
18												18
19												19
20												20
21												21
22												22
23												23

3.

11-3 **APPLICATION PROBLEM, p. 332**

Posting to a general ledger

2.

CASH PAYMENTS JOURNAL

PAGE 11

	DATE	ACCOUNT TITLE	CK. NO.	POST. REF.	1 GENERAL DEBIT	2 GENERAL CREDIT	3 ACCOUNTS PAYABLE DEBIT	4 PURCHASES DISCOUNT CREDIT	5 CASH CREDIT	
1	20-- Nov. 1	Rent Expense	202		1 2 0 0 00				1 2 0 0 00	1
2	2	Prepaid Insurance	203		1 4 4 0 00				1 4 4 0 00	2
10	15	Sales Tax Payable	211		1 6 1 5 20				1 6 1 5 20	10
21	30	Totals			6 0 6 1 00		1 4 6 8 2 00	1 5 4 25	20 5 8 8 75	21
22										22
23										23

GENERAL JOURNAL

PAGE 11

	DATE	ACCOUNT TITLE	DOC. NO.	POST. REF.	DEBIT	CREDIT	
10	28	Supplies—Office	M31		1 2 5 00		10
11		Accounts Payable/Office Center		/240		1 2 5 00	11
12							12
13							13
14							14
15							15
16							16
17							17
18							18

(Note: The ledger accounts used in this problem are also used in Application Problem 11-4.)

1., 2. **GENERAL LEDGER**

ACCOUNT _____   ACCOUNT NO. _____

DATE		ITEM	POST. REF.	DEBIT	CREDIT	BALANCE	
						DEBIT	CREDIT

ACCOUNT _____   ACCOUNT NO. _____

DATE		ITEM	POST. REF.	DEBIT	CREDIT	BALANCE	
						DEBIT	CREDIT

ACCOUNT _____   ACCOUNT NO. _____

DATE		ITEM	POST. REF.	DEBIT	CREDIT	BALANCE	
						DEBIT	CREDIT

ACCOUNT _____   ACCOUNT NO. _____

DATE		ITEM	POST. REF.	DEBIT	CREDIT	BALANCE	
						DEBIT	CREDIT

11-3 **APPLICATION PROBLEM (continued)**

1., 2.   **GENERAL LEDGER**

ACCOUNT _____   ACCOUNT NO. _____

DATE	ITEM	POST. REF.	DEBIT	CREDIT	BALANCE DEBIT	BALANCE CREDIT

ACCOUNT _____   ACCOUNT NO. _____

DATE	ITEM	POST. REF.	DEBIT	CREDIT	BALANCE DEBIT	BALANCE CREDIT

ACCOUNT _____   ACCOUNT NO. _____

DATE	ITEM	POST. REF.	DEBIT	CREDIT	BALANCE DEBIT	BALANCE CREDIT

ACCOUNT _____   ACCOUNT NO. _____

DATE	ITEM	POST. REF.	DEBIT	CREDIT	BALANCE DEBIT	BALANCE CREDIT

ACCOUNT _____ ACCOUNT NO. _____

DATE	ITEM	POST. REF.	DEBIT	CREDIT	BALANCE DEBIT	BALANCE CREDIT

ACCOUNT _____ ACCOUNT NO. _____

DATE	ITEM	POST. REF.	DEBIT	CREDIT	BALANCE DEBIT	BALANCE CREDIT

ACCOUNT _____ ACCOUNT NO. _____

DATE	ITEM	POST. REF.	DEBIT	CREDIT	BALANCE DEBIT	BALANCE CREDIT

11-4 APPLICATION PROBLEM, p. 332

Posting special journal column totals to a general ledger

SALES JOURNAL

PAGE 11

DATE	ACCOUNT DEBITED	SALE NO.	POST. REF.	1 ACCOUNTS RECEIVABLE DEBIT	2 SALES CREDIT	3 SALES TAX PAYABLE CREDIT
30	Totals			9 2 6 2 28	8 7 3 8 00	5 2 4 28

PURCHASES JOURNAL

PAGE 11

DATE	ACCOUNT CREDITED	PURCH. NO.	POST. REF.	PURCHASES DR. ACCTS. PAY. CR.
30	Total			16 1 6 5 80

CASH RECEIPTS JOURNAL

PAGE 11

DATE	ACCOUNT TITLE	DOC. NO.	POST. REF.	1 GENERAL DEBIT	2 GENERAL CREDIT	3 ACCOUNTS RECEIVABLE CREDIT	4 SALES CREDIT	5 SALES TAX PAYABLE CREDIT	6 SALES DISCOUNT DEBIT	7 CASH DEBIT
30	Totals					8 4 20 64	20 5 2 0 00	1 2 3 1 20	1 27 60	30 0 4 4 24

APPLICATION PROBLEM, p. 332

Journalizing and posting correcting entries affecting customer accounts

1., 2.

GENERAL JOURNAL   PAGE

	DATE	ACCOUNT TITLE	DOC. NO.	POST. REF.	DEBIT	CREDIT	
1							1
2							2
3							3
4							4
5							5
6							6
7							7
8							8

11-5 APPLICATION PROBLEM (concluded)

2.   **ACCOUNTS RECEIVABLE LEDGER**

CUSTOMER Mark Ford   CUSTOMER NO. 145

DATE		ITEM	POST. REF.	DEBIT	CREDIT	DEBIT BALANCE
20-- July	1	Balance	✔			9 8 20

CUSTOMER Andrew Forde   CUSTOMER NO. 150

DATE		ITEM	POST. REF.	DEBIT	CREDIT	DEBIT BALANCE
20-- July	1	Balance	✔			1 2 8 00
	5		S12	2 5 3 32		3 8 1 32

CUSTOMER Daniel Patrick   CUSTOMER NO. 185

DATE		ITEM	POST. REF.	DEBIT	CREDIT	DEBIT BALANCE
20-- July	1	Balance	✔			6 0 00
	8		S12	3 8 4 50		4 4 4 50

CUSTOMER Sandy Patterson   CUSTOMER NO. 190

DATE		ITEM	POST. REF.	DEBIT	CREDIT	DEBIT BALANCE
20-- July	1	Balance	✔			1 2 5 00

11-6 MASTERY PROBLEM, p. 333

Posting to general and subsidiary ledgers

1., 2.

SALES JOURNAL

	DATE		ACCOUNT DEBITED	SALE NO.	POST. REF.	ACCOUNTS RECEIVABLE DEBIT (1)	SALES CREDIT (2)	SALES TAX PAYABLE CREDIT (3)	
1	20-- Oct.	4	Jerome Lewis	658		2 2 7 6 88	2 1 4 8 00	1 2 8 88	1
2		12	Douglas Rieves	659		3 7 3 12	3 5 2 00	2 1 12	2
3		15	Amy Carson	660		2 0 6 4 88	1 9 4 8 00	1 1 6 88	3
4		23	John Frazier	661		1 5 6 3 50	1 4 7 5 00	8 8 50	4
5		31	Totals			6 2 7 8 38	5 9 2 3 00	3 5 5 38	5
6									6
7									7
8									8
9									9
10									10
11									11
12									12
13									13
14									14
15									15
16									16
17									17
18									18

11-6 MASTERY PROBLEM (continued)

1., 2.

PURCHASES JOURNAL   PAGE 10

	DATE		ACCOUNT CREDITED	PURCH. NO.	POST. REF.	PURCHASES DR. ACCTS. PAY. CR.	
1	20-- Oct.	5	Harman Supply	345		5 2 1 5 34	1
2		18	Mixon Industries	346		6 2 5 1 38	2
3		22	Alford Salvage	347		8 1 2 5 45	3
4		25	Reliable Auto	348		4 2 1 5 88	4
5		28	Harman Supply	349		3 6 4 8 80	5
6		30	Mixon Industries	350		2 5 1 5 84	6
7		31	Total			29 9 7 2 69	7
8							8
9							9
10							10
11							11
12							12
13							13
14							14
15							15
16							16
17							17
18							18
19							19
20							20
21							21
22							22
23							23
24							24
25							25

11-6 MASTERY PROBLEM (continued)

1.

GENERAL JOURNAL

PAGE 10

	DATE		ACCOUNT TITLE	DOC. NO.	POST. REF.	DEBIT	CREDIT	
1	Oct.	3	John Frazier	M77		8 2 5 00		1
2			Amy Carson				8 2 5 00	2
5		24	Accounts Payable/Alford Salvage	DM97		1 5 0 00		5
6			Purchases Returns and Allowances				1 5 0 00	6
7		25	Sales Returns and Allowances	CM151		3 0 0 00		7
8			Sales Tax Payable			1 8 00		8
9			Accounts Receivable/Jerome Lewis				3 1 8 00	9
10		28	Supplies—Store	M78		2 7 5 00		10
11			Accounts Payable/Mixon Industries				2 7 5 00	11
12								12
13								13

11-6 MASTERY PROBLEM (continued)

1., 2.

CASH RECEIPTS JOURNAL

PAGE 14

	DATE	ACCOUNT TITLE	DOC. NO.	POST. REF.	GENERAL DEBIT	GENERAL CREDIT	ACCOUNTS RECEIVABLE CREDIT	SALES CREDIT	SALES TAX PAYABLE CREDIT	SALES DISCOUNT DEBIT	CASH DEBIT	
1	Oct. 1	Jerome Lewis	R624				854 45				854 45	1
2	3		TS30	✔				5248 00	367 36		5615 36	2
3	10		TS31	✔				6004 00	420 28		6424 28	3
4	12	John Frazier	R625				2170 85			43 42	2127 43	4
5	17		TS32	✔				5495 00	384 65		5879 65	5
6	19	Douglas Rieves	R626				1694 34				1694 34	6
7	24		TS33	✔				5748 00	402 36		6150 36	7
8	26	Amy Carson	R627				420 25			8 41	411 84	8
9	31		TS34	✔				5258 00	368 06		5626 06	9
10	31	Totals					5139 89	27753 00	1942 71	51 83	34783 77	10
11												11
12												12
13												13
14												14

1., 2.

CASH PAYMENTS JOURNAL

PAGE 13

DATE		ACCOUNT TITLE	CK. NO.	POST. REF.	GENERAL DEBIT	GENERAL CREDIT	ACCOUNTS PAYABLE DEBIT	PURCHASES DISCOUNT CREDIT	CASH CREDIT	
20-- Oct.	2	Rent Expense	782		3 0 0 0 00				3 0 0 0 00	1
	4	Utilities Expense	783		7 5 1 25				7 5 1 25	2
	7	Alford Salvage	784				1 5 4 8 45	3 0 97	1 5 1 7 48	3
	8	Mixon Industries	785				2 1 5 8 45	4 3 17	2 1 1 5 28	4
	11	Harman Supply	790				1 4 1 7 25		1 4 1 7 25	5
	12	Reliable Auto	787				3 5 1 5 34	7 0 31	3 4 4 5 03	6
	13	Harman Supply	788				5 2 1 5 34		5 2 1 5 34	7
	14	Advertising Expense	789		2 5 0 0 00				2 5 0 0 00	8
	20	Miscellaneous Expense	786		2 3 4 25				2 3 4 25	9
	24	Supplies—Store	791		3 5 2 25				3 5 2 25	10
	27	Mixon Industries	792				6 2 5 1 38	1 2 5 03	6 1 2 6 35	11
	30	Supplies—Office	793		4 2 5 17				4 2 5 17	12
	31	Totals			7 2 6 2 92		20 1 0 6 21	2 6 9 48	27 0 9 9 65	13
										14
										15

11-6 MASTERY PROBLEM (continued)

1., 2.   **GENERAL LEDGER**

ACCOUNT Cash   ACCOUNT NO. 1110

DATE		ITEM	POST. REF.	DEBIT	CREDIT	BALANCE DEBIT	BALANCE CREDIT
20-- Oct.	1	Balance	✔			20 4 20 25	

ACCOUNT Accounts Receivable   ACCOUNT NO. 1130

DATE		ITEM	POST. REF.	DEBIT	CREDIT	BALANCE DEBIT	BALANCE CREDIT
20-- Oct.	1	Balance	✔			5 1 39 89	

ACCOUNT Supplies—Office   ACCOUNT NO. 1150

DATE		ITEM	POST. REF.	DEBIT	CREDIT	BALANCE DEBIT	BALANCE CREDIT
20-- Oct.	1	Balance	✔			2 5 14 20	

ACCOUNT Supplies—Store   ACCOUNT NO. 1160

DATE		ITEM	POST. REF.	DEBIT	CREDIT	BALANCE DEBIT	BALANCE CREDIT
20-- Oct.	1	Balance	✔			2 5 14 00	

ACCOUNT Accounts Payable   ACCOUNT NO. 2110

DATE		ITEM	POST. REF.	DEBIT	CREDIT	BALANCE DEBIT	BALANCE CREDIT
20-- Oct.	1	Balance	✔				8 6 39 49

ACCOUNT Sales Tax Payable   ACCOUNT NO. 2120

DATE		ITEM	POST. REF.	DEBIT	CREDIT	BALANCE	
						DEBIT	CREDIT
20-- Oct.	1	Balance	✔				8 2 4 25

ACCOUNT Sales   ACCOUNT NO. 4110

DATE		ITEM	POST. REF.	DEBIT	CREDIT	BALANCE	
						DEBIT	CREDIT
20-- Oct.	1	Balance	✔				214 7 1 5 25

ACCOUNT Sales Discount   ACCOUNT NO. 4120

DATE		ITEM	POST. REF.	DEBIT	CREDIT	BALANCE	
						DEBIT	CREDIT
20-- Oct.	1	Balance	✔			5 0 1 35	

ACCOUNT Sales Returns and Allowances   ACCOUNT NO. 4130

DATE		ITEM	POST. REF.	DEBIT	CREDIT	BALANCE	
						DEBIT	CREDIT
20-- Oct.	1	Balance	✔			1 5 9 3 50	

11-6 **MASTERY PROBLEM (continued)**

ACCOUNT Purchases   ACCOUNT NO. 5110

DATE	ITEM	POST. REF.	DEBIT	CREDIT	BALANCE DEBIT	BALANCE CREDIT
20-- Oct. 1	Balance	✔			140 684 34	

ACCOUNT Purchases Discount   ACCOUNT NO. 5120

DATE	ITEM	POST. REF.	DEBIT	CREDIT	BALANCE DEBIT	BALANCE CREDIT
20-- Oct. 1	Balance	✔				2 045 25

ACCOUNT Purchases Returns and Allowances   ACCOUNT NO. 5130

DATE	ITEM	POST. REF.	DEBIT	CREDIT	BALANCE DEBIT	BALANCE CREDIT
20-- Oct. 1	Balance	✔				2 477 00

ACCOUNT Advertising Expense   ACCOUNT NO. 6110

DATE	ITEM	POST. REF.	DEBIT	CREDIT	BALANCE DEBIT	BALANCE CREDIT
20-- Oct. 1	Balance	✔			25 848 45	

ACCOUNT Miscellaneous Expense   ACCOUNT NO. 6140

DATE		ITEM	POST. REF.	DEBIT	CREDIT	BALANCE	
						DEBIT	CREDIT
Oct.	1	Balance	✔			1 5 8 4 00	

ACCOUNT Rent Expense   ACCOUNT NO. 6160

DATE		ITEM	POST. REF.	DEBIT	CREDIT	BALANCE	
						DEBIT	CREDIT
Oct.	1	Balance	✔			30 0 0 0 00	

ACCOUNT Utilities Expense   ACCOUNT NO. 6190

DATE		ITEM	POST. REF.	DEBIT	CREDIT	BALANCE	
						DEBIT	CREDIT
Oct.	1	Balance	✔			8 7 4 5 45	

11-6 **MASTERY PROBLEM (continued)**

1., 3.   **ACCOUNTS RECEIVABLE LEDGER**

CUSTOMER Amy Carson   CUSTOMER NO. 110

DATE		ITEM	POST. REF.	DEBIT	CREDIT	DEBIT BALANCE
20-- Oct.	1	Balance	✔			1 2 4 5 25

CUSTOMER John Frazier   CUSTOMER NO. 120

DATE		ITEM	POST. REF.	DEBIT	CREDIT	DEBIT BALANCE
20-- Oct.	1	Balance	✔			1 3 4 5 85

CUSTOMER Jerome Lewis   CUSTOMER NO. 130

DATE		ITEM	POST. REF.	DEBIT	CREDIT	DEBIT BALANCE
20-- Oct.	1	Balance	✔			8 5 4 45

CUSTOMER Douglas Rieves   CUSTOMER NO. 140

DATE		ITEM	POST. REF.	DEBIT	CREDIT	DEBIT BALANCE
20-- Oct.	1	Balance	✔			1 6 9 4 34

1., 3.   **ACCOUNTS PAYABLE LEDGER**

VENDOR Alford Salvage   VENDOR NO. 210

DATE	ITEM	POST. REF.	DEBIT	CREDIT	CREDIT BALANCE
20-- Oct. 1	Balance	✔			1 5 4 8 45

VENDOR Harman Supply   VENDOR NO. 220

DATE	ITEM	POST. REF.	DEBIT	CREDIT	CREDIT BALANCE
20-- Oct. 1	Balance	✔			1 4 1 7 25

VENDOR Mixon Industries   VENDOR NO. 230

DATE	ITEM	POST. REF.	DEBIT	CREDIT	CREDIT BALANCE
20-- Oct. 1	Balance	✔			2 1 5 8 45

VENDOR Reliable Auto   VENDOR NO. 240

DATE	ITEM	POST. REF.	DEBIT	CREDIT	CREDIT BALANCE
20-- Oct. 1	Balance	✔			3 5 1 5 34

11-7 CHALLENGE PROBLEM, p. 333

Journalizing and posting business transactions

1., 2.

SALES JOURNAL

PAGE

	DATE	ACCOUNT DEBITED	SALE NO.	POST. REF.	1 ACCOUNTS RECEIVABLE DEBIT	2 SALES CREDIT	3 SALES TAX PAYABLE CREDIT	
1								1
2								2
3								3
4								4
5								5

1., 3.

PURCHASES JOURNAL

PAGE

	DATE	ACCOUNT CREDITED	PURCH. NO.	POST. REF.	PURCHASES DR. ACCTS. PAY. CR.	
1						1
2						2
3						3
4						4
5						5

1.

GENERAL JOURNAL

PAGE

	DATE	ACCOUNT TITLE	DOC. NO.	POST. REF.	DEBIT	CREDIT	
1							1
2							2
3							3
4							4
5							5

2. Sales Journal Proof

Col. No.	Column Title	Debit Totals	Credit Totals
1	Accounts Receivable Debit	_____	
2	Sales Credit		_____
3	Sales Tax Payable Credit		_____
	Totals	_____	_____

1., 4., 6.

CASH RECEIPTS JOURNAL

PAGE

DATE	ACCOUNT TITLE	DOC. NO.	POST. REF.	GENERAL DEBIT (1)	GENERAL CREDIT (2)	ACCOUNTS RECEIVABLE CREDIT (3)	SALES CREDIT (4)	SALES TAX PAYABLE CREDIT (5)	CASH DEBIT (6)	
										1
										2
										3
										4
										5
										6
										7
										8
										9
										10
										11

4. Cash Receipts Journal Proof

Col. No.	Column Title	Debit Totals	Credit Totals
1	General Debit		
2	General Credit		
3	Accounts Receivable Credit		
4	Sales Credit		
5	Sales Tax Payable Credit		
6	Cash Debit		
	Totals		

11-7 CHALLENGE PROBLEM (continued)

1., 4., 7.

CASH PAYMENTS JOURNAL

PAGE 5

DATE	ACCOUNT TITLE	CK. NO.	POST. REF.	GENERAL DEBIT	GENERAL CREDIT	ACCOUNTS PAYABLE DEBIT	PURCHASES DISCOUNT CREDIT	CASH CREDIT	
									1
									2
									3
									4
									5
									6
									7
									8
									9
									10
									11
									12
									13
									14

4. Cash Payments Journal Proof

Column Title	Debit Column Totals	Credit Column Totals
General Debit · · · · · · · · · · · · · ·		
General Credit · · · · · · · · · · · · ·		
Accounts Payable Debit · · · · · · ·		
Purchases Discount Credit · · · · · ·		
Cash Credit · · · · · · · · · · · · · ·		
Totals · · · · · · · · · · · · · · · ·		

5.

CASH PROOF

Cash on hand at the beginning of the month .... _____

Plus total cash received during the month .... _____

Equals total .... _____

Less total cash paid during the month .... _____

Equals cash balance on hand at end of the month .... _____

Checkbook balance on the next unused check stub .... _____

8.

11-7 CHALLENGE PROBLEM (continued)

1., 2., 3., 6., 7.   **GENERAL LEDGER**

ACCOUNT Cash   ACCOUNT NO. 1110

DATE	ITEM	POST. REF.	DEBIT	CREDIT	BALANCE DEBIT	BALANCE CREDIT
20-- Oct. 1	Balance	✔			20 2 2 0 00	

ACCOUNT Accounts Receivable   ACCOUNT NO. 1130

DATE	ITEM	POST. REF.	DEBIT	CREDIT	BALANCE DEBIT	BALANCE CREDIT
20-- Oct. 1	Balance	✔			3 4 7 9 40	

ACCOUNT Supplies—Office   ACCOUNT NO. 1150

DATE	ITEM	POST. REF.	DEBIT	CREDIT	BALANCE DEBIT	BALANCE CREDIT
20-- Oct. 1	Balance	✔			3 1 6 2 00	

ACCOUNT Supplies—Store   ACCOUNT NO. 1160

DATE	ITEM	POST. REF.	DEBIT	CREDIT	BALANCE DEBIT	BALANCE CREDIT
20-- Oct. 1	Balance	✔			2 5 9 2 00	

ACCOUNT Accounts Payable   ACCOUNT NO. 2110

DATE	ITEM	POST. REF.	DEBIT	CREDIT	BALANCE DEBIT	BALANCE CREDIT
20-- Oct. 1	Balance	✔				9 6 2 7 60

ACCOUNT Sales Tax Payable   ACCOUNT NO. 2120

DATE	ITEM	POST. REF.	DEBIT	CREDIT	BALANCE DEBIT	BALANCE CREDIT
20-- Oct. 1	Balance	✔				1 5 7 4 40

1., 2., 3., 6., 7. **GENERAL LEDGER**

ACCOUNT Sales   ACCOUNT NO. 4110

DATE		ITEM	POST. REF.	DEBIT	CREDIT	BALANCE DEBIT	BALANCE CREDIT
Oct.	1	Balance	✔				262 49 8 80

ACCOUNT Purchases   ACCOUNT NO. 5110

DATE		ITEM	POST. REF.	DEBIT	CREDIT	BALANCE DEBIT	BALANCE CREDIT
Oct.	1	Balance	✔			135 0 0 0 00	

ACCOUNT Purchases Discount   ACCOUNT NO. 5120

DATE		ITEM	POST. REF.	DEBIT	CREDIT	BALANCE DEBIT	BALANCE CREDIT
Oct.	1	Balance	✔				4 5 8 60

ACCOUNT Advertising Expense   ACCOUNT NO. 6110

DATE		ITEM	POST. REF.	DEBIT	CREDIT	BALANCE DEBIT	BALANCE CREDIT
Oct.	1	Balance	✔			3 5 2 8 00	

ACCOUNT Miscellaneous Expense   ACCOUNT NO. 6140

DATE		ITEM	POST. REF.	DEBIT	CREDIT	BALANCE DEBIT	BALANCE CREDIT
Oct.	1	Balance	✔			1 6 9 2 00	

11-7 CHALLENGE PROBLEM (continued)

1., 2., 3., 6., 7.   **GENERAL LEDGER**

ACCOUNT Rent Expense   ACCOUNT NO. 6160

DATE	ITEM	POST. REF.	DEBIT	CREDIT	BALANCE DEBIT	BALANCE CREDIT
20-- Oct. 1	Balance	✔			10 3 5 0 00	

ACCOUNT Utilities Expense   ACCOUNT NO. 6190

DATE	ITEM	POST. REF.	DEBIT	CREDIT	BALANCE DEBIT	BALANCE CREDIT
20-- Oct. 1	Balance	✔			2 1 4 2 00	

1.   **ACCOUNTS PAYABLE LEDGER**

VENDOR Design Golf   VENDOR NO. 210

DATE	ITEM	POST. REF.	DEBIT	CREDIT	CREDIT BALANCE
20-- Oct. 1	Balance	✔			2 9 1 6 00

VENDOR Eagle Golf Equipment   VENDOR NO. 220

DATE	ITEM	POST. REF.	DEBIT	CREDIT	CREDIT BALANCE
20-- Oct. 1	Balance	✔			2 3 5 8 00

VENDOR Golf Source   VENDOR NO. 230

DATE	ITEM	POST. REF.	DEBIT	CREDIT	CREDIT BALANCE

VENDOR Pro Golf Supply   VENDOR NO. 240

DATE	ITEM	POST. REF.	DEBIT	CREDIT	CREDIT BALANCE
20-- Oct. 1	Balance	✔			1 1 3 7 60

1.

ACCOUNTS PAYABLE LEDGER

VENDOR Vista Golf Co. VENDOR NO. 250

DATE		ITEM	POST. REF.	DEBIT	CREDIT	CREDIT BALANCE
20-- Oct.	1	Balance	✔			3 2 1 6 00

ACCOUNTS RECEIVABLE LEDGER

CUSTOMER David Bench CUSTOMER NO. 110

DATE		ITEM	POST. REF.	DEBIT	CREDIT	DEBIT BALANCE
20-- Oct.	1	Balance	✔			9 7 2 00

CUSTOMER Viola Davis CUSTOMER NO. 120

DATE		ITEM	POST. REF.	DEBIT	CREDIT	DEBIT BALANCE
20-- Oct.	1	Balance	✔			8 2 9 44

CUSTOMER Barry Fuller CUSTOMER NO. 130

DATE		ITEM	POST. REF.	DEBIT	CREDIT	DEBIT BALANCE

CUSTOMER Doris McCarley CUSTOMER NO. 140

DATE		ITEM	POST. REF.	DEBIT	CREDIT	DEBIT BALANCE
20-- Oct.	1	Balance	✔			1 3 9 2 84

CUSTOMER Leona Silva CUSTOMER NO. 150

DATE		ITEM	POST. REF.	DEBIT	CREDIT	DEBIT BALANCE
20-- Oct.	1	Balance	✔			2 8 5 12

11-7 CHALLENGE PROBLEM (concluded)

9. Approaches to Collecting and Paying Sales Taxes

_____

_____

_____

_____

_____

_____

_____

_____

_____

_____

_____

_____

_____

_____

_____

_____

_____

_____

_____

_____

_____

_____

_____

_____

_____

_____

_____

_____

_____

_____

_____

_____

_____

_____

_____

_____

_____

_____

_____

_____

_____

_____

Study Guide 12

Name	Perfect Score	Your Score
Identifying Accounting Terms	12 Pts.	
Analyzing Payroll Procedures	5 Pts.	
Identifying Accounting Practices	23 Pts.	
Total	40 Pts.	

Part One—Identifying Accounting Terms

Directions: Select the one term in Column I that best fits each definition in Column II. Print the letter identifying your choice in the Answers column.

Column I	Column II	Answers
A. employee earnings record	**1.** The money paid for employee services. (p. 340)	1. _____
B. Medicare tax	**2.** The period covered by a salary payment. (p. 340)	2. _____
C. net pay	**3.** The total amount earned by all employees for a pay period. (p. 340)	3. _____
D. pay period	**4.** The total pay due for a pay period before deductions. (p. 343)	4. _____
E. payroll	**5.** Taxes based on the payroll of a business. (p. 345)	5. _____
F. payroll register	**6.** A deduction from total earnings for each person legally supported by a taxpayer, including the employee. (p. 346)	6. _____
G. payroll taxes	**7.** A federal tax paid for old-age, survivors, and disability insurance. (p. 349)	7. _____
H. salary	**8.** A federal tax paid for hospital insurance. (p. 349)	8. _____
I. social security tax	**9.** The maximum amount of earnings on which a tax is calculated. (p. 349)	9. _____
J. tax base	**10.** A business form used to record payroll information. (p. 351)	10. _____
K. total earnings	**11.** The total earnings paid to an employee after payroll taxes and other deductions. (p. 352)	11. _____
L. withholding allowance	**12.** A business form used to record details affecting payments made to an employee. (p. 353)	12. _____

Part Two—Analyzing Payroll Procedures

Directions: For each of the following items, select the choice that best completes the statement. Print the letter of your choice in the Answers column.

1. How many hours were worked by an employee who arrived at 8:10 a.m. and departed at 12:10 p.m.? (A) 4 hours (B) 5 hours (C) 4 hours and 10 minutes (D) none of these. (p. 342)

   1. _____

2. How many hours were worked by an employee who arrived at 7:05 a.m. and departed at 6:05 p.m. with one hour off for lunch? (A) 11 hours (B) 10 hours (C) 12 hours (D) none of these. (p. 342)

   2. _____

3. Employee regular earnings are calculated as (A) regular hours times regular rate (B) total hours divided by regular rate (C) total hours plus overtime rate (D) overtime hours minus overtime rate. (p. 343)

   3. _____

4. Social security tax is calculated on (A) total earnings and marital status (B) number of withholding allowances (C) total earnings and number of withholding allowances (D) employee earnings up to a maximum paid in a calendar year. (p. 349)

   4. _____

5. A separate payroll checking account is used primarily to (A) simplify the payroll accounting system (B) help reduce the cost of preparing a payroll (C) provide additional protection and control payroll payments (D) eliminate employer earnings records. (p. 356)

   5. _____

Part Three—Identifying Accounting Practices

Directions: Place a *T* for True or an *F* for False in the Answers column to
show whether each of the following statements is true or false.

Answers

1. A business may decide to pay employee salaries every week, every two weeks, twice a
   month, or once a month. (p. 340)

   1. _____

2. Businesses use payroll records to inform employees of their annual earnings and to
   prepare payroll reports for the government. (p. 340)

   2. _____

3. Payroll time cards can be used as the basic source of information to prepare a payroll.
   (p. 341)

   3. _____

4. The first task in preparing a payroll is to determine the number of days worked by each
   employee. (p. 342)

   4. _____

5. Total earnings are sometimes referred to as net pay or net earnings. (p. 343)

   5. _____

6. Employee total earnings are calculated as regular hours × regular rate, plus overtime
   hours × overtime rate. (p. 343)

   6. _____

7. Payroll taxes withheld represent a liability for an employer until payment is made to the
   government. (p. 345)

   7. _____

8. A business is required by law to withhold federal income taxes from employee total
   earnings. (p. 345)

   8. _____

9. Employers in many states are required to withhold state, city, or county income tax from
   employee earnings. (p. 345)

   9. _____

10. Employers are required to have a current Form W-4, Employee's Withholding Allowance
    Certificate, for all employees. (p. 346)

    10. _____

11. The amount of income tax withheld from each employee's total earnings is determined
    from the number of withholding allowances and by the employee's marital status.
    (p. 346)

    11. _____

12. A single person will have less income tax withheld than a married employee. (p. 346)

    12. _____

13. The larger the number of withholding allowances claimed, the larger the amount of
    income tax withheld. (p. 346)

    13. _____

14. An employee can be exempt from having federal income tax withheld under certain
    conditions. (p. 346)

    14. _____

    15. _____

15. Social security tax is paid by the employer only. (p. 349)

16. An act of Congress can change the social security tax base and tax rate at any time. (p. 349)

    16. _____

17. When an employee's earnings exceed the tax base, no more social security tax is deducted.
    (p. 349)

    17. _____

18. All deductions from employee wages are recorded in a payroll register. (p. 351)

    18. _____

19. The columns of the employee earnings record consist of the amount columns in a payroll
    register and an accumulated earnings column. (p. 353)

    19. _____

20. A new earnings record is prepared for each employee each year. (p. 353)

    20. _____

21. A check for the total net pay is written and deposited in the payroll checking account. (p. 356)

22. The information used to prepare payroll checks is taken from a payroll register. (p. 357)

23. When EFT is used, the employee does not receive an individual check. (p. 357)

12-1 WORK TOGETHER, p. 344

Calculating total earnings

Employee Number	Hours Worked		Regular Rate	Earnings		Total Earnings
	Regular	Overtime		Regular	Overtime	
1	40	5	$ 9.00	_____	_____	_____
2	40	3	12.50	_____	_____	_____
3	30	0	9.75	_____	_____	_____
4	40	2	11.00	_____	_____	_____

12-1 ON YOUR OWN, p. 344

Calculating total earnings

Employee Number	Hours Worked		Regular Rate	Earnings		Total Earnings
	Regular	Overtime		Regular	Overtime	
1	40	3	$ 8.80	_____	_____	_____
2	30	0	9.00	_____	_____	_____
3	40	3	10.70	_____	_____	_____
4	40	4	12.00	_____	_____	_____

12-2 WORK TOGETHER, p. 350

Determining payroll tax withholding

No.	Name	Marital Status	Number of Withholding Allowances	Total Earnings	Federal Income Tax Withholding	Social Security Tax Withholding	Medicare Tax Withholding
3	Bates, Eric C.	M	2	$1,090.00	_____	_____	_____
4	Cohen, Jason K.	S	1	840.00	_____	_____	_____
1	Grimes, Christi L.	M	3	1,020.00	_____	_____	_____
6	Key, Sharon C.	S	2	980.00	_____	_____	_____

12-2 ON YOUR OWN, p. 350

Determining payroll tax withholding

No.	Name	Marital Status	Number of Withholding Allowances	Total Earnings	Federal Income Tax Withholding	Social Security Tax Withholding	Medicare Tax Withholding
2	Burdine, Ralph C.	S	2	$ 875.00	_____	_____	_____
5	Gibson, Jane L.	M	3	1,080.00	_____	_____	_____
7	Monroy, Tom E.	S	1	1,200.00	_____	_____	_____
9	Tiffin, Andrea P.	M	0	1,030.00	_____	_____	_____

12-3   WORK TOGETHER, p. 355

Preparing payroll records

1., 2.

PAYROLL REGISTER

SEMIMONTHLY PERIOD ENDED _____   DATE OF PAYMENT _____

EMPL. NO.	EMPLOYEE'S NAME	MARI-TAL STATUS	NO. OF ALLOW-ANCES	EARNINGS REGULAR	EARNINGS OVERTIME	EARNINGS TOTAL	DEDUCTIONS FEDERAL INCOME TAX	SOC. SEC. TAX	MEDICARE TAX	HEALTH INSURANCE	OTHER	TOTAL	NET PAY	CHECK NO.
5	Hensley, Judy	M	2	1040 00	39 00									1
9	McCune, Mike	S	1	920 00	51 75									2
														3
22														22

OTHER DEDUCTIONS: B—U.S. SAVINGS BONDS; UW—UNITED WAY

3.

EARNINGS RECORD FOR QUARTER ENDED _____

EMPLOYEE NO. _____   LAST NAME _____   FIRST _____   MIDDLE INITIAL _____   MARITAL STATUS _____   WITHHOLDING ALLOWANCES _____

RATE OF PAY _____ PER HR. _____ SOCIAL SECURITY NO. _____   POSITION _____

PAY PERIOD NO.	ENDED	EARNINGS REGULAR	EARNINGS OVERTIME	EARNINGS TOTAL	DEDUCTIONS FEDERAL INCOME TAX	SOC. SEC. TAX	MEDICARE TAX	HEALTH INSURANCE	OTHER	TOTAL	NET PAY	ACCUMULATED EARNINGS
1												
7	QUARTERLY TOTALS											

OTHER DEDUCTIONS: B—U.S. SAVINGS BONDS; UW—UNITED WAY

Preparing payroll records

1., 2.

PAYROLL REGISTER

SEMIMONTHLY PERIOD ENDED _____ DATE OF PAYMENT _____

EMPL. NO.	EMPLOYEE'S NAME	MARI-TAL STATUS	NO. OF ALLOW-ANCES	EARNINGS			DEDUCTIONS						NET PAY	CHECK NO.
				REGULAR	OVERTIME	TOTAL	FEDERAL INCOME TAX	SOC. SEC. TAX	MEDICARE TAX	HEALTH INSURANCE	OTHER	TOTAL		
				1	2	3	4	5	6	7	8	9	10	
1	4	Best, Allen P.	M	4	1 1 0 0 00										1
2	8	Edwards, Tammy S.	S	1	9 2 4 00	9 4 50									2
3															3
22															22

OTHER DEDUCTIONS: B—U.S. SAVINGS BONDS; UW—UNITED WAY

3.

EARNINGS RECORD FOR QUARTER ENDED _____

EMPLOYEE NO. _____ LAST NAME _____ FIRST _____ MIDDLE INITIAL _____ MARITAL STATUS _____ WITHHOLDING ALLOWANCES _____

RATE OF PAY _____ PER HR. _____ SOCIAL SECURITY NO. _____ POSITION _____

PAY PERIOD		EARNINGS			DEDUCTIONS					NET PAY	ACCUMULATED EARNINGS
NO.	ENDED	REGULAR	OVERTIME	TOTAL	FEDERAL INCOME TAX	SOC. SEC. TAX	MEDICARE TAX	HEALTH INSURANCE	OTHER	TOTAL		
		1	2	3	4	5	6	7	8	9	10	11
1												
7	QUARTERLY TOTALS											

OTHER DEDUCTIONS: B—U.S. SAVINGS BONDS; UW—UNITED WAY

Name _____ Date _____ Class _____

12-4 WORK TOGETHER, p. 358

Preparing payroll checks

1., 2.

NO. **599**				
Date: ___ 20___ $ _____				
To: _____				
_____				
For: _____				
_____				

BAL. BRO'T. FOR'D				
AMT. DEPOSITED				
TOTAL				
AMT. THIS CHECK				
BAL. CAR'D. FOR'D				

GENERAL ACCOUNT   NO. **599**   66-877 / 530

ANTIQUE SHOP   _____ 20 _____

PAY TO THE ORDER OF _____ $ _____

_____ DOLLARS

For Classroom Use Only

Peoples Bank and Trust
Charlotte, NC 28206-8444

⑆053008774⑆ 0639580⑆ 599

CHECK NO. **186**	
PERIOD ENDING	
EARNINGS	$
REG.	$
O.T.	$
DEDUCTIONS	$
INC. TAX	$
SOC. SEC. TAX	$
MED. TAX	$
HEALTH INS.	$
OTHER	$
NET PAY	$

PAYROLL ACCOUNT   66-877 / 530

_____ 20 _____   NO. **186**

PAY TO THE ORDER OF _____ $ _____

_____ DOLLARS

For Classroom Use Only   ANTIQUE SHOP

Peoples Bank and Trust
Charlotte, NC 28206-8444

⑆053008774⑆ 0639583⑆ 186

CHECK NO. **187**	
PERIOD ENDING	
EARNINGS	$
REG.	$
O.T.	$
DEDUCTIONS	$
INC. TAX	$
SOC. SEC. TAX	$
MED. TAX	$
HEALTH INS.	$
OTHER	$
NET PAY	$

PAYROLL ACCOUNT   66-877 / 530

_____ 20 _____   NO. **187**

PAY TO THE ORDER OF _____ $ _____

_____ DOLLARS

For Classroom Use Only   ANTIQUE SHOP

Peoples Bank and Trust
Charlotte, NC 28206-8444

⑆053008774⑆ 0639583⑆ 187

Preparing payroll checks

1., 2.

NO. **824**

Date: _____ 20___ $_____

To: _____

For: _____

_____

BAL. BRO'T. FOR'D			
AMT. DEPOSITED			
TOTAL			
AMT. THIS CHECK			
BAL. CAR'D. FOR'D			

GENERAL ACCOUNT   NO. **824** $\frac{66\text{-}877}{530}$

THE SIGN SHOP

_____ 20 _____

PAY TO THE ORDER OF _____ $ _____

_____ DOLLARS

For Classroom Use Only

Peoples Bank and Trust
Charlotte, NC 28206-8444

⑆053008774⑆ 196223642⑈ 824

____

CHECK NO. **325**

PERIOD ENDING			
EARNINGS	$		
REG.	$		
O.T.	$		
DEDUCTIONS	$		
INC. TAX	$		
SOC. SEC. TAX	$		
MED. TAX	$		
HEALTH INS.	$		
OTHER	$		
NET PAY	$		

PAYROLL ACCOUNT $\frac{66\text{-}877}{530}$

_____ 20 _____   NO. **325**

PAY TO THE ORDER OF _____ $ _____

_____ DOLLARS

For Classroom Use Only

THE SIGN SHOP

Peoples Bank and Trust
Charlotte, NC 28206-8444

⑆053008774⑆ 14672196⑈ 325

____

CHECK NO. **326**

PERIOD ENDING			
EARNINGS	$		
REG.	$		
O.T.	$		
DEDUCTIONS	$		
INC. TAX	$		
SOC. SEC. TAX	$		
MED. TAX	$		
HEALTH INS.	$		
OTHER	$		
NET PAY	$		

PAYROLL ACCOUNT $\frac{66\text{-}877}{530}$

_____ 20 _____   NO. **326**

PAY TO THE ORDER OF _____ $ _____

_____ DOLLARS

For Classroom Use Only

THE SIGN SHOP

Peoples Bank and Trust
Charlotte, NC 28206-8444

⑆053008774⑆ 14672196⑈ 326

12-1   APPLICATION PROBLEM, p. 360

Preparing payroll time cards

1., 2.

EMPLOYEE NO. 14

NAME Marie L. Kerns
PERIOD ENDING April 15, 20 – –

Day	MORNING IN	OUT	AFTERNOON IN	OUT	OVERTIME IN	OUT	HOURS REG	OT
2	759	1201	1256	501				
3	757	1202	1257	502				
4	756	1201	1258	504	701	802		
5	802	1204	101	506				
6	756	1203	1259	500				
9	759	1200	1259	459	559	731		
10	800	1200	1258	501				
11	759	1202	1257	506				
12	756	1159	1256	502	558	732		
13	757	1203	1257	501				

	HOURS	RATE	AMOUNT
REGULAR		11.80	
OVERTIME			
TOTAL HOURS		TOTAL EARNINGS	

EMPLOYEE NO. 11

NAME Henry F. Miller
PERIOD ENDING April 15, 20 – –

Day	MORNING IN	OUT	AFTERNOON IN	OUT	OVERTIME IN	OUT	HOURS REG	OT
2	757	1201	1259	502				
3	757	1202	1258	501				
4	756	1204	100	501	556	659		
5	757	1205	1259	500				
6	759	1205	100	502				
6	757	1204	1259	505				
10	758	1205	1256	504	600	731		
11	756	1202	1257	502				
12	756	1201	1259	501	700	932		
13	757	1200	101	500				

	HOURS	RATE	AMOUNT
REGULAR		9.80	
OVERTIME			
TOTAL HOURS		TOTAL EARNINGS	

EMPLOYEE NO. 16

NAME Sylvia A. Rodriguez
PERIOD ENDING April 15, 20 – –

Day	MORNING IN	OUT	AFTERNOON IN	OUT	OVERTIME IN	OUT	HOURS REG	OT
2	758	1202	1259	503				
3	757	1203	100	500	702	832		
4	800	1200	1259	500				
5	759	1201	1258	504				
6	759	1202	1255	503				
6	758	1201	1256	502				
10	756	1200	1257	501				
11	757	1202	1257	458				
12	758	1200	1259	501				
13	759	1204	1259	500				

	HOURS	RATE	AMOUNT
REGULAR		9.20	
OVERTIME			
TOTAL HOURS		TOTAL EARNINGS	

Determining payroll tax withholding

1., 2.

	Employee		Number of		Federal	Social Security	Medicare
No.	Name	Marital Status	Withholding Allowances	Total Earnings	Income Tax Withholding	Tax Withholding	Tax Withholding
2	Baird, Tony W.	M	2	$1,220.00	_____	_____	_____
6	Delgado, Rudy C.	M	3	1,090.00	_____	_____	_____
3	Garza, Kay H.	S	1	940.00	_____	_____	_____
1	Hess, Monica T.	M	5	1,060.00	_____	_____	_____
8	Levy, Irving S.	S	1	910.00	_____	_____	_____
7	Minick, Esther A.	S	2	990.00	_____	_____	_____
4	Pharr, Angela S.	S	1	900.00	_____	_____	_____
5	Reiner, Greg R.	M	3	1,250.00	_____	_____	_____

12-3 APPLICATION PROBLEM, p. 360

Preparing a payroll register

PAYROLL REGISTER

SEMIMONTHLY PERIOD ENDED _____ DATE OF PAYMENT _____

EMPL. NO.	EMPLOYEE'S NAME	MARI-TAL STATUS	NO. OF ALLOW-ANCES	EARNINGS REGULAR	OVERTIME	TOTAL	DEDUCTIONS FEDERAL INCOME TAX	SOC. SEC. TAX	MEDICARE TAX	HEALTH INSURANCE	OTHER	TOTAL	NET PAY	CHECK NO.
9	Bast, John P.	S	2	1082 40						42 00	10 00			1
2	Clemmons, Jan C.	M	3	1134 00						60 00				2
8	Glazner, Tom S.	S	1	688 00						35 00	20 00			3
1	Holtman, Mark T.	M	4	959 20	65 40					90 00				4
7	Jones, John David	M	2	1364 00						42 00	20 00			5
10	Young, Justin L.	S	1	1040 60						35 00	25 00			6
3	LeBlanc, Patrick G.	M	1	1050 00						35 00				7
6	Pullen, Sharon S.	M	2	1179 20	40 20					42 00				8
11	Shappley, Mary A.	S	2	1249 60						42 00				9
4	Terrell, Terry R.	M	1	903 00						35 00				10
12	Wheat, Andrew P.	M	3	1100 00	93 75					60 00	20 00			11
5	Yates, Gerie V.	S	1	787 50						35 00	25 00			12
13														13
14														14
15														15
16														16
17														17
18														18
19														19
20														20
21														21
22														22
23														23
24														24
25														25

OTHER DEDUCTIONS: B—U.S. SAVINGS BONDS; UW—UNITED WAY

Preparing an employee earnings record
1., 2., 3., 4.

EARNINGS RECORD FOR QUARTER ENDED

EMPLOYEE NO. _____   LAST NAME _____   FIRST _____   MIDDLE INITIAL _____   SOCIAL SECURITY NO. _____

RATE OF PAY _____   PER HR. _____   MARITAL STATUS _____   POSITION _____   WITHHOLDING ALLOWANCES _____

NO.	PAY PERIOD ENDED	EARNINGS REGULAR 1	OVERTIME 2	TOTAL 3	DEDUCTIONS FEDERAL INCOME TAX 4	SOC. SEC. TAX 5	MEDICARE TAX 6	HEALTH INSURANCE 7	OTHER 8	TOTAL 9	NET PAY 10	ACCUMULATED EARNINGS 11
1	7/15	1320 00	45 00	1365 00	87 00	84 63	19 79	60 00	B 20 00	271 42	1093 58	
2	7/31	1200 00	90 00	1290 00	75 00	79 98	18 71	60 00	B 20 00	253 69	1036 31	
3	8/15	1320 00		1320 00	81 00	81 84	19 14	60 00	B 20 00	261 98	1058 02	
4	8/31	1020 00		1020 00	44 00	63 24	14 79	60 00	B 20 00	202 03	817 97	
5	9/15	1320 00	135 00	1455 00								
6	9/30	1200 00		1200 00								
7	QUARTERLY TOTALS											

OTHER DEDUCTIONS: B—U.S. SAVINGS BONDS; UW—UNITED WAY

Name _____ Date _____ Class _____

Preparing payroll checks

1., 2.

NO. **630**		GENERAL ACCOUNT	NO. **630**	$\frac{66\text{-}877}{530}$

NO. **630**

Date: ____ 20___ $_____

To: _____

For: _____

BAL. BRO'T. FOR'D

AMT. DEPOSITED

TOTAL

AMT. THIS CHECK

BAL. CAR'D. FOR'D

GENERAL ACCOUNT

NO. **630** $\frac{66\text{-}877}{530}$

ROYAL APPLIANCES   _____ 20 _____

PAY TO THE
ORDER OF _____ $ _____

_____ DOLLARS

For Classroom Use Only

Peoples Bank and Trust
Charlotte, NC 28206-8444

⑊053008774⑊ 018654210⑊ 630

CHECK NO. **823**

PERIOD ENDING

EARNINGS $

REG. $

O.T. $

DEDUCTIONS $

INC. TAX $

SOC. SEC. TAX $

MEDICARE TAX $

HEALTH INS. $

OTHER $

NET PAY $

PAYROLL ACCOUNT

_____ 20 _____

NO. **823**

PAY TO THE
ORDER OF _____ $ _____

_____ DOLLARS

For Classroom Use Only   ROYAL APPLIANCES

Peoples Bank and Trust
Charlotte, NC 28206-8444

⑊053008774⑊ 018654237⑊ 823

CHECK NO. **827**

PERIOD ENDING

EARNINGS $

REG. $

O.T. $

DEDUCTIONS $

INC. TAX $

SOC. SEC. TAX $

MEDICARE TAX $

HEALTH INS. $

OTHER $

NET PAY $

PAYROLL ACCOUNT

_____ 20 _____

NO. **827**

PAY TO THE
ORDER OF _____ $ _____

_____ DOLLARS

For Classroom Use Only   ROYAL APPLIANCES

Peoples Bank and Trust
Charlotte, NC 28206-8444

⑊053008774⑊ 018654237⑊ 827

Preparing a semimonthly payroll

1.

PAYROLL REGISTER

SEMIMONTHLY PERIOD ENDED _____   DATE OF PAYMENT _____

EMPL. NO.	EMPLOYEE'S NAME	MARI-TAL STATUS	NO. OF ALLOW-ANCES	EARNINGS REGULAR (1)	OVERTIME (2)	TOTAL (3)	DEDUCTIONS FEDERAL INCOME TAX (4)	SOC. SEC. TAX (5)	MEDICARE TAX (6)	HEALTH INSURANCE (7)	OTHER (8)	TOTAL (9)	NET PAY (10)	CHECK NO.
5	Acron, Peter C.	M	3	1126 40	115 20					60 00	10 00			1
7	Barenis, Mary P.	S	1	1155 00						25 00				2
6	Epps, John P.	M	2	792 00						40 00	10 00			3
1	Goforth, Alice A.	S	2	1135 20	77 40					40 00				4
8	Hiett, Franklin B.	M	3	1188 00						60 00	10 00			5
9	Land, Keith	S	1	954 60						25 00	10 00			6
2	Malone, Lillie L.	S	1	1083 60						25 00				7
4	Rivers, Linda K.	M	2	1091 20	93 00					40 00				8
10	Sowell, Jacob S.	M	2	1161 60						40 00	10 00			9
3	Vole, Ryan V.	M	5	1075 00						80 00	10 00			10
														11
														12
														13
														14
														15
														16
														17
														18
														19
														20
														21
														22
														23
														24
														25

OTHER DEDUCTIONS: B—U.S. SAVINGS BONDS; UW—UNITED WAY

12-6 MASTERY PROBLEM (concluded)

2., 3.

NO. **928**

Date: _____ 20___ $ _____

To: _____

For: _____

_____

BAL. BRO'T. FOR'D		
AMT. DEPOSITED		
TOTAL		
AMT. THIS CHECK		
BAL. CAR'D. FOR'D		

GENERAL ACCOUNT　　NO. **928**　　8-8335/430

_____ 20 _____

PAY TO THE ORDER OF _____ $ _____

_____ DOLLARS

For Classroom Use Only

First Security Bank of Pittsburgh
Pittsburgh, PA 15210-3402

⑆043083356⑆ 005972164⑈ 928

CHECK NO. **1692**

PERIOD ENDING	
EARNINGS	$
REG.	$
O.T.	$
DEDUCTIONS	$
INC. TAX	$
SOC. SEC. TAX	$
MED. TAX	$
HEALTH INS.	$
OTHER	$
NET PAY	$

PAYROLL ACCOUNT　　8-8335/430

_____ 20 _____

NO. **1692**

PAY TO THE ORDER OF _____ $ _____

_____ DOLLARS

For Classroom Use Only

First Security Bank of Pittsburgh
Pittsburgh, PA 15210-3402

⑆043083356⑆ 005972165⑈ 1692

CHECK NO. **1696**

PERIOD ENDING	
EARNINGS	$
REG.	$
O.T.	$
DEDUCTIONS	$
INC. TAX	$
SOC. SEC. TAX	$
MED. TAX	$
HEALTH INS.	$
OTHER	$
NET PAY	$

PAYROLL ACCOUNT　　8-8335/430

_____ 20 _____

NO. **1696**

PAY TO THE ORDER OF _____ $ _____

_____ DOLLARS

For Classroom Use Only

First Security Bank of Pittsburgh
Pittsburgh, PA 15210-3402

⑆043083356⑆ 005972165⑈ 1696

Calculating piecework wages

PAYROLL REGISTER

SEMIMONTHLY PERIOD ENDED _____

DATE OF PAYMENT _____

EMPL. NO.	EMPLOYEE'S NAME	MARI-TAL STATUS	NO. OF ALLOW-ANCES	EARNINGS			DEDUCTIONS							NET PAY	CHECK NO.
				1 REGULAR	2 INCENTIVE	3 TOTAL	4 FEDERAL INCOME TAX	5 SOC. SEC. TAX	6 MEDICARE TAX	7 HEALTH INSURANCE	8 OTHER	9 TOTAL		10	
1 C3	Bell, Julie M.	M	4												1
2 C6	Hairston, Gary P.	M	2												2
3 C9	Reeves, John M.	S	1												3
4 A2	Bullock, Amy C.	S	2												4
5 A6	Green, Steven P.	S	1												5
6 A9	Prine, Jacob R.	M	4												6
7 F5	Gerez, Dave A.	M	2												7
8 F2	Kyle, Ryan G.	S	1												8
9															9
10															10
11															11
12															12
13															13
14															14
15															15
16															16
17															17
18															18
19															19
20															20
21															21
22															22
23															23
24															24
25															25

OTHER DEDUCTIONS: B—U.S. SAVINGS BONDS; UW—UNITED WAY

Name	Perfect Score	Your Score
Analyzing Payroll Records	15 Pts.	
Analyzing Transactions Affecting Payroll	5 Pts.	
Analyzing Form W-2	10 Pts.	
Total	30 Pts.	

Part One—Analyzing Payroll Records

Directions: For each of the following items, select the choice that best completes the statement. Print the letter identifying your choice in the Answers column.

Answers

1. All the payroll information needed to prepare a payroll and tax reports is found on (A) Form W-4 and the employee earnings record (B) Form W-4 and the payroll register (C) the payroll register and the employee earnings record (D) Form W-4. (p. 368)

1. _____

2. The payroll journal entry is based on the totals of the (A) Earnings Total column, each deduction column, and the Net Pay column (B) Earnings Total, Earnings Regular, Earnings Overtime, and Deductions Total columns (C) Earnings Regular, Earnings Overtime, and Deductions Total columns (D) Earnings Total, Earnings Regular, and Earnings Overtime Total columns. (p. 369)

2. _____

3. The Earnings Total column total is journalized as a debit to (A) Cash (B) Salary Expense (C) Employee Income Tax Payable (D) Social Security Tax Payable. (p. 370)

3. _____

4. The total of the Federal Income Tax column of a payroll register is credited to (A) a revenue account (B) an expense account (C) a liability account (D) an asset account. (p. 370)

4. _____

5. The total of the Net Pay column of the payroll register is credited to (A) a revenue account (B) an expense account (C) an asset account (D) a liability account. (p. 370)

5. _____

6. When a semimonthly payroll is paid, the credit to Cash is equal to the (A) total earnings of all employees (B) total deductions for income tax and social security tax (C) total deductions (D) net pay of all employees. (p. 370)

6. _____

7. Employer business taxes are (A) assets (B) liabilities (C) revenues (D) expenses. (p. 373)

7. _____

8. Payroll taxes that are paid by both the employer and the employee are (A) federal unemployment tax and social security tax (B) federal unemployment tax and Medicare tax (C) social security tax and Medicare tax (D) federal income tax, social security tax, and Medicare tax. (p. 373)

8. _____

9. A federal tax used for state and federal administrative expenses of the unemployment program is the (A) social security tax (B) Medicare tax (C) federal unemployment tax (D) state unemployment tax. (p. 375)

9. _____

10. A state tax used to pay benefits to unemployed workers is the (A) social security tax (B) Medicare tax (C) unemployment tax (D) state unemployment tax. (p. 375)

10. _____

11. To record the employer payroll taxes expense, the following accounts are credited: (A) Payroll Taxes Expense and Employee Income Tax Payable (B) Employee Income Tax Payable, Social Security Tax Payable, Medicare Tax Payable, Unemployment Tax Payable—Federal, and Unemployment Tax Payable—State (C) Social Security Tax Payable, Medicare Tax Payable, Unemployment Tax Payable—Federal, and Unemployment Tax Payable—State (D) none of these. (p. 376)

11. _____

12. Each employer who withholds income tax, social security tax, and Medicare tax from employee earnings must furnish each employee an (A) IRS Form W-4 (B) IRS Form W-2 (C) IRS Form W-3 (D) IRS Form 941. (p. 378)

12. _____

13. Each employer is required by law to report payroll taxes on an (A) IRS Form W-4 (B) IRS Form 941 (C) IRS Form W-2 (D) IRS Form W-3. (p. 380)

13. _____

14. To record the total federal tax payment for employee income tax, social security tax, and Medicare tax, the account credited is (A) Cash (B) Employee Income Tax Payable (C) Social Security Tax Payable (D) Medicare Tax Payable. (p. 385)

14. _____

15. To record the payment of federal unemployment tax, the account debited is (A) a revenue account (B) an expense account (C) a liability account (D) an asset account. (p. 387)

15. _____

Part Two—Analyzing Transactions Affecting Payroll

Directions: Analyze each of the following transactions into debit and credit parts. Print the letters identifying your choices in the proper Answers column.

Account Title	Transaction	Answers Debit	Credit
A. Cash	**1.** Paid cash for semimonthly payroll. (p. 371)	_____	_____
B. Employee Income Tax Payable	**2.** Recorded employer payroll taxes expense. (p. 376)	_____	_____
C. Health Insurance Premiums Payable	**3.** Paid cash for liability for employee income tax, social security tax, and Medicare tax. (p. 385)	_____	_____
D. Medicare Tax Payable	**4.** Paid cash for federal unemployment tax liability. (p. 387)	_____	_____
E. Payroll Taxes Expense	**5.** Paid cash for state unemployment tax liability. (p. 387)	_____	_____
F. Salary Expense			
G. Social Security Tax Payable			
H. U.S. Savings Bonds Payable			
I. Unemployment Tax Payable—Federal			
J. Unemployment Tax Payable—State			
K. United Way Donations Payable			

Part Three—Analyzing Form W-2

Directions: Analyze the following statements about a Form W-2, Wage and Tax Statement. Use the Form W-2 below to answer the specific questions about Rick Selby. Place a *T* for True or an *F* for False in the Answers column to show whether each of the following statements is true or false. (p. 378)

a Control number 22222 Void ☐	For Official Use Only OMB No. 1545-0008		
b Employer identification number 31-0429632		1 Wages, tips, other compensation 24,843.00	2 Federal income tax withheld 648.00
c Employer's name, address, and ZIP code Hobby Shack, Inc. 1420 College Plaza Atlanta, GA 30337-1726		3 Social security wages 24,843.00	4 Social security tax withheld 1,540.24
		5 Medicare wages and tips 24,843.00	6 Medicare tax withheld 360.21
		7 Social security tips	8 Allocated tips
d Employee's social security number 450-70-6432		9 Advance EIC payment	10 Dependent care benefits
e Employee's first name and initial Rick E. Last name Selby		11 Nonqualified plans	12a See instructions for box 12
1625 Northland Drive Clarkdale, GA 30020-6523		13 Statutory employee ☐ Retirement plan ☐ Third-party sick pay ☐	12b
		14 Other	12c
			12d
f Employee's address and ZIP code			
15 State Employer's state ID number	16 State wages, tips, etc.	17 State income tax	18 Local wages, tips, etc. 19 Local income tax 20 Locality name

Form **W-2** Wage and Tax Statement   20 - -   Department of the Treasury—Internal Revenue Service

Copy A For Social Security Administration — Send this entire page with Form W-3 to the Social Security Administration; photocopies are **not** acceptable.

For Privacy Act and Paperwork Reduction Act Notice, see back of Copy D.

Cat. No. 10134D

Answers

1. Rick Selby's total salary is more than his total social security salary.   1. _____

2. This Form W-2 shows Rick Selby's net pay for the entire year.   2. _____

3. The amount withheld for Mr. Selby's social security and Medicare tax was more than the amount withheld for his federal income tax.   3. _____

4. State income tax was withheld from Mr. Selby's salary.   4. _____

5. All deductions from Mr. Selby's salary are shown on his Form W-2.   5. _____

6. This Form W-2 would indicate whether Mr. Selby had more than one employer during the year.   6. _____

7. If an employee works for several employers during the year, that employee must receive a Form W-2 from each employer.   7. _____

8. An employer is required to provide employees with a Form W-2 no later than January 31 of the year following the one for which the report has been completed.   8. _____

9. When Rick Selby files his federal income tax return, he must attach Copy A of Form W-2 to his return.   9. _____

10. Businesses in states with state income tax must prepare additional copies of Form W-2.   10. _____

13-1 **WORK TOGETHER, p. 372**

Recording a payroll

1.

Salary Expense

Employee Income Tax Payable

Social Security Tax Payable

Medicare Tax Payable

Cash

2.

CASH PAYMENTS JOURNAL

PAGE 15

| | | | | 1 GENERAL | 2 GENERAL | 3 ACCOUNTS PAYABLE | 4 CASH |
DATE	ACCOUNT TITLE	CK. NO.	POST. REF.	DEBIT	CREDIT	DEBIT	CREDIT

Recording a payroll

1.

Salary Expense	
Employee Income Tax Payable	
Social Security Tax Payable	
Medicare Tax Payable	
Cash	

2.

CASH PAYMENTS JOURNAL

PAGE 16

					1	2	3	4
					GENERAL		ACCOUNTS PAYABLE DEBIT	CASH CREDIT
DATE	ACCOUNT TITLE	CK. NO.	POST. REF.		DEBIT	CREDIT		
				1				
				2				
				3				
				4				
				5				
				6				
				7				
				8				
				9				

13-2 WORK TOGETHER, p. 377

Recording employer payroll taxes

1., 2.

Employee Name	Accumulated Earnings, April 30	Total Earnings for May 1–15 Pay Period	Unemployment Taxable Earnings
Beltran, Tamela C.	$5,100.00	$ 637.50	_____
Cintron, Irma V.	7,350.00	920.00	_____
	Totals	_____	_____

Social Security Tax Payable, 6.2%	_____
Medicare Tax Payable, 1.45%	_____
Unemployment Tax Payable—Federal, 0.8%	_____
Unemployment Tax Payable—State, 5.4%	_____
Total Payroll Taxes	_____

3.

GENERAL JOURNAL   PAGE 10

	DATE		ACCOUNT TITLE	DOC. NO.	POST. REF.	DEBIT	CREDIT	
1								1
2								2
3								3
4								4
5								5
6								6
7								7
8								8
9								9
10								10

Recording employer payroll taxes

1., 2.

Employee Name	Accumulated Earnings, May 31	Total Earnings for June 1–15 Pay Period	Unemployment Taxable Earnings
Caldwell, Sarah H.	$6,020.00		_____
Easley, Benjamin P.	5,450.00		_____
Franks, John J.	8,420.00		_____
	Totals	_____	_____

Social Security Tax Payable, 6.2%	_____
Medicare Tax Payable, 1.45%	_____
Unemployment Tax Payable—Federal, 0.8%	_____
Unemployment Tax Payable—State, 5.4%	_____
Total Payroll Taxes	_____

3.

GENERAL JOURNAL   PAGE 12

	DATE	ACCOUNT TITLE	DOC. NO.	POST. REF.	DEBIT	CREDIT	
1							1
2							2
3							3
4							4
5							5
6							6
7							7
8							8
9							9
10							10

13-3 **WORK TOGETHER, p. 382**

Reporting withholding and payroll taxes

1.

Form **941**

Department of the Treasury
Internal Revenue Service (99)

Employer's Quarterly Federal Tax Return

▶ See separate instructions revised January 20-- for information on completing this return.

Please type or print.

Enter state code for state in which deposits were made **only** if different from state in address to the right ▶ [ ]
(see page 2 of separate instructions).

Name (as distinguished from trade name)	Date quarter ended	OMB No. 1545-0029
Trade name, if any	Employer identification number	T
		FF
Address (number and street)	City, state, and ZIP code	FD
		FP
		I
		T

If address is different from prior return, check here ▶ [ ]

IRS Use

1 1 1 1 1 1 1 1 1 1	2	3 3 3 3 3 3 3	4 4 4	5 5 5
6 7 8 8 8 8 8 8 8	9 9 9 9 9	10 10 10 10 10 10 10 10 10		

A If you **do not have to file** returns in the future, check here ▶ [ ] and enter date final wages paid ▶ _____

B If you are a seasonal employer, see **Seasonal employers** on page 1 of the instructions and check here ▶ [ ]

1	Number of employees in the pay period that includes March 12th . ▶	**1**	
2	Total wages and tips, plus other compensation (see separate instructions)	**2**	
3	Total income tax withheld from wages, tips, and sick pay	**3**	
4	Adjustment of withheld income tax for preceding quarters of **this calendar year**	**4**	
5	Adjusted total of income tax withheld (line 3 as adjusted by line 4)	**5**	
6	Taxable social security wages	**6a**	· 12.4% (.124) =	**6b**	
	Taxable social security tips	**6c**	· 12.4% (.124) =	**6d**	
7	Taxable Medicare wages and tips	**7a**	· 2.9% (.029) =	**7b**	
8	Total social security and Medicare taxes (add lines 6b, 6d, and 7b). **Check here if wages are not subject to social security and/or Medicare tax** . . . . ▶ [ ]	**8**	
9	Adjustment of social security and Medicare taxes (see instructions for required explanation) Sick Pay $ _____ ± Fractions of Cents $ _____ ± Other $ _____ =	**9**	
10	Adjusted total of social security and Medicare taxes (line 8 as adjusted by line 9)	**10**	
11	**Total taxes** (add lines 5 and 10)	**11**	
12	Advance earned income credit (EIC) payments made to employees (see instructions) . . .	**12**	
13	Net taxes (subtract line 12 from line 11). **If $2,500 or more, this must equal line 17, column (d) below (or line D of Schedule B (Form 941))**	**13**	
14	Total deposits for quarter, including overpayment applied from a prior quarter	**14**	
15	**Balance due** (subtract line 14 from line 13). See instructions	**15**	
16	**Overpayment.** If line 14 is more than line 13, enter excess here ▶ $ _____ and check if to be: [ ] Applied to next return **or** [ ] Refunded.		

- **All filers:** If line 13 is less than $2,500, **do not** complete line 17 **or** Schedule B (Form 941).
- **Semiweekly schedule depositors:** Complete Schedule B (Form 941) and check here . . . . ▶ [ ]
- **Monthly schedule depositors:** Complete line 17, columns (a) through (d), and check here. . . . . ▶ [ ]

17	**Monthly Summary of Federal Tax Liability.** (Complete **Schedule B (Form 941)** instead, if you were a semiweekly schedule depositor.)		
(a) First month liability	**(b)** Second month liability	**(c)** Third month liability	**(d)** Total liability for quarter

Third Party Designee

Do you want to allow another person to discuss this return with the IRS (see separate instructions)? [ ] **Yes.** Complete the following. [ ] **No**

Designee's name ▶ _____ Phone no. ▶ ( ) _____ Personal identification number (PIN) ▶ [   ]

Sign Here

Under penalties of perjury, I declare that I have examined this return, including accompanying schedules and statements, and to the best of my knowledge and belief, it is true, correct, and complete.

Signature ▶ _____ Print Your Name and Title ▶ _____ Date ▶ _____

For Privacy Act and Paperwork Reduction Act Notice, see back of Payment Voucher.   Cat. No. 17001Z   Form **941**

Reporting withholding and payroll taxes

1.

Form **941**

Department of the Treasury
Internal Revenue Service (99)

Employer's Quarterly Federal Tax Return

▶ See separate instructions revised January 20-- for information on completing this return.

Please type or print.

OMB No. 1545-0029

Enter state code for state in which deposits were made **only** if different from state in address to the right ▶ (see page 2 of separate instructions).

Name (as distinguished from trade name)	Date quarter ended	
Trade name, if any	Employer identification number	
Address (number and street)	City, state, and ZIP code	

T
FF
FD
FP
I
T

If address is different from prior return, check here ▶

IRS Use

1	1	1	1	1	1	1	1	1	1	2	3	3	3	3	3	3	3	4	4	4	5	5	5
6	7		8	8	8	8	8	8	8	9	9	9	9	9	10	10	10	10	10	10	10	10	10

A If you **do not have to file** returns in the future, check here ▶ ☐ and enter date final wages paid ▶

B If you are a seasonal employer, see **Seasonal employers** on page 1 of the instructions and check here ▶ ☐

1	Number of employees in the pay period that includes March 12th . ▶ 1	
2	Total wages and tips, plus other compensation (see separate instructions)	**2**
3	Total income tax withheld from wages, tips, and sick pay	**3**
4	Adjustment of withheld income tax for preceding quarters of **this calendar year**	**4**
5	Adjusted total of income tax withheld (line 3 as adjusted by line 4)	**5**
6	Taxable social security wages . . . . . . **6a** · 12.4% (.124) =	**6b**
	Taxable social security tips . . . . **6c** · 12.4% (.124) =	**6d**
7	Taxable Medicare wages and tips . . . **7a** · 2.9% (.029) =	**7b**
8	Total social security and Medicare taxes (add lines 6b, 6d, and 7b). **Check here if wages are not subject to social security and/or Medicare tax** . . . . ▶ ☐	**8**
9	Adjustment of social security and Medicare taxes (see instructions for required explanation) Sick Pay $ _____ ± Fractions of Cents $ _____ ± Other $ _____ =	**9**
10	Adjusted total of social security and Medicare taxes (line 8 as adjusted by line 9)	**10**
11	**Total taxes** (add lines 5 and 10)	**11**
12	Advance earned income credit (EIC) payments made to employees (see instructions) . . .	**12**
13	Net taxes (subtract line 12 from line 11). **If $2,500 or more, this must equal line 17, column (d) below (or line D of Schedule B (Form 941))**	**13**
14	Total deposits for quarter, including overpayment applied from a prior quarter	**14**
15	**Balance due** (subtract line 14 from line 13). See instructions	**15**
16	**Overpayment.** If line 14 is more than line 13, enter excess here ▶ $ _____ and check if to be: ☐ Applied to next return **or** ☐ Refunded.	

• **All filers:** If line 13 is less than $2,500, **do not** complete line 17 **or** Schedule B (Form 941).
• **Semiweekly schedule depositors:** Complete Schedule B (Form 941) and check here . . . . ▶ ☐
• **Monthly schedule depositors:** Complete line 17, columns (a) through (d), and check here. . . . . ▶ ☐

17	**Monthly Summary of Federal Tax Liability.** (Complete **Schedule B (Form 941)** instead, if you were a semiweekly schedule depositor.)			
	(a) First month liability	**(b)** Second month liability	**(c)** Third month liability	**(d)** Total liability for quarter

Third Party Designee

Do you want to allow another person to discuss this return with the IRS (see separate instructions)? ☐ **Yes.** Complete the following. ☐ **No**

Designee's name ▶

Phone no. ▶ ( )

Personal identification number (PIN) ▶

Sign Here

Under penalties of perjury, I declare that I have examined this return, including accompanying schedules and statements, and to the best of my knowledge and belief, it is true, correct, and complete.

Signature ▶

Print Your Name and Title ▶

Date ▶

For Privacy Act and Paperwork Reduction Act Notice, see back of Payment Voucher.   Cat. No. 17001Z   Form **941**

13-4 WORK TOGETHER, p. 389

Paying withholding and payroll taxes

1., 2.

CASH PAYMENTS JOURNAL

PAGE 14

	DATE	ACCOUNT TITLE	CK. NO.	POST. REF.	GENERAL DEBIT	GENERAL CREDIT	ACCOUNTS PAYABLE DEBIT	PURCHASES DISCOUNT CREDIT	CASH CREDIT	
1										1
2										2
3										3
4										4
5										5
6										6
7										7
8										8
9										9
10										10
11										11
12										12
13										13
14										14
15										15
16										16
17										17
18										18
19										19
20										20
21										21
22										22

Paying withholding and payroll taxes

1., 2.

CASH PAYMENTS JOURNAL

PAGE 19

				1	2	3	4	5
				GENERAL		ACCOUNTS PAYABLE DEBIT	PURCHASES DISCOUNT CREDIT	CASH CREDIT
DATE	ACCOUNT TITLE	CK. NO.	POST. REF.	DEBIT	CREDIT			
1								
2								
3								
4								
5								
6								
7								
8								
9								
10								
11								
12								
13								
14								
15								
16								
17								
18								
19								
20								
21								
22								

13-1 APPLICATION PROBLEM, p. 391

Recording a payroll

CASH PAYMENTS JOURNAL

PAGE 15

DATE	ACCOUNT TITLE	CK. NO.	POST. REF.	GENERAL DEBIT (1)	GENERAL CREDIT (2)	ACCOUNTS PAYABLE DEBIT (3)	PURCHASES DISCOUNT CREDIT (4)	CASH CREDIT (5)
1								
2								
3								
4								
5								
6								
7								
8								
9								
10								
11								
12								
13								
14								
15								
16								
17								
18								
19								
20								
21								
22								
23								

APPLICATION PROBLEM, p. 391

Recording employer payroll taxes

1., 2., 4.

Employee Name	Accumulated Earnings, March 31	Total Earnings for April 1–15 Pay Period	Unemployment Taxable Earnings, April 15	Accumulated Earnings, April 15	Total Earnings for April 16–30 Pay Period	Unemployment Taxable Earnings, April 30
Bolser, Frank T.	$4,860.00	$ 810.00	_____	_____	$ 795.00	_____
Denham, Beth R.	5,670.00	945.00	_____	_____	980.00	_____
Harjo, Teresa S.	7,500.00	1,250.00	_____	_____	1,250.00	_____
Knutzen, John L.	3,720.00	620.00	_____	_____	635.00	_____
Prescott, Laura F.	4,560.00	760.00	_____	_____	740.00	_____
Schmidt, Ian T.	6,900.00	1,150.00	_____	_____	1,125.00	_____
	Totals	_____	_____	Totals	_____	_____

Social Security Tax Payable	_____	Social Security Tax Payable	_____
Medicare Tax Payable	_____	Medicare Tax Payable	_____
Unemployment Tax Payable—Federal	_____	Unemployment Tax Payable—Federal	_____
Unemployment Tax Payable—State	_____	Unemployment Tax Payable—State	_____

3., 5.

GENERAL JOURNAL

PAGE 16

	DATE	ACCOUNT TITLE	DOC. NO.	POST. REF.	DEBIT	CREDIT	
1							1
2							2
3							3
4							4
5							5
6							6
7							7
8							8
9							9
10							10
11							11
12							12
13							13

Name _____ Date _____ Class _____

13-3 APPLICATION PROBLEM, p. 392

Reporting withholding and payroll taxes

Form **941**

Department of the Treasury
Internal Revenue Service (99)

Employer's Quarterly Federal Tax Return

▶ See separate instructions revised January 20-- for information on completing this return.

Please type or print.

Enter state code for state in which deposits were made **only** if different from state in address to the right ▶ [ ] (see page 2 of separate instructions).

Name (as distinguished from trade name)	Date quarter ended
Trade name, if any	Employer identification number
Address (number and street)	City, state, and ZIP code

OMB No. 1545-0029

T	
FF	
FD	
FP	
I	
T	

If address is different from prior return, check here ▶ [ ]

IRS Use

1 1 1 1 1 1 1 1 1 1   2   3 3 3 3 3 3 3 3   4 4 4   5 5 5

6   7   8 8 8 8 8 8 8   9 9 9 9 9   10 10 10 10 10 10 10 10 10 10

A If you **do not have to file** returns in the future, check here ▶ [ ] and enter date final wages paid ▶

B If you are a seasonal employer, see **Seasonal employers** on page 1 of the instructions and check here ▶ [ ]

1	Number of employees in the pay period that includes March 12th ▶	1		
2	Total wages and tips, plus other compensation (see separate instructions)		**2**	
3	Total income tax withheld from wages, tips, and sick pay		**3**	
4	Adjustment of withheld income tax for preceding quarters of **this calendar year**		**4**	
5	Adjusted total of income tax withheld (line 3 as adjusted by line 4)		**5**	

6	Taxable social security wages	**6a**		· 12.4% (.124) =	**6b**	
	Taxable social security tips	**6c**		· 12.4% (.124) =	**6d**	
7	Taxable Medicare wages and tips . . .	**7a**		· 2.9% (.029) =	**7b**	

8	Total social security and Medicare taxes (add lines 6b, 6d, and 7b). **Check here if wages are not subject to social security and/or Medicare tax** . . . . ▶ [ ]		**8**	
9	Adjustment of social security and Medicare taxes (see instructions for required explanation) Sick Pay $ _____ ± Fractions of Cents $ _____ ± Other $ _____ =		**9**	
10	Adjusted total of social security and Medicare taxes (line 8 as adjusted by line 9)		**10**	
11	**Total taxes** (add lines 5 and 10)		**11**	
12	Advance earned income credit (EIC) payments made to employees (see instructions) . . .		**12**	
13	Net taxes (subtract line 12 from line 11). **If $2,500 or more, this must equal line 17, column (d) below (or line D of Schedule B (Form 941))**		**13**	
14	Total deposits for quarter, including overpayment applied from a prior quarter		**14**	
15	**Balance due** (subtract line 14 from line 13). See instructions		**15**	

16 **Overpayment.** If line 14 is more than line 13, enter excess here ▶ $ _____

and check if to be: [ ] Applied to next return **or** [ ] Refunded.

- **All filers:** If line 13 is less than $2,500, **do not** complete line 17 **or** Schedule B (Form 941).
- **Semiweekly schedule depositors:** Complete Schedule B (Form 941) and check here . . . . ▶ [ ]
- **Monthly schedule depositors:** Complete line 17, columns (a) through (d), and check here. . . . . ▶ [ ]

17	Monthly Summary of Federal Tax Liability. (Complete **Schedule B (Form 941)** instead, if you were a semiweekly schedule depositor.)			
	(a) First month liability	**(b)** Second month liability	**(c)** Third month liability	**(d)** Total liability for quarter

Third Party Designee

Do you want to allow another person to discuss this return with the IRS (see separate instructions)? [ ] **Yes.** Complete the following. [ ] **No**

Designee's name ▶   Phone no. ▶ ( )   Personal identification number (PIN) ▶ [ ][ ][ ][ ][ ][ ]

Sign Here

Under penalties of perjury, I declare that I have examined this return, including accompanying schedules and statements, and to the best of my knowledge and belief, it is true, correct, and complete.

Signature ▶   Print Your Name and Title ▶   Date ▶

For Privacy Act and Paperwork Reduction Act Notice, see back of Payment Voucher.   Cat. No. 17001Z   Form **941**

Paying withholding and payroll taxes

1., 2., 3.

CASH PAYMENTS JOURNAL

PAGE 8

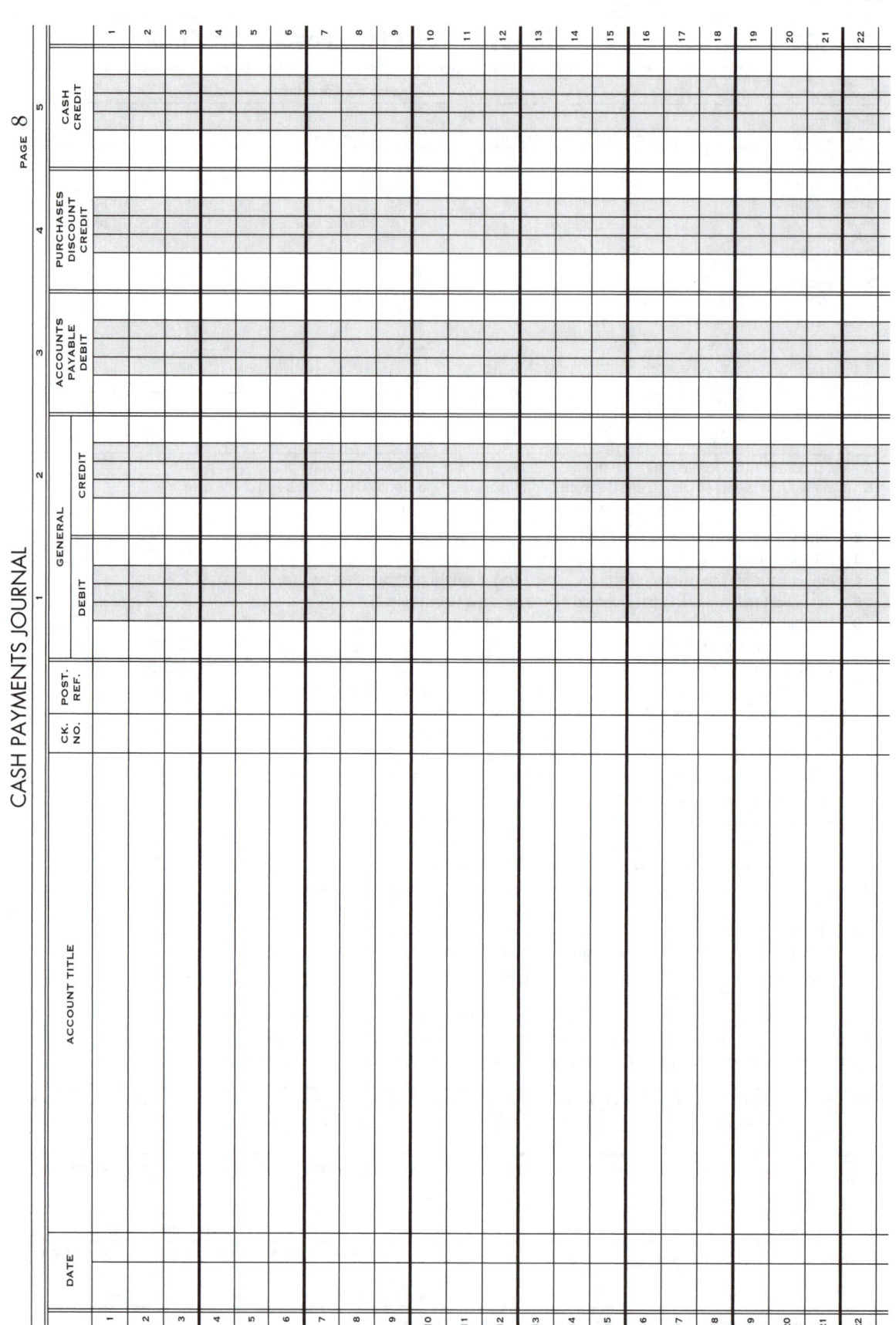

13-5 MASTERY PROBLEM, p. 393

Journalizing payroll transactions

1., 2.

CASH PAYMENTS JOURNAL

PAGE 14

	DATE	ACCOUNT TITLE	CK. NO.	POST. REF.	GENERAL DEBIT	GENERAL CREDIT	ACCOUNTS PAYABLE DEBIT	PURCHASES DISCOUNT CREDIT	CASH CREDIT	
1										1
2										2
3										3
4										4
5										5
6										6
7										7
8										8
9										9
10										10
11										11
12										12
13										13
14										14
15										15
16										16
17										17
18										18
19										19
20										20
21										21
22										22
23										23
24										24
25										25

1.

GENERAL JOURNAL   PAGE 10

	DATE		ACCOUNT TITLE	DOC. NO.	POST. REF.	DEBIT	CREDIT	
1								1
2								2
3								3
4								4
5								5
6								6
7								7
8								8
9								9
10								10
11								11
12								12
13								13
14								14
15								15
16								16
17								17
18								18
19								19
20								20
21								21
22								22
23								23
24								24
25								25

13-6 CHALLENGE PROBLEM, p. 393

Journalizing and posting payroll transactions

1., 2.

CASH PAYMENTS JOURNAL

PAGE 1

DATE	ACCOUNT TITLE	CK. NO.	POST. REF.	GENERAL DEBIT	GENERAL CREDIT	ACCOUNTS PAYABLE DEBIT	PURCHASES DISCOUNT CREDIT	CASH CREDIT	
									1
									2
									3
									4
									5
									6
									7
									8
									9
									10
									11
									12
									13
									14
									15
									16
									17
									18
									19
									20

1., 3.

GENERAL JOURNAL

PAGE 1

DATE	ACCOUNT TITLE	DOC. NO.	POST. REF.	DEBIT	CREDIT	
						1
						2
						3
						4
						5
						6
						7
						8
						9
						10
						11
						12
						13
						14
						15
						16
						17
						18
						19
						20
						21
						22
						23
						24
						25

13-6 CHALLENGE PROBLEM (continued)

2., 3., 4.

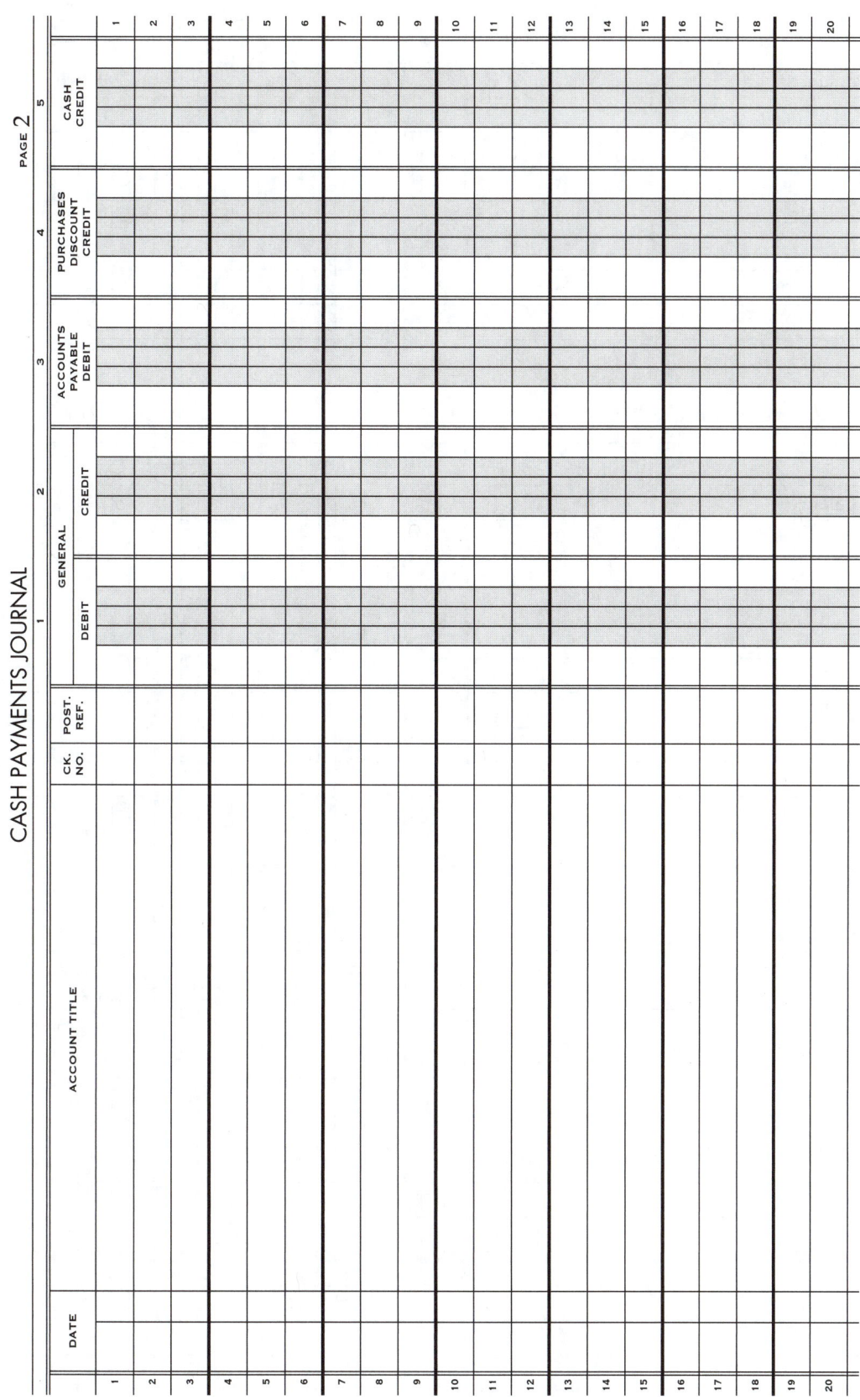

CASH PAYMENTS JOURNAL

PAGE 2

1., 3.   **GENERAL LEDGER**

ACCOUNT Employee Income Tax Payable   ACCOUNT NO. 2120

DATE		ITEM	POST. REF.	DEBIT	CREDIT	BALANCE	
						DEBIT	CREDIT
Jan. 20--	1	Balance	✔				1 2 9 2 00

ACCOUNT Social Security Tax Payable   ACCOUNT NO. 2130

DATE		ITEM	POST. REF.	DEBIT	CREDIT	BALANCE	
						DEBIT	CREDIT
Jan. 20--	1	Balance	✔				1 5 2 7 50

ACCOUNT Medicare Tax Payable   ACCOUNT NO. 2140

DATE		ITEM	POST. REF.	DEBIT	CREDIT	BALANCE	
						DEBIT	CREDIT
Jan. 20--	1	Balance	✔				1 7 6 25

13-6 CHALLENGE PROBLEM (concluded)

ACCOUNT Unemployment Tax Payable—Federal   ACCOUNT NO. 2150

DATE	ITEM	POST. REF.	DEBIT	CREDIT	BALANCE DEBIT	BALANCE CREDIT
20-- Jan. 1	Balance	✔				2 6 4 00

ACCOUNT Unemployment Tax Payable—State   ACCOUNT NO. 2160

DATE	ITEM	POST. REF.	DEBIT	CREDIT	BALANCE DEBIT	BALANCE CREDIT
20-- Jan. 1	Balance	✔				1 7 8 2 00

ACCOUNT U.S. Savings Bonds Payable   ACCOUNT NO. 2180

DATE	ITEM	POST. REF.	DEBIT	CREDIT	BALANCE DEBIT	BALANCE CREDIT
20-- Jan. 1	Balance	✔				3 7 5 00

ACCOUNT Payroll Taxes Expense   ACCOUNT NO. 6150

DATE	ITEM	POST. REF.	DEBIT	CREDIT	BALANCE DEBIT	BALANCE CREDIT

ACCOUNT Salary Expense   ACCOUNT NO. 6170

DATE	ITEM	POST. REF.	DEBIT	CREDIT	BALANCE DEBIT	BALANCE CREDIT

REINFORCEMENT ACTIVITY 2   PART A, p. 398

An Accounting Cycle for a Corporation: Journalizing and Posting Transactions
1., 4., 5.

SALES JOURNAL   PAGE 12

	DATE	ACCOUNT DEBITED	SALE NO.	POST. REF.	1 ACCOUNTS RECEIVABLE DEBIT	2 SALES CREDIT	3 SALES TAX PAYABLE CREDIT	
1								1
2								2
3								3
4								4
5								5
6								6
7								7
8								8
9								9
10								10
11								11
12								12
13								13
14								14
15								15
16								16
17								17
18								18
19								19

REINFORCEMENT ACTIVITY 2 PART A (continued)

1., 4., 6.

PURCHASES JOURNAL   PAGE 12

	DATE	ACCOUNT CREDITED	PURCH. NO.	POST. REF.	PURCHASES DR. ACCTS. PAY. CR.	
1						1
2						2
3						3
4						4
5						5
6						6
7						7
8						8
9						9
10						10
11						11
12						12
13						13
14						14
15						15
16						16
17						17
18						18
19						19
20						20
21						21
22						22
23						23
24						24
25						25

REINFORCEMENT ACTIVITY 2 PART A (continued)

1., 4.

GENERAL JOURNAL

	DATE	ACCOUNT TITLE	DOC. NO.	POST. REF.	DEBIT	CREDIT	
1							1
2							2
3							3
4							4
5							5
6							6
7							7
8							8
9							9
10							10
11							11
12							12
13							13
14							14
15							15
16							16
17							17
18							18
19							19
20							20
21							21
22							22
23							23
24							24
25							25
26							26
27							27
28							28
29							29
30							30
31							31
32							32

1., 4., 7., 9.

CASH RECEIPTS JOURNAL

PAGE 12

	DATE	ACCOUNT TITLE	DOC. NO.	POST. REF.	GENERAL DEBIT	GENERAL CREDIT	ACCOUNTS RECEIVABLE CREDIT	SALES CREDIT	SALES TAX PAYABLE CREDIT	SALES DISCOUNT DEBIT	CASH DEBIT	
					1	2	3	4	5	6	7	
1												1
2												2
3												3
4												4
5												5
6												6
7												7
8												8
9												9
10												10
11												11
12												12
13												13
14												14
15												15
16												16
17												17
18												18
19												19
20												20
21												21
22												22
23												23

REINFORCEMENT ACTIVITY 2 PART A (continued)

1., 2.

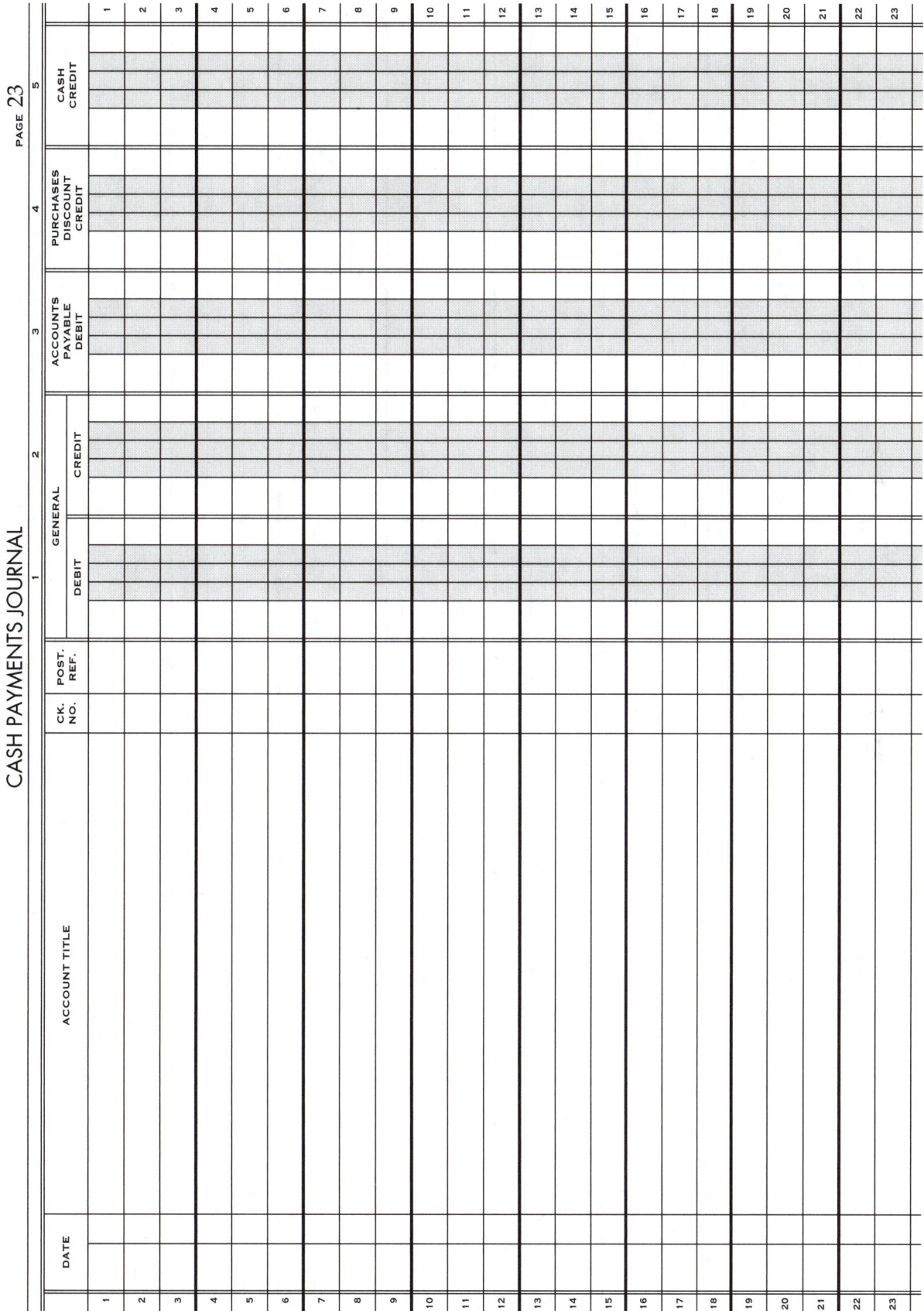

CASH PAYMENTS JOURNAL

PAGE 23

3., 4., 7., 10.

CASH PAYMENTS JOURNAL

PAGE 24

	DATE	ACCOUNT TITLE	CK. NO.	POST. REF.	GENERAL DEBIT	GENERAL CREDIT	ACCOUNTS PAYABLE DEBIT	PURCHASES DISCOUNT CREDIT	CASH CREDIT	
					1	2	3	4	5	
1										1
2										2
3										3
4										4
5										5
6										6
7										7
8										8
9										9
10										10
11										11
12										12
13										13
14										14
15										15
16										16
17										17
18										18
19										19
20										20
21										21
22										22
23										23
24										24

REINFORCEMENT ACTIVITY 2 PART A (continued)

1., 4.   **ACCOUNTS RECEIVABLE LEDGER**

customer Bratton Clinic   customer no. 110

DATE	ITEM	POST. REF.	DEBIT	CREDIT	DEBIT BALANCE
20-- Dec. 1	Balance	✔			4 9 6 7 60

customer Clegg Medical Center   customer no. 120

DATE	ITEM	POST. REF.	DEBIT	CREDIT	DEBIT BALANCE
20-- Dec. 1	Balance	✔			4 1 3 40

customer Glenmore School   customer no. 130

DATE	ITEM	POST. REF.	DEBIT	CREDIT	DEBIT BALANCE

customer Jamacus Clinic   customer no. 140

DATE	ITEM	POST. REF.	DEBIT	CREDIT	DEBIT BALANCE
20-- Dec. 1	Balance	✔			1 6 4 3 00

customer Odom Daycare   customer no. 150

DATE	ITEM	POST. REF.	DEBIT	CREDIT	DEBIT BALANCE

customer Treet Retirement Home   customer no. 160

DATE	ITEM	POST. REF.	DEBIT	CREDIT	DEBIT BALANCE
20-- Dec. 1	Balance	✔			8 0 0 1 52

REINFORCEMENT ACTIVITY 2 PART A (continued)

1., 4.   **ACCOUNTS PAYABLE LEDGER**

VENDOR Armstrong Medical   VENDOR NO. 210

DATE		ITEM	POST. REF.	DEBIT	CREDIT	CREDIT BALANCE
20-- Dec.	1	Balance	✔			1 2 7 2 00

VENDOR Cross Office Supply   VENDOR NO. 220

DATE		ITEM	POST. REF.	DEBIT	CREDIT	CREDIT BALANCE
20-- Dec.	1	Balance	✔			1 4 1 7 25

VENDOR Evans Supply   VENDOR NO. 230

DATE		ITEM	POST. REF.	DEBIT	CREDIT	CREDIT BALANCE
20-- Dec.	1	Balance	✔			1 3 9 6 00

VENDOR Ogden Instruments   VENDOR NO. 240

DATE		ITEM	POST. REF.	DEBIT	CREDIT	CREDIT BALANCE
20-- Dec.	1	Balance	✔			2 2 0 0 00

VENDOR Spencer Industries   VENDOR NO. 250

DATE		ITEM	POST. REF.	DEBIT	CREDIT	CREDIT BALANCE
20-- Dec.	1	Balance	✔			5 8 0 00

VENDOR Ziegler, Inc.   VENDOR NO. 260

DATE		ITEM	POST. REF.	DEBIT	CREDIT	CREDIT BALANCE

REINFORCEMENT ACTIVITY 2 PART A (continued)

11.

REINFORCEMENT ACTIVITY 2 PART A (continued)

GENERAL LEDGER

ACCOUNT Cash   ACCOUNT NO. 1110

DATE		ITEM	POST. REF.	DEBIT	CREDIT	BALANCE DEBIT	BALANCE CREDIT
20-- Dec.	1	Balance	✔			1 9 9 6 4 82	

ACCOUNT Petty Cash   ACCOUNT NO. 1120

DATE		ITEM	POST. REF.	DEBIT	CREDIT	BALANCE DEBIT	BALANCE CREDIT
20-- Dec.	1	Balance	✔			2 5 0 00	

ACCOUNT Accounts Receivable   ACCOUNT NO. 1130

DATE		ITEM	POST. REF.	DEBIT	CREDIT	BALANCE DEBIT	BALANCE CREDIT
20-- Dec.	1	Balance	✔			1 5 0 2 5 52	

ACCOUNT Allowance for Uncollectible Accounts   ACCOUNT NO. 1135

DATE		ITEM	POST. REF.	DEBIT	CREDIT	BALANCE DEBIT	BALANCE CREDIT
20-- Dec.	1	Balance	✔				1 0 2 12

ACCOUNT Merchandise Inventory   ACCOUNT NO. 1140

DATE		ITEM	POST. REF.	DEBIT	CREDIT	BALANCE DEBIT	BALANCE CREDIT
20-- Dec.	1	Balance	✔			3 4 5 2 1 56	

REINFORCEMENT ACTIVITY 2 PART A (continued)

ACCOUNT Supplies—Office   ACCOUNT NO. 1145

DATE		ITEM	POST. REF.	DEBIT	CREDIT	BALANCE	
						DEBIT	CREDIT
Dec. 20--	1	Balance	✔			3 7 5 6 00	

ACCOUNT Supplies—Store   ACCOUNT NO. 1150

DATE		ITEM	POST. REF.	DEBIT	CREDIT	BALANCE	
						DEBIT	CREDIT
Dec. 20--	1	Balance	✔			4 2 1 0 00	

ACCOUNT Prepaid Insurance   ACCOUNT NO. 1160

DATE		ITEM	POST. REF.	DEBIT	CREDIT	BALANCE	
						DEBIT	CREDIT
Dec. 20--	1	Balance	✔			8 0 0 0 00	

ACCOUNT Office Equipment   ACCOUNT NO. 1210

DATE		ITEM	POST. REF.	DEBIT	CREDIT	BALANCE	
						DEBIT	CREDIT
Dec. 20--	1	Balance	✔			1 3 7 5 2 00	

ACCOUNT Accumulated Depreciation—Office Equipment   ACCOUNT NO. 1220

DATE		ITEM	POST. REF.	DEBIT	CREDIT	BALANCE	
						DEBIT	CREDIT
Dec. 20--	1	Balance	✔				2 2 1 0 00

REINFORCEMENT ACTIVITY 2 PART A (continued)

ACCOUNT Store Equipment   ACCOUNT NO. 1230

DATE	ITEM	POST. REF.	DEBIT	CREDIT	BALANCE DEBIT	BALANCE CREDIT
20-- Dec. 1	Balance	✔			10 259 00	

ACCOUNT Accumulated Depreciation—Store Equipment   ACCOUNT NO. 1240

DATE	ITEM	POST. REF.	DEBIT	CREDIT	BALANCE DEBIT	BALANCE CREDIT
20-- Dec. 1	Balance	✔				5 844 00

ACCOUNT Accounts Payable   ACCOUNT NO. 2110

DATE	ITEM	POST. REF.	DEBIT	CREDIT	BALANCE DEBIT	BALANCE CREDIT
20-- Dec. 1	Balance	✔				6 865 25

ACCOUNT Federal Income Tax Payable   ACCOUNT NO. 2115

DATE	ITEM	POST. REF.	DEBIT	CREDIT	BALANCE DEBIT	BALANCE CREDIT

ACCOUNT Employee Income Tax Payable   ACCOUNT NO. 2120

DATE	ITEM	POST. REF.	DEBIT	CREDIT	BALANCE DEBIT	BALANCE CREDIT
20-- Dec. 1	Balance	✔				342 00

REINFORCEMENT ACTIVITY 2 PART A (continued)

ACCOUNT Social Security Tax Payable   ACCOUNT NO. 2130

DATE		ITEM	POST. REF.	DEBIT	CREDIT	BALANCE	
						DEBIT	CREDIT
Dec.²⁰⁻⁻	1	Balance	✔				7 6 7 00

ACCOUNT Medicare Tax Payable   ACCOUNT NO. 2135

DATE		ITEM	POST. REF.	DEBIT	CREDIT	BALANCE	
						DEBIT	CREDIT
Dec.²⁰⁻⁻	1	Balance	✔				1 7 9 38

ACCOUNT Sales Tax Payable   ACCOUNT NO. 2140

DATE		ITEM	POST. REF.	DEBIT	CREDIT	BALANCE	
						DEBIT	CREDIT
Dec.²⁰⁻⁻	1	Balance	✔				1 5 9 25

ACCOUNT Unemployment Tax Payable—Federal   ACCOUNT NO. 2150

DATE		ITEM	POST. REF.	DEBIT	CREDIT	BALANCE	
						DEBIT	CREDIT
Dec.²⁰⁻⁻	1	Balance	✔				1 2 00

ACCOUNT Unemployment Tax Payable—State   ACCOUNT NO. 2160

DATE		ITEM	POST. REF.	DEBIT	CREDIT	BALANCE	
						DEBIT	CREDIT
Dec.²⁰⁻⁻	1	Balance	✔				8 1 00

ACCOUNT Health Insurance Premiums Payable   ACCOUNT NO. 2170

DATE	ITEM	POST. REF.	DEBIT	CREDIT	BALANCE DEBIT	BALANCE CREDIT

ACCOUNT U.S. Savings Bonds Payable   ACCOUNT NO. 2180

DATE	ITEM	POST. REF.	DEBIT	CREDIT	BALANCE DEBIT	BALANCE CREDIT

ACCOUNT United Way Donations Payable   ACCOUNT NO. 2190

DATE	ITEM	POST. REF.	DEBIT	CREDIT	BALANCE DEBIT	BALANCE CREDIT

ACCOUNT Dividends Payable   ACCOUNT NO. 2195

DATE	ITEM	POST. REF.	DEBIT	CREDIT	BALANCE DEBIT	BALANCE CREDIT
20-- Dec. 1	Balance	✔				7 5 0 0 00

ACCOUNT Capital Stock   ACCOUNT NO. 3110

DATE	ITEM	POST. REF.	DEBIT	CREDIT	BALANCE DEBIT	BALANCE CREDIT
20-- Dec. 1	Balance	✔				1 0 0 0 0 00

ACCOUNT Retained Earnings   ACCOUNT NO. 3120

DATE	ITEM	POST. REF.	DEBIT	CREDIT	BALANCE DEBIT	BALANCE CREDIT
20-- Dec. 1	Balance	✔				3 8 7 1 8 01

REINFORCEMENT ACTIVITY 2 PART A (continued)

ACCOUNT Dividends   ACCOUNT NO. 3130

DATE		ITEM	POST. REF.	DEBIT	CREDIT	BALANCE	
						DEBIT	CREDIT
20-- Dec.	1	Balance	✔			3 0 0 0 00	

ACCOUNT Income Summary   ACCOUNT NO. 3140

DATE		ITEM	POST. REF.	DEBIT	CREDIT	BALANCE	
						DEBIT	CREDIT

ACCOUNT Sales   ACCOUNT NO. 4110

DATE		ITEM	POST. REF.	DEBIT	CREDIT	BALANCE	
						DEBIT	CREDIT
20-- Dec.	1	Balance	✔				310 1 5 9 00

ACCOUNT Sales Discount   ACCOUNT NO. 4120

DATE		ITEM	POST. REF.	DEBIT	CREDIT	BALANCE	
						DEBIT	CREDIT
20-- Dec.	1	Balance	✔			2 5 3 00	

ACCOUNT Sales Returns and Allowances   ACCOUNT NO. 4130

DATE		ITEM	POST. REF.	DEBIT	CREDIT	BALANCE	
						DEBIT	CREDIT
20-- Dec.	1	Balance	✔			1 5 6 0 00	

ACCOUNT Purchases   ACCOUNT NO. 5110

DATE		ITEM	POST. REF.	DEBIT	CREDIT	BALANCE	
						DEBIT	CREDIT
20-- Dec.	1	Balance	✔			123 5 7 8 10	

ACCOUNT Purchases Discount

ACCOUNT NO. 5120

DATE	ITEM	POST. REF.	DEBIT	CREDIT	BALANCE DEBIT	BALANCE CREDIT
20-- Dec. 1	Balance	✔				1 8 9 7 35

ACCOUNT Purchases Returns and Allowances

ACCOUNT NO. 5130

DATE	ITEM	POST. REF.	DEBIT	CREDIT	BALANCE DEBIT	BALANCE CREDIT
20-- Dec. 1	Balance	✔				2 2 8 4 50

ACCOUNT Advertising Expense

ACCOUNT NO. 6110

DATE	ITEM	POST. REF.	DEBIT	CREDIT	BALANCE DEBIT	BALANCE CREDIT
20-- Dec. 1	Balance	✔			1 6 5 2 3 00	

ACCOUNT Cash Short and Over

ACCOUNT NO. 6115

DATE	ITEM	POST. REF.	DEBIT	CREDIT	BALANCE DEBIT	BALANCE CREDIT
20-- Dec. 1	Balance	✔			8 43	

ACCOUNT Credit Card Fee Expense

ACCOUNT NO. 6120

DATE	ITEM	POST. REF.	DEBIT	CREDIT	BALANCE DEBIT	BALANCE CREDIT
20-- Dec. 1	Balance	✔			1 9 8 2 55	

ACCOUNT Depreciation Expense—Office Equipment

ACCOUNT NO. 6125

DATE	ITEM	POST. REF.	DEBIT	CREDIT	BALANCE DEBIT	BALANCE CREDIT

REINFORCEMENT ACTIVITY 2   PART A (continued)

ACCOUNT Depreciation Expense—Store Equipment   ACCOUNT NO. 6130

DATE	ITEM	POST. REF.	DEBIT	CREDIT	BALANCE DEBIT	BALANCE CREDIT

ACCOUNT Insurance Expense   ACCOUNT NO. 6135

DATE	ITEM	POST. REF.	DEBIT	CREDIT	BALANCE DEBIT	BALANCE CREDIT

ACCOUNT Miscellaneous Expense   ACCOUNT NO. 6140

DATE	ITEM	POST. REF.	DEBIT	CREDIT	BALANCE DEBIT	BALANCE CREDIT
20-- Dec. 1	Balance	✔			1 5 3 8 00	

ACCOUNT Payroll Taxes Expense   ACCOUNT NO. 6150

DATE	ITEM	POST. REF.	DEBIT	CREDIT	BALANCE DEBIT	BALANCE CREDIT
20-- Dec. 1	Balance	✔			6 5 8 7 43	

ACCOUNT Rent Expense   ACCOUNT NO. 6160

DATE	ITEM	POST. REF.	DEBIT	CREDIT	BALANCE DEBIT	BALANCE CREDIT
20-- Dec. 1	Balance	✔			10 8 0 0 00	

ACCOUNT Repairs Expense   ACCOUNT NO. 6165

DATE	ITEM	POST. REF.	DEBIT	CREDIT	BALANCE DEBIT	BALANCE CREDIT
20-- Dec. 1	Balance	✔			2 4 4 6 00	

REINFORCEMENT ACTIVITY 2 PART A (concluded)

ACCOUNT Salary Expense   ACCOUNT NO. 6170

DATE		ITEM	POST. REF.	DEBIT	CREDIT	BALANCE	
						DEBIT	CREDIT
20-- Dec.	1	Balance	✔			63 3 6 0 00	

ACCOUNT Supplies Expense—Office   ACCOUNT NO. 6175

DATE		ITEM	POST. REF.	DEBIT	CREDIT	BALANCE	
						DEBIT	CREDIT

ACCOUNT Supplies Expense—Store   ACCOUNT NO. 6180

DATE		ITEM	POST. REF.	DEBIT	CREDIT	BALANCE	
						DEBIT	CREDIT

ACCOUNT Uncollectible Accounts Expense   ACCOUNT NO. 6185

DATE		ITEM	POST. REF.	DEBIT	CREDIT	BALANCE	
						DEBIT	CREDIT

ACCOUNT Utilities Expense   ACCOUNT NO. 6190

DATE		ITEM	POST. REF.	DEBIT	CREDIT	BALANCE	
						DEBIT	CREDIT
20-- Dec.	1	Balance	✔			8 7 4 5 45	

ACCOUNT Federal Income Tax Expense   ACCOUNT NO. 7105

DATE		ITEM	POST. REF.	DEBIT	CREDIT	BALANCE	
						DEBIT	CREDIT
20-- Dec.	1	Balance	✔			10 0 0 0 00	

Study Guide 14

Name	Perfect Score	Your Score
Identifying Accounting Concepts and Practices	25 Pts.	
Analyzing Adjustments on a Work Sheet	12 Pts.	
Analyzing Work Sheet Extensions	38 Pts.	
Total	75 Pts.	

Part One—Identifying Accounting Concepts and Practices

Directions: Place a *T* for True or an *F* for False in the Answers column to show whether each of the following statements is true or false.

Answers

1. A stockholder is an owner of one of more shares of a corporation. (p. 405)

1. _____

2. Owners' equity accounts for a corporation normally are listed under a major chart of accounts division titled Capital Stock. (p. 405)

2. _____

3. Retained earnings are earnings distributed to stockholders. (p. 405)

3. _____

4. A dividend is an amount earned by a corporation and not yet distributed to stockholders. (p. 405)

4. _____

5. A dividends account has a normal debit balance and is increased by a debit. (p. 405)

5. _____

6. A group of persons elected by the stockholders to manage a corporation is called a board of directors. (p. 406)

6. _____

7. A board of directors distributes earnings of a corporation to stockholders by declaring a dividend. (p. 406)

7. _____

8. A declared dividend is classified as an expense. (p. 406)

8. _____

9. The accounts used to record the declaration of a dividend are Dividends Payable and Dividends Expense. (p. 406)

9. _____

10. When a declared dividend is paid, Dividends Payable is debited. (p. 407)

10. _____

11. The purpose of a work sheet is to plan adjustments and summarize the information necessary to prepare financial statements. (p. 409)

11. _____

12. The steps for preparing a work sheet are similar for proprietorships and corporations. (p. 409)

12. _____

13. The general ledger account balances are changed when the adjustments are entered on the work sheet. (p. 409)

13. _____

14. The adjustment for merchandise inventory is common for all businesses. (p. 409)

14. _____

15. The Supplies—Office account must be adjusted to show the expense of the supplies that are used during the year. (p. 411)

15. _____

16. The Prepaid Insurance account is adjusted to show the value of insurance that has been used. (p. 413)

16. _____

17. During a fiscal period, the amount of merchandise on hand increases and decreases. (p. 415)

17. _____

18. Most accounts needing adjustment at the end of a fiscal period have a related temporary account. (p. 416)

18. _____

19. The risk of uncollectible accounts should be recorded as an expense in the same accounting period that the revenue is earned. (p. 419)

19. _____

20. The account Allowance for Uncollectible Accounts is a contra account. (p. 419)

20. _____

21. Many businesses use a percentage of total sales on account to estimate uncollectible accounts expense. (p. 420)

22. Assets that will be used for a number of years in the operation of a business are called current assets. (p. 423)

23. Accumulated depreciation is the depreciation expense that has been recorded since the purchase of a plant asset. (p. 424)

24. Federal income tax is an expense of a corporation. (p. 427)

25. When a corporation makes the quarterly payment of estimated federal income tax, the cash account is credited. (p. 427)

Part Two—Analyzing Adjustments on a Work Sheet

Directions: For each of the following items, select the choice that best completes the statement. Print the letter identifying your choice in the Answers column.

Answers

1. The Supplies—Office amount in a work sheet's Trial Balance Debit column represents the value of supplies (A) at the beginning of a fiscal period (B) used during a fiscal period (C) at the beginning of a fiscal period plus office supplies bought during the fiscal period (D) bought during a fiscal period. (p. 411)

1. _____

2. The two accounts used to adjust the Office Supplies account are (A) Supplies and Purchases (B) Supplies—Office and Income Summary (C) Supplies—Office and Supplies Expense—Office (D) Supplies Expense—Office and Income Summary. (p. 411)

2. _____

3. The portion of the insurance premiums that has expired during a fiscal period is classified as (A) a liability (B) an asset (C) an expense (D) capital. (p. 413)

3. _____

4. The two accounts used to adjust the Prepaid Insurance account are (A) Insurance Expense and Income Summary (B) Prepaid Insurance and Insurance Expense (C) Prepaid Insurance and Income Summary (D) Prepaid Insurance Expense and Income Summary. (p. 413)

4. _____

5. The amount of goods on hand for sale to customers is called (A) inventory (B) purchases (C) sales (D) merchandise inventory. (p. 415)

5. _____

6. The Merchandise Inventory amount in a work sheet's Trial Balance Debit column represents the merchandise inventory (A) at the end of a fiscal period (B) at the beginning of a fiscal period (C) purchased during a fiscal period (D) available during a fiscal period. (p. 416)

6. _____

7. The two accounts used to adjust the Merchandise Inventory account are (A) Merchandise Inventory and Supplies (B) Merchandise Inventory and Purchases (C) Merchandise Inventory and Income Summary (D) Merchandise Inventory and Sales. (p. 416)

7. _____

8. The Income Summary amount in a work sheet's Adjustments Debit column represents the (A) decrease in Merchandise Inventory (B) increase in Merchandise Inventory (C) beginning Merchandise Inventory (D) ending Merchandise Inventory. (p. 416)

8. _____

9. Recording expenses in the accounting period in which the expenses contribute to earning revenue is an application of the accounting concept (A) Matching Expenses with Revenue (B) Consistent Reporting (C) Historical Cost (D) Adequate Disclosure. (p. 419)

9. _____

10. The two accounts used to adjust the uncollectible accounts are (A) Uncollectible Accounts Expense and Allowance for Uncollectible Accounts (B) Accounts Receivable and Uncollectible Accounts Expense (C) Accounts Receivable and Allowance for Uncollectible Accounts (D) Accounts Receivable and Accounts Receivable Expense. (p. 421)

10. _____

11. The two accounts used to adjust the depreciation of store equipment are (A) Store Equipment and Store Equipment Expense (B) Accumulated Depreciation—Store Equipment and Accumulated Depreciation Expense (C) Accumulated Depreciation—Store Equipment and Store Equipment Expense (D) Accumulated Depreciation—Store Equipment and Depreciation Expense—Store Equipment. (p. 425)

11. _____

12. The two accounts used to record the adjustment for federal income tax are (A) Federal Income Tax Expense and Taxes Payable (B) Federal Income Tax Payable and Federal Income Tax Expense (C) Federal Income Tax Expense and Allowance for Federal Tax Expense (D) Federal Income Tax Expense and Federal Income Tax Adjustments. (p. 429)

12. _____

Part Three—Analyzing Work Sheet Extensions (pp. 432–433)

Directions: For each account listed below, place a check mark in the column to which amounts are extended on a work sheet.

Account Title	Income Statement Debit	Credit	Balance Sheet Debit	Credit
1. Accounts Payable	___	___	___	___
2. Accounts Receivable	___	___	___	___
3. Accumulated Depreciation—Office Equipment	___	___	___	___
4. Accumulated Depreciation—Store Equipment	___	___	___	___
5. Advertising Expense	___	___	___	___
6. Allowance for Uncollectible Accounts	___	___	___	___
7. Capital Stock	___	___	___	___
8. Cash	___	___	___	___
9. Credit Card Fee Expense	___	___	___	___
10. Dividends	___	___	___	___
11. Employee Income Tax Payable	___	___	___	___
12. Health Insurance Premiums Payable	___	___	___	___
13. Income Summary (ending inventory smaller than beginning inventory)	___	___	___	___
14. Insurance Expense	___	___	___	___
15. Medicare Tax Payable	___	___	___	___
16. Merchandise Inventory	___	___	___	___
17. Miscellaneous Expense	___	___	___	___
18. Office Equipment	___	___	___	___
19. Payroll Taxes Expense	___	___	___	___
20. Petty Cash	___	___	___	___
21. Prepaid Insurance	___	___	___	___
22. Purchases	___	___	___	___
23. Rent Expense	___	___	___	___
24. Retained Earnings	___	___	___	___
25. Salary Expense	___	___	___	___
26. Sales	___	___	___	___
27. Sales Tax Payable	___	___	___	___
28. Social Security Tax Payable	___	___	___	___
29. Store Equipment	___	___	___	___
30. Supplies Expense—Office	___	___	___	___
31. Supplies Expense—Store	___	___	___	___
32. Supplies—Office	___	___	___	___
33. Supplies—Store	___	___	___	___
34. Unemployment Tax Payable—Federal	___	___	___	___
35. Unemployment Tax Payable—State	___	___	___	___
36. United Way Donations Payable	___	___	___	___
37. U.S. Savings Bonds Payable	___	___	___	___
38. Utilities Expense	___	___	___	___

Name _____ Date _____ Class _____

14-1 WORK TOGETHER, p. 408

Journalizing dividends

1.

GENERAL JOURNAL PAGE 14

	DATE	ACCOUNT TITLE	DOC. NO.	POST. REF.	DEBIT	CREDIT	
1							1
2							2
3							3
4							4
5							5

2.

CASH PAYMENTS JOURNAL

PAGE 21

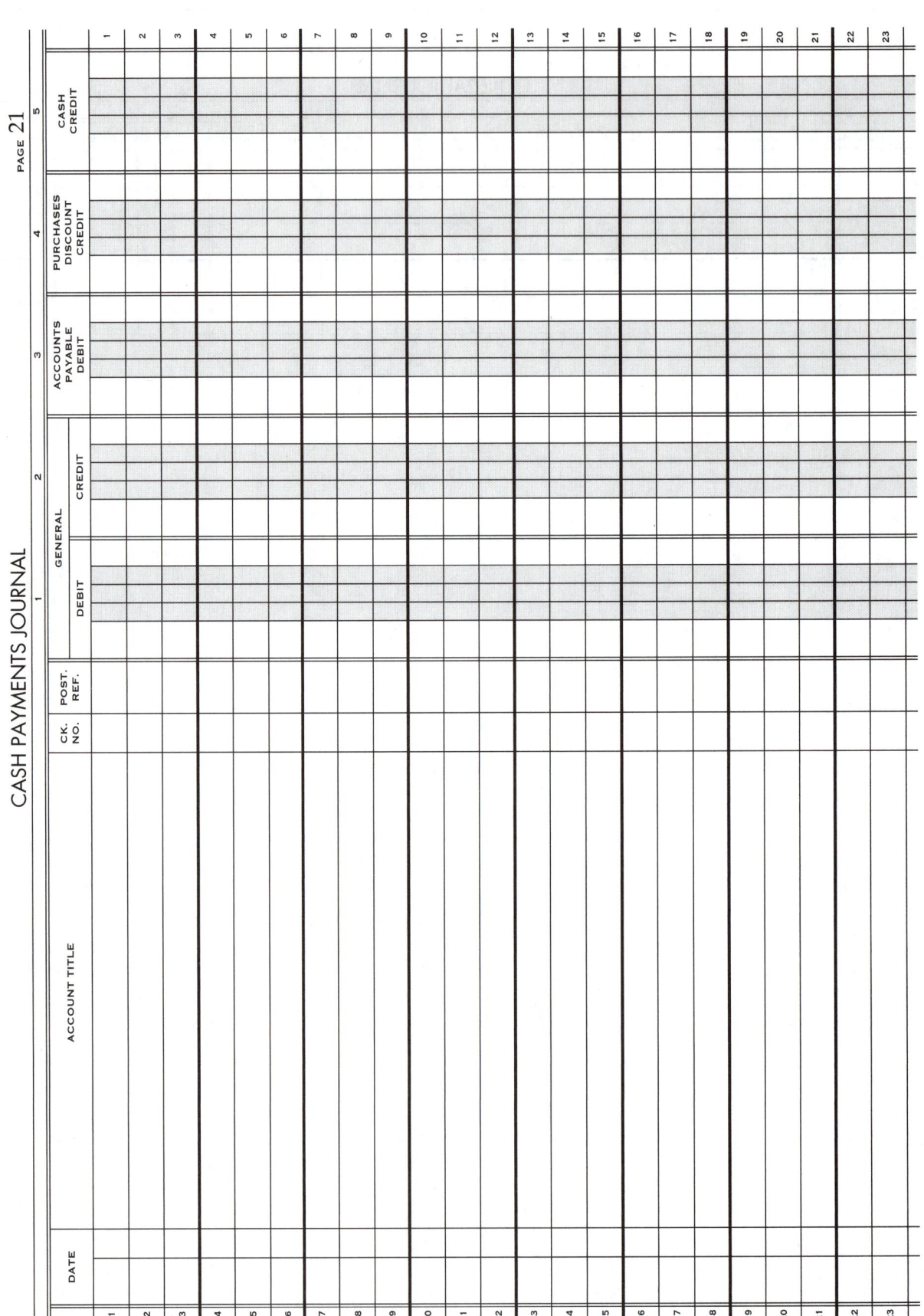

14-1 ON YOUR OWN, p. 408

Journalizing dividends

1.

GENERAL JOURNAL

PAGE 22

	DATE	ACCOUNT TITLE	DOC. NO.	POST. REF.	DEBIT	CREDIT	
1							1
2							2
3							3
4							4
5							5
6							6
7							7
8							8
9							9
10							10
11							11
12							12
13							13
14							14
15							15
16							16
17							17
18							18
19							19
20							20
21							21
22							22
23							23
24							24
25							25
26							26
27							27
28							28
29							29
30							30
31							31
32							32

2.

CASH PAYMENTS JOURNAL

PAGE 24

	DATE	ACCOUNT TITLE	CK. NO.	POST. REF.	GENERAL DEBIT	GENERAL CREDIT	ACCOUNTS PAYABLE DEBIT	PURCHASES DISCOUNT CREDIT	CASH CREDIT	
1										1
2										2
3										3
4										4
5										5
6										6
7										7
8										8
9										9
10										10
11										11
12										12
13										13
14										14
15										15
16										16
17										17
18										18
19										19
20										20
21										21
22										22
23										23
24										24

[This page left blank intentionally]

14-2 Beginning an 8-column work sheet for a merchandising business
14-3 Analyzing and recording an adjustment for merchandise inventory
14-4 Analyzing and recording an adjustment for uncollectible accounts expense
14-5 Planning and recording adjustments for depreciation
14-6 Completing an 8-column work sheet for a merchandising business organized as a corporation

Coastal Aquatics
Work Sheet
For Year Ended December 31, 20 – –

#	ACCOUNT TITLE	TRIAL BALANCE DEBIT	TRIAL BALANCE CREDIT
1	Cash	18 4 8 5 00	
2	Petty Cash	3 0 0 00	
3			
4	Allow. for Uncoll. Accts.		5 2 4 84
5	Merchandise Inventory	248 7 5 2 25	
6	Supplies—Office	5 4 8 5 25	
7	Supplies—Store	4 5 7 8 36	
8	Prepaid Insurance	6 2 0 0 00	
9	Office Equipment	35 4 8 7 25	
10	Acc. Depr.—Office Equipment		12 4 8 5 25
11	Store Equipment	40 8 4 9 50	
12	Acc. Depr.—Store Equipment		15 4 8 3 25
13	Federal Income Tax Payable		
14	Emp. Income Tax Pay.		9 9 8 00
15	Social Security Tax Payable		7 7 4 07
16	Medicare Tax Payable		1 8 1 03
17	Sales Tax Payable		1 8 4 8 35
18	Unemployment Tax Pay.—Fed.		2 4 00
19	Unemployment Tax Pay.—State		1 6 2 00
20	Health Ins. Premiums Pay.		9 5 0 00
21	U.S. Savings Bonds Payable		8 0 00
22	United Way Donations Pay.		7 5 00
23	Dividends Payable		10 0 0 0 00
24	Capital Stock		175 0 0 0 00
25	Retained Earnings		12 5 7 7 45
26			

(Additional column headings across the work sheet: ADJUSTMENTS — Debit / Credit; INCOME STATEMENT — Debit / Credit; BALANCE SHEET — Debit / Credit)

Before Federal Income Tax

Total of Income Statement Credit column	_____
Total of Income Statement Debit column	_____
Net Income Before Federal Income Tax	_____

Coastal Aquatics

Work Sheet

For Year Ended December 31, 20 – –

| | 1 TRIAL BALANCE DEBIT | 2 TRIAL BALANCE CREDIT | 3 ADJUSTMENTS DEBIT | 4 ADJUSTMENTS CREDIT | 5 INCOME STATEMENT DEBIT | 6 INCOME STATEMENT CREDIT | 7 BALANCE SHEET DEBIT | 8 BALANCE SHEET CREDIT | |
ACCOUNT TITLE									
Dividends	21 000 00								27
Income Summary									28
									29
Sales Discount	6 48 25								30
Sales Returns and Allowances	8 157 27								31
									32
Purchases Discount		4 615 25							33
Purch. Returns and Allowances		9 497 00							34
Advertising Expense	15 280 00								35
Cash Short and Over	12 85								36
Credit Card Fee Expense	6 482 27								37
Depr. Exp.—Office Equipment									38
Depr. Exp.—Store Equipment									39
Insurance Expense									40
Miscellaneous Expense	4 568 97								41
Payroll Taxes Expense	16 184 25								42
Rent Expense	24 000 00								43
Salary Expense	204 180 85								44
Supplies Expense—Office									45
Supplies Expense—Store									46
Uncollectible Accounts Exp.									47
Utilities Expense	4 264 28								48
Fed. Income Tax Expense	40 000 00								49
									50
									51
									52

Federal Income Tax   Rate   Tax

First $50,000 _____ _____

Next $25,000 _____ _____

Next $25,000 _____ _____

_____ – $100,000.00 = _____ _____ _____

Total Federal Income Tax _____

14-2 Beginning an 8-column work sheet for a merchandising business
14-3 Analyzing and recording an adjustment for merchandise inventory
14-4 Analyzing and recording an adjustment for uncollectible accounts expense
14-5 Planning and recording adjustments for depreciation
14-6 Completing an 8-column work sheet for a merchandising business organized as a corporation

Sonoma Treasures
Work Sheet
For Year Ended December 31, 20 - -

	ACCOUNT TITLE	TRIAL BALANCE DEBIT	TRIAL BALANCE CREDIT	ADJUSTMENTS DEBIT	ADJUSTMENTS CREDIT	INCOME STATEMENT DEBIT	INCOME STATEMENT CREDIT	BALANCE SHEET DEBIT	BALANCE SHEET CREDIT	
1	Cash	17 0 5 8 25								1
2	Petty Cash	5 0 0 00								2
3	Accounts Receivable	25 6 0 9 70								3
4	Allow. for Uncoll. Accts.		6 48 29							4
5	Merchandise Inventory	264 2 4 8 84								5
6	Supplies—Office	2 4 8 3 28								6
7	Supplies—Store	5 1 8 1 94								7
8										8
9	Office Equipment	32 1 8 4 25								9
10	Acc. Depr.—Office Equipment		18 4 7 4 00							10
11	Store Equipment	45 1 8 4 98								11
12	Acc. Depr.—Store Equipment		21 4 4 8 00							12
13	Accounts Payable		22 1 5 4 17							13
14	Federal Income Tax Payable									14
15	Emp. Income Tax Pay.—Federal		1 2 1 5 00							15
16	Social Security Tax Payable		8 77 42							16
17	Medicare Tax Payable		2 05 20							17
18	Sales Tax Payable		3 5 1 5 00							18
19	Unemployment Tax Pay.—Fed.		24 00							19
20	Unemployment Tax Pay.—State		1 62 00							20
21	Health Ins. Premiums Pay.		1 0 2 0 00							21
22	U.S. Savings Bonds Payable		1 00 00							22
23	United Way Donations Pay.		1 20 00							23
24	Dividends Payable		12 0 0 0 00							24
25										25
26	Retained Earnings		90 9 6 2 38							26

Before Federal Income Tax
Total of Income Statement Credit column   _____
Total of Income Statement Debit column   _____
Net Income Before Federal Income Tax   _____

14-2, 14-3, 14-4, 14-5, and 14-6 ON YOUR OWN (concluded)

Sonoma Treasures

Work Sheet

For Year Ended December 31, 20 - -

	ACCOUNT TITLE	TRIAL BALANCE DEBIT	TRIAL BALANCE CREDIT	ADJUSTMENTS DEBIT	ADJUSTMENTS CREDIT	INCOME STATEMENT DEBIT	INCOME STATEMENT CREDIT	BALANCE SHEET DEBIT	BALANCE SHEET CREDIT	
27	Dividends	84 0 0 0 00								27
28	Income Summary									28
29	Sales		925 1 8 3 20							29
30										30
31	Sales Returns and Allowances	6 9 4 2 28								31
32	Purchases	482 1 0 1 66								32
33	Purchases Discount		4 2 1 5 35							33
34	Purch. Returns and Allowances		8 1 4 8 99							34
35	Advertising Expense	13 2 5 0 00								35
36	Cash Short and Over	1 1 18								36
37	Credit Card Fee Expense	12 4 5 1 27								37
38	Depr. Exp.—Office Equipment									38
39	Depr. Exp.—Store Equipment									39
40	Insurance Expense									40
41	Miscellaneous Expense	8 4 0 2 00								41
42	Payroll Taxes Expense	21 4 8 2 88								42
43										43
44	Salary Expense	234 1 8 2 25								44
45	Supplies Expense—Office									45
46	Supplies Expense—Store									46
47	Uncollectible Accounts Exp.									47
48	Utilities Expense	6 4 8 2 99								48
49	Fed. Income Tax Expense	16 0 0 0 00								49
50										50
51										51
52										52

Federal Income Tax   Rate   Tax

First $50,000   ____   _____

Next $25,000   ____   _____

_____ − $75,000.00 = _____   ____   _____

Total Federal Income Tax   _____

Planning and recording adjustments for depreciation

1.

Original Cost _____
Estimated Salvage Value _____
Estimated Total Depreciation Expense _____ ÷ _____ Years of Estimated Useful Life = _____ Annual Depreciation Expense

2.

Original Cost _____
Depreciation: Year 1 _____
                Year 2 _____

Book Value _____

Planning and recording adjustments for depreciation

1.

Original Cost _____
Estimated Salvage Value _____
Estimated Total Depreciation Expense _____ ÷ _____ Years of Estimated Useful Life = _____ Annual Depreciation Expense

2.

Original Cost _____
Depreciation: Year 1 _____
                Year 2 _____
                Year 3 _____

Book Value _____

14-1 APPLICATION PROBLEM, p. 438

Journalizing dividends

1.

GENERAL JOURNAL

	DATE	ACCOUNT TITLE	DOC. NO.	POST. REF.	DEBIT	CREDIT	
1							1
2							2
3							3
4							4
5							5
6							6
7							7

2.

CASH PAYMENTS JOURNAL

PAGE 28

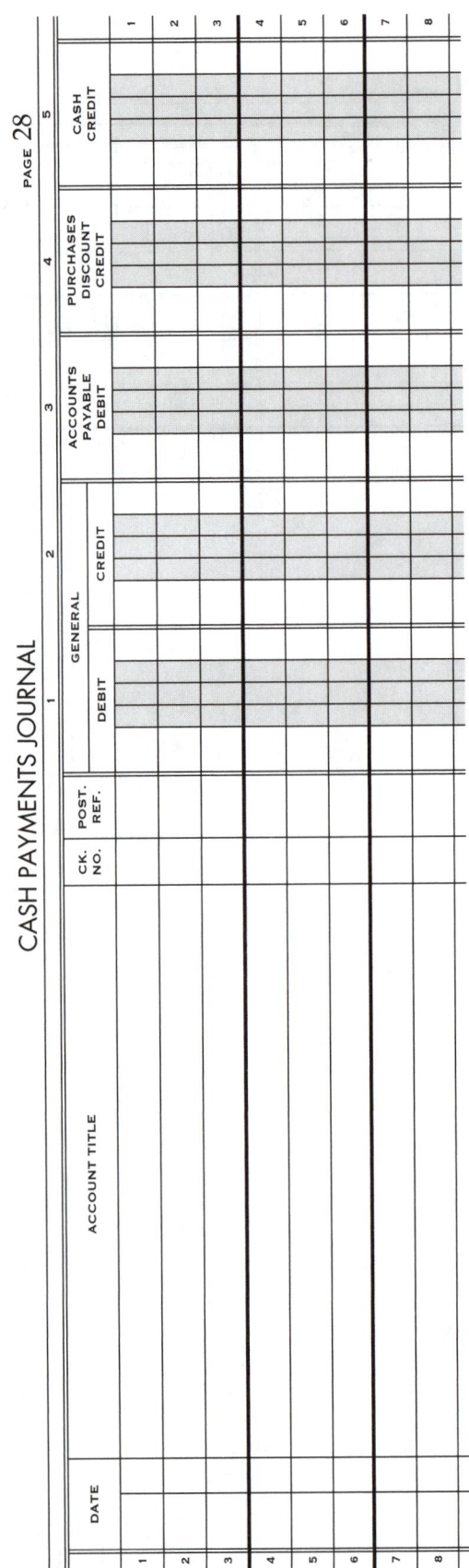

[This page left blank intentionally]

14-2 Beginning an 8-column work sheet for a merchandising business
14-3 Analyzing and recording a merchandise inventory adjustment on a work sheet
14-4 Analyzing and recording an allowance for uncollectible accounts adjustment on a work sheet
14-5 Planning and recording adjustments for depreciation
14-6 Calculating federal income tax and completing an 8-column work sheet for a merchandising business

Branson Amusement Company

Work Sheet

For Year Ended December 31, 20 – –

	TRIAL BALANCE DEBIT	TRIAL BALANCE CREDIT	ADJUSTMENTS DEBIT	ADJUSTMENTS CREDIT	INCOME STATEMENT DEBIT	INCOME STATEMENT CREDIT	BALANCE SHEET DEBIT	BALANCE SHEET CREDIT
1 Cash	17560 75							
2 Petty Cash	300 00							
3 Accounts Receivable	14710 98							
4 Allow. for Uncoll. Accts.		498 59						
5 Merchandise Inventory	236314 63							
6								
7 Supplies—Store	4349 44							
8 Prepaid Insurance	6000 00							
9 Office Equipment	33712 88							
10 Acc. Depr.—Office Equipment		11860 98						
11 Store Equipment	38807 02							
12 Acc. Depr.—Store Equipment		14709 08						
13								
14 Federal Income Tax Payable								
15 Emp. Income Tax Pay.		948 10						
16 Social Security Tax Payable		724 41						
17 Medicare Tax Payable		169 42						
18 Sales Tax Payable		1755 93						
19 Unemployment Tax Pay.—Fed.		24 00						
20 Unemployment Tax Pay.—State		162 00						
21 Health Ins. Premiums Pay.		902 50						
22 U.S. Savings Bonds Payable		76 00						
23 United Way Donations Pay.		71 25						
24 Dividends Payable		3150 00						
25 Capital Stock		525000 00						
26 Retained Earnings		96689 21						

Before Federal Income Tax

Total of Income Statement Credit column _____

Total of Income Statement Debit column _____

Net Income Before Federal Income Tax _____

14-2, 14-3, 14-4, 14-5, and 14-6 — APPLICATION PROBLEMS (concluded)

Branson Amusement Company

Work Sheet

For Year Ended December 31, 20 --

		ACCOUNT TITLE	TRIAL BALANCE DEBIT	TRIAL BALANCE CREDIT	ADJUSTMENTS DEBIT	ADJUSTMENTS CREDIT	INCOME STATEMENT DEBIT	INCOME STATEMENT CREDIT	BALANCE SHEET DEBIT	BALANCE SHEET CREDIT	
27		Dividends	126000 00								27
28		Income Summary									28
29		Sales		843536 68							29
30		Sales Discount	2515 25								30
31		Sales Returns and Allowances	8482 25								31
32		Purchases	369724 80								32
33											33
34		Purch. Returns and Allowances		9022 15							34
35		Advertising Expense	14516 00								35
36		Cash Short and Over	7 72								36
37		Credit Card Fee Expense	6158 15								37
38		Depr. Exp.—Office Equipment									38
39		Depr. Exp.—Store Equipment									39
40		Insurance Expense									40
41		Miscellaneous Expense	4345 00								41
42		Payroll Taxes Expense	15375 03								42
43		Rent Expense	22800 00								43
44											44
45		Supplies Expense—Office									45
46		Supplies Expense—Store									46
47		Uncollectible Accounts Exp.									47
48		Utilities Expense	4051 06								48
49		Fed. Income Tax Expense	48000 00								49
50											50
51											51
52											52

Federal Income Tax   Rate   Tax

First $50,000   ____ ____

Next $25,000   ____ ____

Next $25,000   ____ ____

_____ − $100,000.00 = _____   ____ ____

Total Federal Income Tax   ____

APPLICATION PROBLEM, p. 439

Planning and recording adjustments for depreciation

Wave Diving company scuba testing equipment:

1.

Original Cost _____

Estimated Salvage Value _____

Estimated Total Depreciation Expense _____ ÷ ____ Years of Estimated Useful Life = _____ Annual Depreciation Expense

2.

Original Cost _____

Depreciation: Year 1 _____

           Year 2 _____

Book Value _____

[This page left blank intentionally]

14-7 MASTERY PROBLEM, p. 440

Preparing an 8-column work sheet for a merchandising business

Carol's Closet

Work Sheet

For Year Ended December 31, 20 – –

	ACCOUNT TITLE	TRIAL BALANCE DEBIT	TRIAL BALANCE CREDIT	ADJUSTMENTS DEBIT	ADJUSTMENTS CREDIT	INCOME STATEMENT DEBIT	INCOME STATEMENT CREDIT	BALANCE SHEET DEBIT	BALANCE SHEET CREDIT	
1	Cash	28 5 4 8 25								1
2	Petty Cash	5 0 0 00								2
3	Accounts Receivable	32 5 1 8 28								3
4	Allow. for Uncoll. Accts.		1 5 5 25							4
5	Merchandise Inventory	229 2 8 2 36								5
6	Supplies—Office	6 1 2 8 25								6
7	Supplies—Store	4 2 1 8 36								7
8	Prepaid Insurance	12 0 0 0 00								8
9	Office Equipment	28 1 8 7 25								9
10	Acc. Depr.—Office Equipment		5 1 5 8 25							10
11	Store Equipment	42 8 4 1 05								11
12	Acc. Depr.—Store Equipment		12 4 8 3 25							12
13	Accounts Payable		21 5 4 3 20							13
14	Federal Income Tax Payable									14
15	Emp. Income Tax Pay.		1 2 4 8 25							15
16	Social Security Tax Payable		8 2 2 00							16
17	Medicare Tax Payable		1 9 2 24							17
18	Sales Tax Payable		2 4 1 5 25							18
19	Unemployment Tax Pay.—Fed.		3 3 60							19
20	Unemployment Tax Pay.—State		2 2 6 80							20
21	Health Ins. Premiums Pay.		9 6 0 00							21
22	U.S. Savings Bonds Payable		7 5 00							22
23	United Way Donations Pay.		1 0 0 00							23
24	Dividends Payable		11 0 0 0 00							24
25	Capital Stock		55 0 0 0 00							25
26	Retained Earnings		172 9 8 0 13							26

Before Federal Income Tax

Total of Income Statement Credit column   _____

Total of Income Statement Debit column   _____

Net Income Before Federal Income Tax   _____

14-7 MASTERY PROBLEM (concluded)

Carol's Closet

Work Sheet

For Year Ended December 31, 20 - -

	ACCOUNT TITLE	TRIAL BALANCE DEBIT	TRIAL BALANCE CREDIT	ADJUSTMENTS DEBIT	ADJUSTMENTS CREDIT	INCOME STATEMENT DEBIT	INCOME STATEMENT CREDIT	BALANCE SHEET DEBIT	BALANCE SHEET CREDIT	
27	Dividends	44 000 00								27
28	Income Summary									28
29	Sales		948 484 25							29
30	Sales Discount	3 154 15								30
31	Sales Returns and Allowances	7 148 15								31
32	Purchases	489 335 54								32
33	Purchases Discount		5 015 25							33
34	Purch. Returns and Allowances		7 058 05							34
35	Advertising Expense	16 025 00								35
36	Cash Short and Over	7 25								36
37	Credit Card Fee Expense	7 015 95								37
38	Depr. Exp.—Office Equipment									38
39	Depr. Exp.—Store Equipment									39
40	Insurance Expense									40
41	Miscellaneous Expense	5 098 00								41
42	Payroll Taxes Expense	18 152 25								42
43	Rent Expense	28 000 00								43
44	Salary Expense	193 971 80								44
45	Supplies Expense—Office									45
46	Supplies Expense—Store									46
47	Uncollectible Accounts Exp.									47
48	Utilities Expense	4 818 88								48
49	Fed. Income Tax Expense	44 000 00								49
50										50
51										51
52										52

Federal Income Tax	Rate	Tax
First $50,000	____	_____
Next $25,000	____	_____
Next $25,000	____	_____
_____ − $100,000.00 = _____	____	_____
Total Federal Income Tax		_____

Preparing a 10-column work sheet for a merchandising business

Hillside Ski Shop

Work Sheet

For Year Ended December 31, 20 – –

	ACCOUNT TITLE	TRIAL BALANCE		ADJUSTMENTS	
		DEBIT	CREDIT	DEBIT	CREDIT
1	Cash	14 2 5 8 25			
2	Petty Cash	2 5 0 00			
3	Accounts Receivable	16 4 8 5 25			
4	Allow. for Uncoll. Accts.		2 5 1 25		
5	Merchandise Inventory	169 1 5 8 66			
6	Supplies—Office	3 1 8 4 67			
7	Supplies—Store	2 4 1 5 29			
8	Prepaid Insurance	12 0 0 0 00			
9	Office Equipment	28 1 8 7 25			
10	Acc. Depr.—Office Equipment		12 1 8 2 00		
11	Store Equipment	32 1 8 4 84			
12	Acc. Depr.—Store Equipment		16 1 8 4 00		
13	Accounts Payable		12 4 8 2 36		
14	Federal Income Tax Payable				
15	Emp. Income Tax Pay.—Federal		1 2 4 8 25		
16	Social Security Tax Payable		5 1 1 83		
17	Medicare Tax Payable		1 1 9 70		
18	Sales Tax Payable		1 2 1 5 25		
19	Unemployment Tax Pay.—Fed.		2 5 60		
20	Unemployment Tax Pay.—State		1 7 2 80		
21	Health Ins. Premiums Pay.		5 6 0 00		
22	U.S. Savings Bonds Payable		2 0 00		
23	United Way Donations Pay.		6 0 00		
24	Dividends Payable		12 0 0 0 00		
25	Capital Stock		150 0 0 0 00		
26	Retained Earnings		22 1 0 8 43		

Before Federal Income Tax

Total of Income Statement Credit column   _____

Total of Income Statement Debit column   _____

Net Income Before Federal Income Tax   _____

14-8 **CHALLENGE PROBLEM (continued)**

_____
_____
_____

	5		6		7		8		9		10		
	ADJUSTED TRIAL BALANCE				INCOME STATEMENT				BALANCE SHEET				
	DEBIT		CREDIT		DEBIT		CREDIT		DEBIT		CREDIT		
													1
													2
													3
													4
													5
													6
													7
													8
													9
													10
													11
													12
													13
													14
													15
													16
													17
													18
													19
													20
													21
													22
													23
													24
													25
													26

Hillside Ski Shop

Work Sheet

For Year Ended December 31, 20 – –

	ACCOUNT TITLE	TRIAL BALANCE DEBIT	TRIAL BALANCE CREDIT	ADJUSTMENTS DEBIT	ADJUSTMENTS CREDIT
27	Dividends	48 0 0 0 00			
28	Income Summary				
29	Sales		508 2 1 8 88		
30	Sales Discount	1 5 4 8 81			
31	Sales Returns and Allowances	2 1 8 4 94			
32	Purchases	204 8 4 0 10			
33	Purchases Discount		2 4 8 9 05		
34	Purch. Returns and Allowances		3 1 4 8 08		
35	Advertising Expense	12 5 0 0 00			
36	Cash Short and Over	8 04			
37	Credit Card Fee Expense	2 4 8 4 10			
38	Depr. Exp.—Office Equipment				
39	Depr. Exp.—Store Equipment				
40	Insurance Expense				
41	Miscellaneous Expense	4 1 5 0 00			
42	Payroll Taxes Expense	12 1 8 4 20			
43	Rent Expense	24 0 0 0 00			
44	Salary Expense	130 1 5 4 20			
45	Supplies Expense—Office				
46	Supplies Expense—Store				
47	Uncollectible Accounts Exp.				
48	Utilities Expense	4 8 1 8 88			
49	Fed. Income Tax Expense	18 0 0 0 00			
50					
51					
52					

Federal Income Tax	Rate	Tax
First $50,000	____	_____
Next $25,000	____	_____
_____ − $75,000.00 = _____	____	_____
Total Federal Income Tax		_____

14-8 CHALLENGE PROBLEM (concluded)

	5	6	7	8	9	10	
	ADJUSTED TRIAL BALANCE		INCOME STATEMENT		BALANCE SHEET		
	DEBIT	CREDIT	DEBIT	CREDIT	DEBIT	CREDIT	
							27
							28
							29
							30
							31
							32
							33
							34
							35
							36
							37
							38
							39
							40
							41
							42
							43
							44
							45
							46
							47
							48
							49
							50
							51
							52

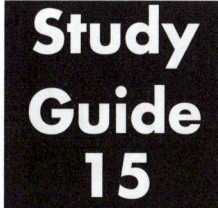

Study Guide 15

Name	Perfect Score	Your Score
Identifying Accounting Terms	11 Pts.	
Analyzing Acceptable Component Percentages	8 Pts.	
Analyzing Financial Statements for a Merchandising Business	21 Pts.	
Total	40 Pts.	

Part One—Identifying Accounting Terms

Directions: Select the one term in Column I that best fits each definition in Column II. Print the letter identifying your choice in the Answers column.

Column I	Column II	Answers
A. cost of merchandise sold	1. Total sales less sales discount and sales returns and allowances. (p. 449)	1. _____
B. current liabilities	2. The original price of all merchandise sold during a fiscal period. (p. 450)	2. _____
C. earnings per share	3. The revenue remaining after cost of merchandise sold has been deducted. (p. 452)	3. _____
D. financial ratio	4. A comparison between two items of financial information. (p. 459)	4. _____
E. gross profit on sales	5. The amount of net income after federal income tax belonging to a single share of stock. (p. 459)	5. _____
F. long-term liabilities	6. The relationship between the market value per share and earnings per share of a stock. (p. 459)	6. _____
G. net sales	7. A financial statement that shows changes in a corporation's ownership for a fiscal period. (p. 461)	7. _____
H. par value	8. A value assigned to a share of stock and printed on the stock certificate. (p. 461)	8. _____
I. price-earnings ratio	9. Liabilities due within a short time, usually within a year. (p. 467)	9. _____
J. statement of stockholders' equity	10. Liabilities owed for more than a year. (p. 467)	10. _____
K. supporting schedule	11. A report prepared to give details about an item on a principal financial statement. (p. 470)	11. _____

Part Two—Analyzing Acceptable Component Percentages

Directions: For each of the income statement component percentages given, write a *U* in the Answers column if it is Unacceptable and write an *A* in the Answers column if it is Acceptable. (pp. 455–456)

Acceptable Component Percentages	
Sales	100%
Cost of merchandise sold	Not more than 48.6%
Gross profit on sales	Not less than 51.4%
Total expenses	Not more than 34.9%
Net income	Not less than 16.5%

Answers

1. The component percentage for total expenses is 42.8% this year.

   1. _____

2. The component percentage for cost of merchandise sold is 51.0% this year.

   2. _____

3. The component percentage for gross profit on sales is 52.8% this year.

   3. _____

4. The component percentage for total expenses is 34.3% this year.

   4. _____

5. The component percentage for gross profit on sales is 51.4% this year.

   5. _____

6. The component percentage for net income is 17.0% this year.

   6. _____

7. The component percentage for cost of merchandise sold is 48.7% this year.

   7. _____

8. The component percentage for net income is 10.4% this year.

   8. _____

Part Three—Analyzing Financial Statements for a Merchandising Business

Directions: Place a *T* for True or an *F* for False in the Answers column to show whether each of the following statements is true or false.

Answers

1. Financial statements provide the primary source of information needed by owners and managers to make decisions on the future activity of a business. (p. 446)

1. _____

2. Reporting financial information the same way from one fiscal period to the next is an application of the accounting concept Adequate Disclosure. (p. 446)

2. _____

3. An income statement is used to report a business's financial progress. (p. 448)

3. _____

4. An income statement for a merchandising business has three main sections: revenue section, cost of merchandise sold section, and expenses section. (p. 448)

4. _____

5. Cost of merchandise sold is also known as cost of goods sold. (p. 450)

5. _____

6. Revenue less cost of merchandise sold equals net income. (p. 452)

6. _____

7. Calculating a ratio between gross profit on sales and net sales enables management to compare its performance to prior fiscal periods. (pp. 452–453)

7. _____

8. Total expenses on an income statement are deducted from the gross profit on sales to find net income before federal income tax. (p. 453)

8. _____

9. For a merchandising business, every sales dollar reported on the income statement includes only three components: gross profit on sales, total expenses, and net income. (p. 455)

9. _____

10. When a business's expenses are less than the gross profit on sales, the difference is known as a net loss. (p. 457)

10. _____

11. Increasing sales revenue while keeping cost of merchandise sold the same will increase gross profit on sales. (p. 458)

11. _____

12. Most businesses correct an unacceptable component percentage for gross profit by simply increasing the markup on merchandise purchased for sale because an increased selling price will always increase profit. (p. 458)

12. _____

13. Individual amounts reported on an income statement have little meaning without being compared to another amount. (p. 459)

13. _____

14. A statement of stockholders' equity contains two major sections: (1) capital stock and (2) retained earnings. (p. 461)

14. _____

15. The beginning balance of the capital stock account is the amount of capital stock issued at the beginning of the year. (p. 461)

15. _____

16. The amounts in the capital stock section of the statement of stockholders' equity are obtained from the general ledger account, Capital Stock. (p. 461)

16. _____

17. Net income is shown on the last line of a statement of stockholders' equity. (p. 462)

17. _____

18. Some income may be distributed as dividends to provide stockholders with a return on their investments. (p. 462)

18. _____

19. Data needed to prepare the liabilities section of a balance sheet are obtained from a work sheet. (p. 467)

19. _____

20. Ruled double lines across both amount columns below the Assets section and below the Stockholders' Equity section show that the assets equal liabilities plus owners' equity. (p. 468)

21. When more detailed information about an item on a financial statement is needed, a supporting schedule may be prepared. (p. 470)

Preparing an income statement for a merchandising business

Interstate Tires, Inc.

Work Sheet

For Year Ended December 31, 20 - -

ACCOUNT TITLE	TRIAL BALANCE DEBIT	TRIAL BALANCE CREDIT	ADJUSTMENTS DEBIT	ADJUSTMENTS CREDIT	INCOME STATEMENT DEBIT	INCOME STATEMENT CREDIT	BALANCE SHEET DEBIT	BALANCE SHEET CREDIT	
Cash	12 848 00						12 848 00		1
Petty Cash	3 000 00						3 000 00		2
Accounts Receivable	18 438 90						18 438 90		3
Allow. for Uncoll. Accts.		847 29		(e) 1 680 00				2 527 29	4
Merchandise Inventory	198 480 33			(d) 9 481 08			188 999 25		5
Supplies—Office	3 341 58			(a) 2 486 99			854 59		6
Supplies—Store	4 248 96			(b) 2 948 28			1 300 68		7
Prepaid Insurance	9 000 00			(c) 6 000 00			3 000 00		8
Office Equipment	18 486 38						18 486 38		9
Acc. Depr.—Office Equip.		9 485 25		(f) 4 260 00				13 745 25	10
Store Equipment	32 184 07						32 184 07		11
Acc. Depr.—Store Equip.		18 486 45		(g) 5 750 00				24 236 45	12
Accounts Payable		16 107 08						16 107 08	13
Federal Income Tax Payable				(h) 2 603 79				2 603 79	14
Emp. Income Tax Payable		840 00						840 00	15
Social Security Tax Payable		529 98						529 98	16
Medicare Tax Payable		123 95						123 95	17
Sales Tax Payable		1 848 25						1 848 25	18
Unemploy. Tax Payable—Fed.		32 00						32 00	19
Unemploy. Tax Payable—State		216 00						216 00	20
Health Insur. Premiums Payable		620 00						620 00	21
U.S. Savings Bonds Payable		35 00						35 00	22
United Way Donations Payable		40 00						40 00	23
Dividends Payable		2 200 00						2 200 00	24
Capital Stock		110 000 00						110 000 00	25
Retained Earnings		46 599 48						46 599 48	26

(Note: Work sheet is continued on next page.)

Interstate Tires, Inc.

Work Sheet

For Year Ended December 31, 20 - -

	ACCOUNT TITLE	TRIAL BALANCE DEBIT	TRIAL BALANCE CREDIT	ADJUSTMENTS DEBIT	ADJUSTMENTS CREDIT	INCOME STATEMENT DEBIT	INCOME STATEMENT CREDIT	BALANCE SHEET DEBIT	BALANCE SHEET CREDIT	
27	Dividends	8 8 0 0 00						8 8 0 0 00		27
28	Income Summary			(d) 9 4 8 1 08		9 4 8 1 08				28
29	Sales		548 9 8 9 25				548 9 8 9 25			29
30	Sales Discount	6 6 1 69				6 6 1 69				30
31	Sales Returns and Allowances	3 5 1 2 84				3 5 1 2 84				31
32	Purchases	278 4 5 2 39				278 4 5 2 39				32
33	Purchases Discount		1 8 4 5 78				1 8 4 5 78			33
34	Purch. Returns and Allowances		3 5 4 8 65				3 5 4 8 65			34
35	Advertising Expense	9 3 2 0 00				9 3 2 0 00				35
36	Cash Short and Over	5 27				5 27				36
37	Credit Card Fee Expense	9 4 5 4 45				9 4 5 4 45				37
38	Depr. Exp.—Office Equipment			(f) 4 2 6 0 00		4 2 6 0 00				38
39	Depr. Exp.—Store Equipment			(g) 5 7 5 0 00		5 7 5 0 00				39
40	Insurance Expense			(c) 6 0 0 0 00		6 0 0 0 00				40
41	Miscellaneous Expense	6 4 8 0 00				6 4 8 0 00				41
42	Payroll Taxes Expense	9 3 1 5 66				9 3 1 5 66				42
43	Rent Expense	18 0 0 0 00				18 0 0 0 00				43
44	Salary Expense	102 5 7 6 00				102 5 7 6 00				44
45	Supplies Expense—Office			(a) 2 4 8 6 99		2 4 8 6 99				45
46	Supplies Expense—Store			(b) 2 9 4 8 28		2 9 4 8 28				46
47	Uncollectible Accounts Expense			(e) 1 6 8 0 00		1 6 8 0 00				47
48	Utilities Expense	6 4 8 7 89				6 4 8 7 89				48
49	Federal Income Tax Expense	120 0 0 0 00		(h) 2 6 0 3 79		1460 3 79				49
50		762 3 9 4 41	762 3 9 4 41	35 2 1 0 14	35 2 1 0 14	491 4 7 6 33	554 3 8 3 68	285 2 1 1 87	222 3 0 4 52	50
51	Net Income after Fed. Income Tax					62 9 0 7 35			62 9 0 7 35	51
52						554 3 8 3 68	554 3 8 3 68	285 2 1 1 87	285 2 1 1 87	52
53										53

15-1 WORK TOGETHER (concluded)

1., 2.

							*% OF NET SALES

*Rounded to the nearest 0.1%

Preparing an income statement for a merchandising business

Osborn Corporation

Work Sheet

For Year Ended December 31, 20 – –

	TRIAL BALANCE		ADJUSTMENTS		INCOME STATEMENT		BALANCE SHEET	
ACCOUNT TITLE	DEBIT	CREDIT	DEBIT	CREDIT	DEBIT	CREDIT	DEBIT	CREDIT
1 Cash	15 2 1 8 25						15 2 1 8 25	
2 Petty Cash	2 5 0 00						2 5 0 00	
3 Accounts Receivable	22 4 8 5 28						22 4 8 5 28	
4 Allow. for Uncoll. Accts.		1 0 5 2 05		(e) 1 7 2 00				2 7 7 2 05
5 Merchandise Inventory	228 1 8 9 80			(d) 8 4 2 4 00			219 7 6 5 80	
6 Supplies—Office	3 1 5 8 15			(a) 2 7 4 9 00			4 0 9 15	
7 Supplies—Store	3 8 1 9 74			(b) 3 0 4 3 35			7 7 6 39	
8 Prepaid Insurance	8 0 0 0 00			(c) 7 2 0 0 00			8 0 0 00	
9 Office Equipment	22 1 8 3 08						22 1 8 3 08	
10 Acc. Depr.—Office Equip.		8 4 8 3 00		(f) 4 5 8 0 00				13 0 6 3 00
11 Store Equipment	45 1 8 4 98						45 1 8 4 98	
12 Acc. Depr.—Store Equip.		11 2 5 0 00		(g) 4 8 9 0 00				16 1 4 0 00
13 Accounts Payable		22 1 5 4 17						22 1 5 4 17
14 Federal Income Tax Payable				(h) 1 5 4 1 19				1 5 4 1 19
15 Emp. Income Tax Payable		1 0 2 5 00						1 0 2 5 00
16 Social Security Tax Payable		7 5 3 80						7 5 3 80
17 Medicare Tax Payable		1 7 6 29						1 7 6 29
18 Sales Tax Payable		2 4 8 7 00						2 4 8 7 00
19 Unemploy. Tax Payable—Fed.		2 4 00						2 4 00
20 Unemploy. Tax Payable—State		1 6 2 00						1 6 2 00
21 Health Insur. Premiums Payable		8 0 0 00						8 0 0 00
22 U.S. Savings Bonds Payable		6 0 00						6 0 00
23 United Way Donations Payable		7 0 00						7 0 00
24 Dividends Payable		7 5 0 0 00						7 5 0 0 00
25 Capital Stock		200 0 0 0 00						200 0 0 0 00
26 Retained Earnings		19 7 3 5 06						19 7 3 5 06

(Note: Work sheet is continued on next page.)

15-1 ON YOUR OWN (continued)

Osborn Corporation

Work Sheet

For Year Ended December 31, 20 – –

#	ACCOUNT TITLE	TRIAL BALANCE DEBIT	TRIAL BALANCE CREDIT	ADJUSTMENTS DEBIT	ADJUSTMENTS CREDIT	INCOME STATEMENT DEBIT	INCOME STATEMENT CREDIT	BALANCE SHEET DEBIT	BALANCE SHEET CREDIT
27	Dividends	30 0 0 0 00						30 0 0 0 00	
28	Income Summary			(d) 8 4 2 4 00		8 4 2 4 00			
29	Sales		704 8 0 9 54				704 8 0 9 54		
30	Sales Discount	6 1 5 25				6 1 5 25			
31	Sales Returns and Allowances	4 7 8 9 84				4 7 8 9 84			
32	Purchases	369 4 8 5 04				369 4 8 5 04			
33	Purchases Discount		3 0 5 8 89				3 0 5 8 89		
34	Purch. Returns and Allowances		4 8 0 0 85				4 8 0 0 85		
35	Advertising Expense	8 5 0 0 00				8 5 0 0 00			
36	Cash Short and Over	9 33				9 33			
37	Credit Card Fee Expense	12 4 5 8 22				12 4 5 8 22			
38	Depr. Exp.—Office Equipment			(f) 4 5 8 0 00		4 5 8 0 00			
39	Depr. Exp.—Store Equipment			(g) 4 8 9 0 00		4 8 9 0 00			
40	Insurance Expense			(e) 7 2 0 0 00		7 2 0 0 00			
41	Miscellaneous Expense	7 4 8 0 00				7 4 8 0 00			
42	Payroll Taxes Expense	13 1 3 0 64				13 1 3 0 64			
43	Rent Expense	24 0 0 0 00				24 0 0 0 00			
44	Salary Expense	145 8 9 6 00				145 8 9 6 00			
45	Supplies Expense—Office			(a) 2 7 4 9 00		2 7 4 9 00			
46	Supplies Expense—Store			(b) 3 0 4 3 35		3 0 4 3 35			
47	Uncollectible Accounts Expense			(c) 1 7 2 0 00		1 7 2 0 00			
48	Utilities Expense	7 5 4 8 05				7 5 4 8 05			
49	Federal Income Tax Expense	16 0 0 0 00		(h) 1 5 4 1 19		17 5 4 1 19			
50		988 4 0 1 65	988 4 0 1 65	34 1 4 7 54	34 1 4 7 54	644 0 5 9 91	712 6 6 9 28	357 0 7 2 93	288 4 6 3 56
51	Net Income after Fed. Income Tax					68 6 0 9 37			68 6 0 9 37
52						712 6 6 9 28	712 6 6 9 28	357 0 7 2 93	357 0 7 2 93
53									

1., 2.

								*% OF NET SALES

*Rounded to the nearest 0.1%

15-2 WORK TOGETHER, p. 460

Analyzing an income statement

1., 2., 3.

Component	Acceptable Percentage	Actual Percentage	Acceptable Result		Recommended Action If Needed
			Yes	No	
Cost of merchandise sold	No more than 53.0%				
Gross profit on sales	No less than 47.0%				

Earnings per Share

Net Income after Federal Income Tax		Number of Shares Outstanding		Earnings per Share
$	÷		=	
	÷		=	$

Price-Earnings Ratio

Market Price per Share		Earnings per Share		Price-Earnings Ratio
$	÷		=	
	÷	$	=	

Analyzing an income statement

1., 2., 3.

Component	Acceptable Percentage	Actual Percentage	Acceptable Result		Recommended Action If Needed
			Yes	No	
Total expenses	No more than 30.0%				
Net income before federal income tax	No less than 15.0%				

Earnings per Share

Net Income after Federal Income Tax		Number of Shares Outstanding		Earnings per Share
$	÷		=	
	÷		=	$

Price-Earnings Ratio

Market Price per Share		Earnings per Share		Price-Earnings Ratio
	÷		=	
$	÷	$	=	

15-3 WORK TOGETHER, p. 463

Preparing a statement of stockholders' equity

1.

Preparing a statement of stockholders' equity

1.

15-4 WORK TOGETHER, p. 471

Preparing a balance sheet for a corporation

1.

Preparing a balance sheet for a corporation

1.

15-1 APPLICATION PROBLEM, p. 473

Preparing an income statement for a merchandising business

Historical Doors, Inc.

Work Sheet

For Year Ended December 31, 20 – –

	Trial Balance Debit	Trial Balance Credit	Adjustments Debit	Adjustments Credit	Income Statement Debit	Income Statement Credit	Balance Sheet Debit	Balance Sheet Credit	
5 Merchandise Inventory	201 184 25			(d) 2 548 25			198 636 00		5
29 Sales		615 258 25				615 258 25			29
30 Sales Discount	1 184 25				1 184 25				30
31 Sales Returns and Allowances	4 152 88				4 152 88				31
32 Purchases	301 525 80				301 525 80				32
33 Purchases Discount		2 151 81				2 151 81			33
34 Purch. Returns and Allowances		4 150 08				4 150 08			34
35 Advertising Expense	12 500 00				12 500 00				35
36 Cash Short and Over	2 88				2 88				36
37 Credit Card Fee Expense	8 428 25				8 428 25				37
38 Depr. Exp.—Office Equipment			(f) 4 515 00		4 515 00				38
39 Depr. Exp.—Store Equipment			(g) 2 815 00		2 815 00				39
40 Insurance Expense			(c) 8 000 00		8 000 00				40
41 Miscellaneous Expense	7 450 00				7 450 00				41
42 Payroll Taxes Expense	9 415 25				9 415 25				42
43 Rent Expense	24 000 00				24 000 00				43
44 Salary Expense	108 482 25				108 482 25				44
45 Supplies Expense—Office			(a) 1 482 25		1 482 25				45
46 Supplies Expense—Store			(b) 3 018 28		3 018 28				46
47 Uncollectible Accounts Expense			(e) 1 720 00		1 720 00				47
48 Utilities Expense	7 158 22				7 158 22				48
49 Federal Income Tax Expense	26 000 00		(h) 1 383 02		27 383 02				49
50	819 131 92	819 131 92	25 481 80	25 481 80	535 781 58	621 560 14	293 783 36	208 004 80	50
51 Net Income after Fed. Income Tax					85 778 56			85 778 56	51
52					621 560 14	621 560 14	293 783 36	293 783 36	52

1., 2.

					*% OF NET SALES

*Rounded to the nearest 0.1%

15-2 APPLICATION PROBLEM, p. 473

Analyzing component percentages and financial ratios

Custom Jewelry, Inc.

Income Statement

For Year Ended December 31, 20 – –

					*% OF NET SALES
Revenue:					
Sales			915 4 8 2 15		
Less: Sales Discount		2 1 5 8 28			
Sales Ret. and Allow.		6 1 4 8 25	8 3 0 6 53		
Net Sales				907 1 7 5 62	100.0
Cost of Merchandise Sold:					
Merchandise Inventory, January 1, 20 – –			201 1 8 4 25		
Purchases		331 2 5 8 25			
Less: Purchases Discount	4 1 5 8 25				
Purch. Ret. and Allow.	2 4 1 8 29	6 5 7 6 54			
Net Purchases			324 6 8 1 71		
Total Cost of Mdse. Avail. for Sale			525 8 6 5 96		
Less Mdse. Inventory, Dec. 31, 20 – –			198 6 3 6 00		
Cost of Merchandise Sold				327 2 2 9 96	36.1
Gross Profit on Sales				579 9 4 5 66	63.9
Expenses:					
Advertising Expense			52 4 0 0 00		
Credit Card Fee Expense			12 4 8 2 88		
Depr. Exp.—Office Equipment			3 4 8 5 00		
Depr. Exp.—Store Equipment			8 4 5 0 00		
Insurance Expense			12 0 0 0 00		
Miscellaneous Expense			14 1 8 4 29		
Payroll Taxes Expense			21 4 8 2 27		
Rent Expense			36 0 0 0 00		
Salary Expense			201 4 8 2 80		
Supplies Expense—Office			2 4 8 1 05		
Supplies Expense—Store			6 0 8 1 80		
Uncollectible Accounts Expense			5 8 4 0 00		
Utilities Expense			8 4 0 8 09		
Total Expenses				384 7 7 8 18	42.4
Net Income before Federal Income Tax				195 1 6 7 48	21.5
Less Federal Income Tax Expense				59 3 6 5 32	
Net Income after Federal Income Tax				135 8 0 2 16	

*Rounded to the nearest 0.1%

1.

Component	Acceptable Percentage	Actual Percentage	Acceptable Result Yes	Acceptable Result No	Recommended Action If Needed
Cost of merchandise sold	No more than 35.0%				
Gross profit on sales	No less than 65.0%				
Total expenses	No more than 40.0%				
Net income before federal income tax	No less than 25.0%				

2.

Earnings per Share

Net Income after Federal Income Tax		Number of Shares Outstanding		Earnings per Share
$	÷		=	$

Price-Earnings Ratio

Market Price per Share		Earnings per Share		Price-Earnings Ratio
$	÷	$	=	

15-3 APPLICATION PROBLEM, p. 473

Preparing a statement of stockholders' equity

15-4   APPLICATION PROBLEM, p. 474

Preparing a balance sheet for a corporation

Henderson Corporation

Work Sheet

For Year Ended December 31, 20 - -

	TRIAL BALANCE		ADJUSTMENTS		INCOME STATEMENT		BALANCE SHEET	
ACCOUNT TITLE	DEBIT	CREDIT	DEBIT	CREDIT	DEBIT	CREDIT	DEBIT	CREDIT
1 Cash	22 154 00						22 154 00	
2 Petty Cash	300 00						300 00	
3 Accounts Receivable	35 158 25						35 158 25	
4 Allow. for Uncoll. Accts.		91 25		(e) 4 150 00				4 241 25
5 Merchandise Inventory	251 018 80			(d) 1 548 25			249 470 55	
6 Supplies—Office	4 215 89			(a) 3 818 04			397 85	
7 Supplies—Store	5 184 69			(b) 4 818 77			365 92	
8 Prepaid Insurance	14 000 00			(c) 12 000 00			2 000 00	
9 Office Equipment	19 485 28						19 485 28	
10 Acc. Depr.—Office Equip.		4 185 00		(f) 4 260 00				8 445 00
11 Store Equipment	38 481 50						38 481 50	
12 Acc. Depr.—Store Equip.		12 158 00		(g) 5 750 00				17 908 00
13 Accounts Payable		23 154 50						23 154 50
14 Federal Income Tax Payable				(h) 881 17				881 17
15 Emp. Income Tax Payable		1 548 00						1 548 00
16 Social Security Tax Payable		815 30						815 30
17 Medicare Tax Payable		190 68						190 68
18 Sales Tax Payable		3 154 20						3 154 20
19 Unemploy. Tax Payable—Fed.		33 60						33 60
20 Unemploy. Tax Payable—State		226 80						226 80
21 Health Insur. Premiums Payable		750 00						750 00
22 U.S. Savings Bonds Payable		100 00						100 00
23 United Way Donations Payable		70 00						70 00
24 Dividends Payable		9 000 00						9 000 00
25 Capital Stock		200 000 00						200 000 00
26 Retained Earnings		57 966 71						57 966 71
27 Dividends	28 000 00						28 000 00	
28 Income Summary			(d) 1 548 25		1 548 25			

15-4 **APPLICATION PROBLEM (concluded)**

Preparing financial statements

Lighting Center, Inc.

Work Sheet

For Year Ended December 31, 20 – –

| | TRIAL BALANCE | | ADJUSTMENTS | | INCOME STATEMENT | | BALANCE SHEET | |
ACCOUNT TITLE	DEBIT	CREDIT	DEBIT	CREDIT	DEBIT	CREDIT	DEBIT	CREDIT
1 Cash	14258 00						14258 00	
2 Petty Cash	500 00						500 00	
3 Accounts Receivable	22318 25						22318 25	
4 Allow. for Uncoll. Accts.		1088 80		(e) 1525 00				2613 80
5 Merchandise Inventory	219248 25			(d) 2154 25			217094 00	
6 Supplies—Office	3510 15			(a) 3015 12			495 03	
7 Supplies—Store	4828 19			(b) 3815 32			1012 87	
8 Prepaid Insurance	12000 00			(c) 10000 00			2000 00	
9 Office Equipment	23185 00						23185 00	
10 Acc. Depr.—Office Equip.		8450 00		(f) 4050 00				12500 00
11 Store Equipment	46184 00						46184 00	
12 Acc. Depr.—Store Equip.		12280 00		(g) 6025 00				18305 00
13 Accounts Payable		24158 20						24158 20
14 Federal Income Tax Payable				(h) 52 86				52 86
15 Emp. Income Tax Payable		1055 00						1055 00
16 Social Security Tax Payable		747 60						747 60
17 Medicare Tax Payable		174 84						174 84
18 Sales Tax Payable		2248 25						2248 25
19 Unemploy. Tax Payable—Fed.		25 60						25 60
20 Unemploy. Tax Payable—State		172 80						172 80
21 Health Insur. Premiums Payable		750 00						750 00
22 U.S. Savings Bonds Payable		100 00						100 00
23 United Way Donations Payable		70 00						70 00
24 Dividends Payable		10000 00						10000 00
25 Capital Stock		100000 00						100000 00
26 Retained Earnings		107246 92						107246 92

(Note: Work sheet is continued on next page.)

Lighting Center, Inc.
Work Sheet
For Year Ended December 31, 20 — —

#	ACCOUNT TITLE	TB Debit	TB Credit	Adj. Debit	Adj. Credit	IS Debit	IS Credit	BS Debit	BS Credit
27	Dividends	40 000 00						40 000 00	
28	Income Summary			(d) 2 154 25		2 154 25			
29	Sales		745 824 50				745 824 50		
30	Sales Discount	1 154 25				1 154 25			
31	Sales Returns and Allowances	3 481 25				3 481 25			
32	Purchases	368 482 22				368 482 22			
33	Purchases Discount		1 548 00				1 548 00		
34	Purch. Returns and Allowances		3 848 77				3 848 77		
35	Advertising Expense	12 510 00				12 510 00			
36	Cash Short and Over	14 02				14 02			
37	Credit Card Fee Expense	9 182 22				9 182 22			
38	Depr. Exp.—Office Equipment			(f) 4 050 00		4 050 00			
39	Depr. Exp.—Store Equipment			(g) 6 025 00		6 025 00			
40	Insurance Expense			(c) 10 000 00		10 000 00			
41	Miscellaneous Expense	12 140 00				12 140 00			
42	Payroll Taxes Expense	15 482 98				15 482 98			
43	Rent Expense	36 000 00				36 000 00			
44	Salary Expense	139 158 47				139 158 47			
45	Supplies Expense—Office			(a) 3 015 12		3 015 12			
46	Supplies Expense—Store			(b) 3 815 32		3 815 32			
47	Uncollectible Accounts Expense			(e) 1 525 00		1 525 00			
48	Utilities Expense	8 152 03				8 152 03			
49	Federal Income Tax Expense	28 000 00		(h) 52 86		28 052 86			
50		1019 789 28	1019 789 28	30 637 55	30 637 55	664 394 99	751 221 27	367 047 15	280 220 87
51	Net Income after Fed. Income Tax					86 826 28			86 826 28
52						751 221 27	751 221 27	367 047 15	367 047 15

1.

										*% OF NET SALES

15-5 **MASTERY PROBLEM (continued)**

2.

4.

Earnings per Share

Net Income after Federal Income Tax	÷	Number of Shares Outstanding	=	Earnings per Share
$	÷		=	$

Price-Earnings Ratio

Market Price per Share	÷	Earnings per Share	=	Price-Earnings Ratio
$	÷	$	=	

3.

Name	Perfect Score	Your Score
Analyzing Accounts Affected by Adjusting and Closing Entries	24 Pts.	
Examining Adjusting and Closing Entries	18 Pts.	
Analyzing the Accounting Cycle for a Merchandising Business Organized as a Corporation	9 Pts.	
Total	51 Pts.	

Part One—Analyzing Accounts Affected by Adjusting and Closing Entries

Directions: For each adjusting or closing entry described, decide which accounts are debited and credited. Print the letter identifying your choice in the proper Answers column.

Account Title	Transaction	Accounts to Be Debited	Credited
A. Accumulated Depreciation—Office Equipment	**1–2.** Adjusting entry for allowance for uncollectible accounts. (p. 482)	_____	_____
B. Accumulated Depreciation—Store Equipment	**3–4.** Adjusting entry for a decrease in merchandise inventory. (p. 482)	_____	_____
C. Allowance for Uncollectible Accounts	**5–6.** Adjusting entry for office supplies. (p. 483)	_____	_____
D. Dividends	**7–8.** Adjusting entry for store supplies. (p. 483)	_____	_____
E. Depreciation Expense—Office Equipment	**9–10.** Adjusting entry for prepaid insurance. (p. 484)	_____	_____
F. Depreciation Expense—Store Equipment	**11–12.** Adjusting entry for depreciation of office equipment. (p. 484)	_____	_____
G. Federal Income Tax Expense	**13–14.** Adjusting entry for depreciation of store equipment. (p. 485)	_____	_____
H. Federal Income Tax Payable	**15–16.** Adjusting entry for federal income taxes. (p. 485)	_____	_____
I. Income Summary	**17–18.** Closing entry for the sales account. (p. 488)	_____	_____
J. Insurance Expense	**19–20.** Closing entry for the purchases account. (p. 490)	_____	_____
K. Merchandise Inventory	**21–22.** Closing entry for the income summary account with a net income. (p. 491)	_____	_____
L. Prepaid Insurance	**23–24.** Closing entry for dividends. (p. 491)	_____	_____
M. Purchases			
N. Retained Earnings			
O. Sales			
P. Supplies—Office			
Q. Supplies—Store			
R. Supplies Expense—Office			
S. Supplies Expense—Store			
T. Uncollectible Accounts Expense			

Part Two—Examining Adjusting and Closing Entries

Directions: Place a *T* for True or an *F* for False in the Answers column to show whether each of the following statements is true or false.

1. General ledger account balances are changed only by posting journal entries. (p. 481) 1. _____

2. Adjusting entries bring subsidiary ledger accounts up to date. (p. 481) 2. _____

3. Hobby Shack records the adjusting entries in the general journal on the next line following the last daily transaction. (p. 481) 3. _____

4. Indicating a source document is not necessary when journalizing adjusting entries. (p. 481) 4. _____

5. Temporary accounts are closed at the end of a fiscal period to prepare the general ledger for the next fiscal period. (p. 487) 5. _____

6. Closing the temporary accounts at the end of a fiscal period is an application of the accounting concept Matching Expenses with Revenue. (p. 487) 6. _____

7. A temporary account is closed by recording an equal amount on the side opposite the balance. (p. 487) 7. _____

8. The Trial Balance columns of a work sheet and an income statement contain the information needed to journalize closing entries. (p. 487) 8. _____

9. Permanent accounts are sometimes referred to as nominal accounts. (p. 487) 9. _____

10. The ending account balances of permanent accounts for one fiscal period are the beginning account balances for the next fiscal period. (p. 487) 10. _____

11. Contra accounts with credit balances are closed by debiting the accounts and crediting Income Summary. (p. 488) 11. _____

12. Expense accounts are closed by debiting the expense accounts and crediting Income Summary. (p. 489) 12. _____

13. The Income Summary account is closed into the Retained Earnings account. (p. 491) 13. _____

14. Dividends increase the earnings retained by a corporation. (p. 491) 14. _____

15. After the closing entry for the dividends account is posted, the Dividends account has a zero balance. (p. 491) 15. _____

16. After all closing entries are posted, the income statement accounts are the only general ledger accounts that have balances. (p. 494) 16. _____

17. When the general ledger is ready for the next fiscal period, this is an application of the Business Entity accounting concept. (p. 494) 17. _____

18. The purpose of the post-closing trial balance is to prove the general ledger equality of debits and credits. (p. 496) 18. _____

Part Three—Analyzing the Accounting Cycle for a Merchandising Business Organized as a Corporation

Directions: Write a number from 1 to 9 to the left of each step to indicate the correct sequence of all the steps in the accounting cycle. (p. 497)

Answers

1. _____ Post journal entries to the subsidiary ledgers and the general ledger.

2. _____ Check source documents for accuracy, and analyze transactions into debit and credit parts.

3. _____ Journalize adjusting and closing entries from the work sheet.

4. _____ Record transactions in journals, using information on source documents.

5. _____ Prepare the schedules of accounts payable and accounts receivable, using information from the subsidiary ledgers.

6. _____ Prepare a post-closing trial balance of the general ledger.

7. _____ Prepare financial statements from the work sheet.

8. _____ Post adjusting and closing entries to the general ledger.

9. _____ Prepare a work sheet, including a trial balance, from the general ledger.

16-1 WORK TOGETHER, p. 486

Journalizing adjusting entries

Discount Books, Inc.

Work Sheet

For Year Ended December 31, 20 – –

	ACCOUNT TITLE	TRIAL BALANCE DEBIT	TRIAL BALANCE CREDIT	ADJUSTMENTS DEBIT	ADJUSTMENTS CREDIT	INCOME STATEMENT DEBIT	INCOME STATEMENT CREDIT	BALANCE SHEET DEBIT	BALANCE SHEET CREDIT	
1	Cash	5148 25						5148 25		1
2	Petty Cash	200 00						200 00		2
3	Accounts Receivable	14158 22						14158 22		3
4	Allow. for Uncoll. Accts.		21 20		(e) 1500 00				1521 20	4
5	Merchandise Inventory	84815 20		(d) 1848 25				86663 45		5
6	Supplies—Office	1648 85			(a) 1448 55			200 30		6
7	Supplies—Store	3481 12			(b) 3248 11			233 01		7
8	Prepaid Insurance	1200 00			(c) 1100 00			100 00		8
9	Office Equipment	14154 55						14154 55		9
10	Acc. Depr.—Office Equipment		4154 25		(f) 3410 00				7564 25	10
11	Store Equipment	42158 15						42158 15		11
12	Acc. Depr.—Store Equipment		8480 00		(g) 6420 00				14900 00	12
13	Accounts Payable		12458 51						12458 51	13
14	Federal Income Tax Payable				(h) 3948 91				3948 91	14
15	Emp. Income Tax Pay.		465 00						465 00	15
16	Social Security Tax Payable		496 00						496 00	16
17	Medicare Tax Payable		116 00						116 00	17
18	Sales Tax Payable		1548 00						1548 00	18
19	Unemployment Tax Pay.—Fed.		8 00						8 00	19
20	Unemployment Tax Pay.—State		54 00						54 00	20
21	Health Ins. Premiums Pay.		500 00						500 00	21
22	U.S. Savings Bonds Payable		50 00						50 00	22
23	United Way Donations Pay.		60 00						60 00	23
24	Dividends Payable		4000 00						4000 00	24
25	Capital Stock		24000 00						24000 00	25
26	Retained Earnings		34942 87						34942 87	26

(Note: Work sheet is continued on next page.)

Discount Books, Inc.

Work Sheet

For Year Ended December 31, 20 – –

	ACCOUNT TITLE	TRIAL BALANCE DEBIT	TRIAL BALANCE CREDIT	ADJUSTMENTS DEBIT	ADJUSTMENTS CREDIT	INCOME STATEMENT DEBIT	INCOME STATEMENT CREDIT	BALANCE SHEET DEBIT	BALANCE SHEET CREDIT	
27	Dividends	16 000 00						16 000 00		27
28	Income Summary				(d) 1 848 25		1 848 25			28
29	Sales		430 521 58				430 521 58			29
30	Sales Discount	2 155 00				2 155 00				30
31	Sales Returns and Allowances	4 153 28				4 153 28				31
32	Purchases	174 481 20				174 481 20				32
33	Purchases Discount		3 455 25				3 455 25			33
34	Purch. Returns and Allowances		5 548 74				5 548 74			34
35	Advertising Expense	6 000 00				6 000 00				35
36	Cash Short and Over	4 84				4 84				36
37	Credit Card Fee Expense	5 148 25				5 148 25				37
38	Depr. Exp.—Office Equipment			(f) 3 410 00		3 410 00				38
39	Depr. Exp.—Store Equipment			(g) 6 420 00		6 420 00				39
40	Insurance Expense			(c) 11 000 00		11 000 00				40
41	Miscellaneous Expense	4 150 00				4 150 00				41
42	Payroll Taxes Expense	8 745 25				8 745 25				42
43	Rent Expense	12 000 00				12 000 00				43
44	Salary Expense	97 458 84				97 458 84				44
45	Supplies Expense—Office			(a) 1 448 55		1 448 55				45
46	Supplies Expense—Store			(b) 3 248 11		3 248 11				46
47	Uncollectible Accounts Exp.			(e) 1 500 00		1 500 00				47
48	Utilities Expense	5 648 40				5 648 40				48
49	Fed. Income Tax Expense	16 000 00		(h) 3 948 91		19 948 91				49
50		527 769 40	527 769 40	32 823 82	32 823 82	364 980 63	438 263 82	179 915 93	106 632 74	50
51	Net Income after Fed. Income Tax					73 283 19			73 283 19	51
52						438 263 82	438 263 82	179 915 93	179 915 93	52

16-1 WORK TOGETHER (concluded)

1.

GENERAL JOURNAL   PAGE 18

	DATE	ACCOUNT TITLE	DOC. NO.	POST. REF.	DEBIT	CREDIT	
1							1
2							2
3							3
4							4
5							5
6							6
7							7
8							8
9							9
10							10
11							11
12							12
13							13
14							14
15							15
16							16
17							17
18							18
19							19
20							20
21							21
22							22
23							23
24							24
25							25
26							26
27							27
28							28
29							29
30							30
31							31
32							32
33							33

Journalizing adjusting entries

Sturgis Supply, Inc.

Work Sheet

For Year Ended December 31, 20 – –

#	ACCOUNT TITLE	TRIAL BALANCE DEBIT	TRIAL BALANCE CREDIT	ADJUSTMENTS DEBIT	ADJUSTMENTS CREDIT	INCOME STATEMENT DEBIT	INCOME STATEMENT CREDIT	BALANCE SHEET DEBIT	BALANCE SHEET CREDIT
1	Cash	20 158 25						20 158 25	
2	Petty Cash	5 000 00						5 000 00	
3	Accounts Receivable	42 488 25						42 488 25	
4	Allow. for Uncoll. Accts.		1 088 18		(e) 3 250 00				4 338 18
5	Merchandise Inventory	315 418 25			(d) 1 648 22			313 770 03	
6	Supplies—Office	7 148 48			(a) 6 847 15			301 33	
7	Supplies—Store	6 154 88			(b) 5 548 11			606 77	
8	Prepaid Insurance	18 000 00			(c) 16 000 00			2 000 00	
9	Office Equipment	41 484 89						41 484 89	
10	Acc. Depr.—Office Equipment		16 180 00		(f) 8 450 00				24 630 00
11	Store Equipment	90 184 11						90 184 11	
12	Acc. Depr.—Store Equipment		22 180 00		(g) 8 600 00				30 780 00
13	Accounts Payable		22 154 17						22 154 17
14	Federal Income Tax Payable				(h) 24 163 72				24 163 72
15	Emp. Income Tax Pay.		3 210 00						3 210 00
16	Social Security Tax Payable		945 50						945 50
17	Medicare Tax Payable		221 13						221 13
18	Sales Tax Payable		4 215 02						4 215 02
19	Unemployment Tax Pay.—Fed.		32 00						32 00
20	Unemployment Tax Pay.—State		216 00						216 00
21	Health Ins. Premiums Pay.		1 200 00						1 200 00
22	U.S. Savings Bonds Payable		120 00						120 00
23	United Way Donations Pay.		140 00						140 00
24	Dividends Payable		9 000 00						9 000 00
25	Capital Stock		225 000 00						225 000 00
26	Retained Earnings		38 179 53						38 179 53

(Note: Work sheet is continued on next page.)

16-1 ON YOUR OWN (continued)

Sturgis Supply, Inc.

Work Sheet

For Year Ended December 31, 20 – –

| | TRIAL BALANCE | | ADJUSTMENTS | | INCOME STATEMENT | | BALANCE SHEET | |
ACCOUNT TITLE	DEBIT	CREDIT	DEBIT	CREDIT	DEBIT	CREDIT	DEBIT	CREDIT
27 Dividends	36000.00						36000.00	
28 Income Summary			(d) 16484.22		16484.22			
29 Sales		998148.15				998148.15		
30 Sales Discount	1248.22				1248.22			
31 Sales Returns and Allowances	6488.95				6488.95			
32 Purchases	442518.25				442518.25			
33 Purchases Discount		7154.25				7154.25		
34 Purch. Returns and Allowances		6448.94				6448.94		
35 Advertising Expense	15000.00				15000.00			
36 Cash Short and Over	5.25				5.25			
37 Credit Card Fee Expense	18487.15				18487.15			
38 Depr. Exp.—Office Equipment			(f) 8450.00		8450.00			
39 Depr. Exp.—Store Equipment			(g) 8600.00		8600.00			
40 Insurance Expense			(c) 16000.00		16000.00			
41 Miscellaneous Expense	9480.00				9480.00			
42 Payroll Taxes Expense	18486.69				18486.69			
43 Rent Expense	24000.00				24000.00			
44 Salary Expense	183000.00				183000.00			
45 Supplies Expense—Office			(a) 6847.15		6847.15			
46 Supplies Expense—Store			(b) 5548.11		5548.11			
47 Uncollectible Accounts Exp.			(e) 3250.00		3250.00			
48 Utilities Expense	9581.25				9581.25			
49 Fed. Income Tax Expense	50000.00		(h) 24163.72		74163.72			
50	1,355832.87	1,355832.87	74507.20	74507.20	852802.96	1,011751.34	493163.88	345525
51 Net Income after Fed. Income Tax					158948.38			158948.38
52					1,011751.34	1,011751.34	493163.88	493163.88

1.

GENERAL JOURNAL   PAGE 24

	DATE	ACCOUNT TITLE	DOC. NO.	POST. REF.	DEBIT	CREDIT	
1							1
2							2
3							3
4							4
5							5
6							6
7							7
8							8
9							9
10							10
11							11
12							12
13							13
14							14
15							15
16							16
17							17
18							18
19							19
20							20
21							21
22							22
23							23
24							24
25							25
26							26
27							27
28							28
29							29
30							30
31							31
32							32
33							33

16-2 WORK TOGETHER, p. 493

Journalizing closing entries

1.

GENERAL JOURNAL   PAGE 19

	DATE	ACCOUNT TITLE	DOC. NO.	POST. REF.	DEBIT	CREDIT	
1							1
2							2
3							3
4							4
5							5
6							6
7							7
8							8
9							9
10							10
11							11
12							12
13							13
14							14
15							15
16							16
17							17
18							18
19							19
20							20
21							21
22							22
23							23
24							24
25							25
26							26
27							27
28							28
29							29
30							30
31							31
32							32

Journalizing closing entries

1.

GENERAL JOURNAL PAGE 25

	DATE		ACCOUNT TITLE	DOC. NO.	POST. REF.	DEBIT	CREDIT	
1								1
2								2
3								3
4								4
5								5
6								6
7								7
8								8
9								9
10								10
11								11
12								12
13								13
14								14
15								15
16								16
17								17
18								18
19								19
20								20
21								21
22								22
23								23
24								24
25								25
26								26
27								27
28								28
29								29
30								30
31								31
32								32

16-3 **WORK TOGETHER, p. 498**

Preparing a post-closing trial balance

1.

ACCOUNT TITLE	DEBIT	CREDIT

1.

ACCOUNT TITLE	DEBIT	CREDIT

16-1 APPLICATION PROBLEM, p. 500

Journalizing adjusting entries

Cellar Books, Inc.
Work Sheet
For Year Ended December 31, 20 – –

	ACCOUNT TITLE	TRIAL BALANCE DEBIT	TRIAL BALANCE CREDIT	ADJUSTMENTS DEBIT	ADJUSTMENTS CREDIT	INCOME STATEMENT DEBIT	INCOME STATEMENT CREDIT	BALANCE SHEET DEBIT	BALANCE SHEET CREDIT	
1	Cash	16485 00						16485 00		1
2	Petty Cash	400 00						400 00		2
3	Accounts Receivable	41483 15						41483 15		3
4	Allow. for Uncoll. Accts.		948 15		(e) 1458 00				2406 15	4
5	Merchandise Inventory	248752 30			(d) 2154 25			246598 05		5
6	Supplies—Office	6148 28			(a) 5818 66			329 62		6
7	Supplies—Store	5174 85			(b) 4848 04			326 81		7
8	Prepaid Insurance	14000 00			(c) 12000 00			2000 00		8
9	Office Equipment	38458 25						38458 25		9
10	Acc. Depr.—Office Equipment		17480 00		(f) 6480 00				23960 00	10
11	Store Equipment	41478 50						41478 50		11
12	Acc. Depr.—Store Equipment		23450 00		(g) 7650 00				31100 00	12
13	Accounts Payable		19948 80						19948 80	13
14	Federal Income Tax Payable				(h) 3660 23				3660 23	14
26	Retained Earnings		170024 63						170024 63	26
27	Dividends	12000 00						12000 00		27
28	Income Summary			(d) 2154 25		2154 25				28
29	Sales		668742 20				668742 20			29
30	Sales Discount	1454 85				1454 85				30
31	Sales Returns and Allow.	4215 48				4215 48				31
32	Purchases	284835 25				284835 25				32

(Note: Work sheet is continued on next page.)

Cellar Books, Inc.

Work Sheet

For Year Ended December 31, 20 – –

	ACCOUNT TITLE	TRIAL BALANCE		ADJUSTMENTS		INCOME STATEMENT		BALANCE SHEET	
		DEBIT	CREDIT	DEBIT	CREDIT	DEBIT	CREDIT	DEBIT	CREDIT
33	Purchases Discount		2 4 1 8 81				2 4 1 8 81		
34	Purch. Returns and Allow.		4 1 5 8 41				4 1 5 8 41		
35	Advertising Expense	12 5 4 0 00				12 5 4 0 00			
36	Cash Short and Over	8 08				8 08			
37	Credit Card Fee Expense	9 4 8 1 10				9 4 8 1 10			
38	Depr. Exp. —Office Equip.			(f) 6 4 8 0 00		6 4 8 0 00			
39	Depr. Exp. —Store Equip.			(g) 7 6 5 0 00		7 6 5 0 00			
40	Insurance Expense			(c) 12 0 0 0 00		12 0 0 0 00			
41	Miscellaneous Expense	5 4 1 0 00				5 4 1 0 00			
42	Payroll Taxes Expense	15 8 4 1 20				15 8 4 1 20			
43	Rent Expense	18 0 0 0 00				18 0 0 0 00			
44	Salary Expense	174 9 6 0 33				174 9 6 0 33			
45	Supplies Expense—Office			(a) 5 8 1 8 66		5 8 1 8 66			
46	Supplies Expense—Store			(b) 4 8 4 8 04		4 8 4 8 04			
47	Uncollectible Accounts Exp.			(e) 1 4 5 8 00		1 4 5 8 00			
48	Utilities Expense	4 5 4 8 20				4 5 4 8 20			
49	Fed. Income Tax Expense	20 0 0 0 00		(h) 3 6 6 0 23		23 6 6 0 23			
50		975 6 7 4 82	975 6 7 4 82	44 0 6 9 18	44 0 6 9 18	595 3 6 3 67	675 3 1 9 42	399 5 5 9 38	319 6 0 3 63
51	Net Income after Fed. Income Tax					79 9 5 5 75			79 9 5 5 75
52						675 3 1 9 42	675 3 1 9 42	399 5 5 9 38	399 5 5 9 38

16-1 **APPLICATION PROBLEM (concluded)**

1.

GENERAL JOURNAL PAGE 22

	DATE		ACCOUNT TITLE	DOC. NO.	POST. REF.	DEBIT	CREDIT	
1								1
2								2
3								3
4								4
5								5
6								6
7								7
8								8
9								9
10								10
11								11
12								12
13								13
14								14
15								15
16								16
17								17
18								18
19								19
20								20
21								21
22								22
23								23
24								24
25								25
26								26
27								27
28								28
29								29
30								30
31								31
32								32

Journalizing closing entries

1., 2., 3.

GENERAL JOURNAL   PAGE 23

	DATE	ACCOUNT TITLE	DOC. NO.	POST. REF.	DEBIT	CREDIT	
1							1
2							2
3							3
4							4
5							5
6							6
7							7
8							8
9							9
10							10
11							11
12							12
13							13
14							14
15							15
16							16
17							17
18							18
19							19
20							20
21							21
22							22
23							23
24							24
25							25
26							26
27							27
28							28
29							29
30							30
31							31
32							32

16-3 APPLICATION PROBLEM, p. 500

Preparing a post-closing trial balance

1.

ACCOUNT TITLE	DEBIT	CREDIT

APPLICATION PROBLEM, p. 500

Journalizing and posting adjusting and closing entries; preparing a post-closing trial balance

1., 2.

GENERAL JOURNAL   PAGE 22

	DATE		ACCOUNT TITLE	DOC. NO.	POST. REF.	DEBIT	CREDIT	
1								1
2								2
3								3
4								4
5								5
6								6
7								7
8								8
9								9
10								10
11								11
12								12
13								13
14								14
15								15
16								16
17								17
18								18
19								19
20								20
21								21
22								22
23								23
24								24
25								25
26								26
27								27
28								28
29								29
30								30
31								31

16-4 APPLICATION PROBLEM (continued)

3., 4.

GENERAL JOURNAL   PAGE 23

	DATE	ACCOUNT TITLE	DOC. NO.	POST. REF.	DEBIT	CREDIT	
1							1
2							2
3							3
4							4
5							5
6							6
7							7
8							8
9							9
10							10
11							11
12							12
13							13
14							14
15							15
16							16
17							17
18							18
19							19
20							20
21							21
22							22
23							23
24							24
25							25
26							26
27							27
28							28
29							29
30							30
31							31
32							32
33							33

2., 4.   **GENERAL LEDGER**

ACCOUNT Cash   ACCOUNT NO. 1110

DATE		ITEM	POST. REF.	DEBIT	CREDIT	BALANCE	
						DEBIT	CREDIT
Dec.	31	Balance	✔			15 4 8 2 00	

ACCOUNT Petty Cash   ACCOUNT NO. 1120

DATE		ITEM	POST. REF.	DEBIT	CREDIT	BALANCE	
						DEBIT	CREDIT
Dec.	31	Balance	✔			5 0 0 00	

ACCOUNT Accounts Receivable   ACCOUNT NO. 1130

DATE		ITEM	POST. REF.	DEBIT	CREDIT	BALANCE	
						DEBIT	CREDIT
Dec.	31	Balance	✔			42 1 5 8 80	

ACCOUNT Allow. for Uncoll. Accts.   ACCOUNT NO. 1135

DATE		ITEM	POST. REF.	DEBIT	CREDIT	BALANCE	
						DEBIT	CREDIT
Dec.	31	Balance	✔				6 8 4 20

ACCOUNT Merchandise Inventory   ACCOUNT NO. 1140

DATE		ITEM	POST. REF.	DEBIT	CREDIT	BALANCE	
						DEBIT	CREDIT
Dec.	31	Balance	✔			274 5 3 5 33	

16-4 APPLICATION PROBLEM (continued)

ACCOUNT Supplies—Office   ACCOUNT NO. 1145

DATE	ITEM	POST. REF.	DEBIT	CREDIT	BALANCE DEBIT	BALANCE CREDIT
Dec. 31	Balance	✔			6 1 5 8 84	

ACCOUNT Supplies—Store   ACCOUNT NO. 1150

DATE	ITEM	POST. REF.	DEBIT	CREDIT	BALANCE DEBIT	BALANCE CREDIT
Dec. 31	Balance	✔			5 5 4 8 55	

ACCOUNT Prepaid Insurance   ACCOUNT NO. 1160

DATE	ITEM	POST. REF.	DEBIT	CREDIT	BALANCE DEBIT	BALANCE CREDIT
Dec. 31	Balance	✔			8 0 0 0 00	

ACCOUNT Office Equipment   ACCOUNT NO. 1205

DATE	ITEM	POST. REF.	DEBIT	CREDIT	BALANCE DEBIT	BALANCE CREDIT
Dec. 31	Balance	✔			22 1 5 8 66	

ACCOUNT Acc. Depr. —Office Equipment   ACCOUNT NO. 1210

DATE	ITEM	POST. REF.	DEBIT	CREDIT	BALANCE DEBIT	BALANCE CREDIT
Dec. 31	Balance	✔				4 8 4 8 00

ACCOUNT Store Equipment   ACCOUNT NO. 1215

DATE	ITEM	POST. REF.	DEBIT	CREDIT	BALANCE DEBIT	BALANCE CREDIT
Dec. 31	Balance	✔			34 1 5 8 11	

ACCOUNT Acc. Depr. —Store Equipment   ACCOUNT NO. 1220

DATE	ITEM	POST. REF.	DEBIT	CREDIT	BALANCE DEBIT	BALANCE CREDIT
20-- Dec. 31	Balance	✔				12 4 8 0 00

ACCOUNT Accounts Payable   ACCOUNT NO. 2110

DATE	ITEM	POST. REF.	DEBIT	CREDIT	BALANCE DEBIT	BALANCE CREDIT
20-- Dec. 31	Balance	✔				15 4 8 7 99

ACCOUNT Federal Income Tax Payable   ACCOUNT NO. 2120

DATE	ITEM	POST. REF.	DEBIT	CREDIT	BALANCE DEBIT	BALANCE CREDIT

ACCOUNT Employee Income Tax Payable   ACCOUNT NO. 2130

DATE	ITEM	POST. REF.	DEBIT	CREDIT	BALANCE DEBIT	BALANCE CREDIT
20-- Dec. 31	Balance	✔				1 1 2 5 58

ACCOUNT Social Security Tax Payable   ACCOUNT NO. 2135

DATE	ITEM	POST. REF.	DEBIT	CREDIT	BALANCE DEBIT	BALANCE CREDIT
20-- Dec. 31	Balance	✔				9 0 3 96

ACCOUNT Medicare Tax Payable   ACCOUNT NO. 2140

DATE	ITEM	POST. REF.	DEBIT	CREDIT	BALANCE DEBIT	BALANCE CREDIT
20-- Dec. 31	Balance	✔				2 1 1 41

16-4 APPLICATION PROBLEM (continued)

ACCOUNT Sales Tax Payable   ACCOUNT NO. 2145

DATE	ITEM	POST. REF.	DEBIT	CREDIT	BALANCE DEBIT	BALANCE CREDIT
20-- Dec. 31	Balance	✔				2 3 4 5 99

ACCOUNT Unemployment Tax Payable—Federal   ACCOUNT NO. 2150

DATE	ITEM	POST. REF.	DEBIT	CREDIT	BALANCE DEBIT	BALANCE CREDIT
20-- Dec. 31	Balance	✔				2 5 60

ACCOUNT Unemployment Tax Payable—State   ACCOUNT NO. 2155

DATE	ITEM	POST. REF.	DEBIT	CREDIT	BALANCE DEBIT	BALANCE CREDIT
20-- Dec. 31	Balance	✔				1 7 2 80

ACCOUNT Health Insurance Premiums Payable   ACCOUNT NO. 2160

DATE	ITEM	POST. REF.	DEBIT	CREDIT	BALANCE DEBIT	BALANCE CREDIT
20-- Dec. 31	Balance	✔				3 5 0 00

ACCOUNT U.S. Savings Bonds Payable   ACCOUNT NO. 2165

DATE	ITEM	POST. REF.	DEBIT	CREDIT	BALANCE DEBIT	BALANCE CREDIT
20-- Dec. 31	Balance	✔				5 0 00

ACCOUNT United Way Donations Payable   ACCOUNT NO. 2170

DATE	ITEM	POST. REF.	DEBIT	CREDIT	BALANCE DEBIT	BALANCE CREDIT
20-- Dec. 31	Balance	✔				6 0 00

ACCOUNT Dividends Payable   ACCOUNT NO. 2180

DATE	ITEM	POST. REF.	DEBIT	CREDIT	BALANCE DEBIT	BALANCE CREDIT
20-- Dec. 31	Balance	✔				5 0 0 0 00

ACCOUNT Capital Stock   ACCOUNT NO. 3110

DATE	ITEM	POST. REF.	DEBIT	CREDIT	BALANCE DEBIT	BALANCE CREDIT
20-- Dec. 31	Balance	✔				125 0 0 0 00

ACCOUNT Retained Earnings   ACCOUNT NO. 3120

DATE	ITEM	POST. REF.	DEBIT	CREDIT	BALANCE DEBIT	BALANCE CREDIT
20-- Dec. 1	Balance	✔				136 8 4 3 68

ACCOUNT Dividends   ACCOUNT NO. 3130

DATE	ITEM	POST. REF.	DEBIT	CREDIT	BALANCE DEBIT	BALANCE CREDIT
20-- Dec. 31	Balance	✔			20 0 0 0 00	

ACCOUNT Income Summary   ACCOUNT NO. 3140

DATE	ITEM	POST. REF.	DEBIT	CREDIT	BALANCE DEBIT	BALANCE CREDIT

16-4 APPLICATION PROBLEM (continued)

ACCOUNT Sales   ACCOUNT NO. 4110

DATE		ITEM	POST. REF.	DEBIT	CREDIT	BALANCE DEBIT	BALANCE CREDIT
20-- Dec.	31	Balance	✔				724 1 8 3 99

ACCOUNT Sales Discount   ACCOUNT NO. 4120

DATE		ITEM	POST. REF.	DEBIT	CREDIT	BALANCE DEBIT	BALANCE CREDIT
20-- Dec.	31	Balance	✔			1 6 9 4 48	

ACCOUNT Sales Returns and Allowances   ACCOUNT NO. 4130

DATE		ITEM	POST. REF.	DEBIT	CREDIT	BALANCE DEBIT	BALANCE CREDIT
20-- Dec.	31	Balance	✔			4 1 8 9 64	

ACCOUNT Purchases   ACCOUNT NO. 5110

DATE		ITEM	POST. REF.	DEBIT	CREDIT	BALANCE DEBIT	BALANCE CREDIT
20-- Dec.	31	Balance	✔			331 8 0 5 18	

ACCOUNT Purchases Discount   ACCOUNT NO. 5120

DATE		ITEM	POST. REF.	DEBIT	CREDIT	BALANCE DEBIT	BALANCE CREDIT
20-- Dec.	31	Balance	✔				3 4 1 8 47

ACCOUNT Purch. Returns and Allowances   ACCOUNT NO. 5130

DATE	ITEM	POST. REF.	DEBIT	CREDIT	BALANCE DEBIT	BALANCE CREDIT
20-- Dec. 31	Balance	✔				4 6 8 4 69

ACCOUNT Advertising Expense   ACCOUNT NO. 6105

DATE	ITEM	POST. REF.	DEBIT	CREDIT	BALANCE DEBIT	BALANCE CREDIT
20-- Dec. 31	Balance	✔			14 5 1 8 00	

ACCOUNT Cash Short and Over   ACCOUNT NO. 6110

DATE	ITEM	POST. REF.	DEBIT	CREDIT	BALANCE DEBIT	BALANCE CREDIT
20-- Dec. 31	Balance	✔			4 60	

ACCOUNT Credit Card Fee Expense   ACCOUNT NO. 6115

DATE	ITEM	POST. REF.	DEBIT	CREDIT	BALANCE DEBIT	BALANCE CREDIT
20-- Dec. 31	Balance	✔			12 1 8 0 00	

ACCOUNT Depr. Exp. —Office Equipment   ACCOUNT NO. 6120

DATE	ITEM	POST. REF.	DEBIT	CREDIT	BALANCE DEBIT	BALANCE CREDIT

ACCOUNT Depr. Exp. —Store Equipment   ACCOUNT NO. 6125

DATE	ITEM	POST. REF.	DEBIT	CREDIT	BALANCE DEBIT	BALANCE CREDIT

16-4 APPLICATION PROBLEM (continued)

ACCOUNT Insurance Expense   ACCOUNT NO. 6130

DATE	ITEM	POST. REF.	DEBIT	CREDIT	BALANCE DEBIT	BALANCE CREDIT

ACCOUNT Miscellaneous Expense   ACCOUNT NO. 6135

DATE	ITEM	POST. REF.	DEBIT	CREDIT	BALANCE DEBIT	BALANCE CREDIT
20-- Dec. 31	Balance	✔			6 4 8 1 00	

ACCOUNT Payroll Taxes Expense   ACCOUNT NO. 6140

DATE	ITEM	POST. REF.	DEBIT	CREDIT	BALANCE DEBIT	BALANCE CREDIT
20-- Dec. 31	Balance	✔			14 1 8 4 60	

ACCOUNT Rent Expense   ACCOUNT NO. 6145

DATE	ITEM	POST. REF.	DEBIT	CREDIT	BALANCE DEBIT	BALANCE CREDIT
20-- Dec. 31	Balance	✔			20 1 5 0 00	

ACCOUNT Salary Expense   ACCOUNT NO. 6150

DATE	ITEM	POST. REF.	DEBIT	CREDIT	BALANCE DEBIT	BALANCE CREDIT
20-- Dec. 31	Balance	✔			168 4 8 3 60	

ACCOUNT Supplies Expense—Office   ACCOUNT NO. 6155

DATE	ITEM	POST. REF.	DEBIT	CREDIT	BALANCE DEBIT	BALANCE CREDIT

ACCOUNT Supplies Expense—Store   ACCOUNT NO. 6160

DATE	ITEM	POST. REF.	DEBIT	CREDIT	BALANCE DEBIT	BALANCE CREDIT

ACCOUNT Uncollectible Accounts Expense   ACCOUNT NO. 6165

DATE	ITEM	POST. REF.	DEBIT	CREDIT	BALANCE DEBIT	BALANCE CREDIT

ACCOUNT Utilities Expense   ACCOUNT NO. 6170

DATE	ITEM	POST. REF.	DEBIT	CREDIT	BALANCE DEBIT	BALANCE CREDIT
20-- Dec. 31	Balance	✔			5 4 8 4 97	

ACCOUNT Federal Income Tax Expense   ACCOUNT NO. 7105

DATE	ITEM	POST. REF.	DEBIT	CREDIT	BALANCE DEBIT	BALANCE CREDIT
20-- Dec. 31	Balance	✔			30 0 0 0 00	

16-4 APPLICATION PROBLEM (concluded)

5.

ACCOUNT TITLE	DEBIT	CREDIT

Journalizing and posting adjusting and closing entries; preparing a post-closing trial balance

1., 2.

GENERAL JOURNAL   PAGE 18

	DATE		ACCOUNT TITLE	DOC. NO.	POST. REF.	DEBIT	CREDIT	
1								1
2								2
3								3
4								4
5								5
6								6
7								7
8								8
9								9
10								10
11								11
12								12
13								13
14								14
15								15
16								16
17								17
18								18
19								19
20								20
21								21
22								22
23								23
24								24
25								25
26								26
27								27
28								28
29								29
30								30
31								31

16-5 **MASTERY PROBLEM (continued)**

3., 4.

GENERAL JOURNAL   PAGE 19

	DATE		ACCOUNT TITLE	DOC. NO.	POST. REF.	DEBIT	CREDIT	
1								1
2								2
3								3
4								4
5								5
6								6
7								7
8								8
9								9
10								10
11								11
12								12
13								13
14								14
15								15
16								16
17								17
18								18
19								19
20								20
21								21
22								22
23								23
24								24
25								25
26								26
27								27
28								28
29								29
30								30
31								31
32								32
33								33

2., 4.   **GENERAL LEDGER**

ACCOUNT Cash   ACCOUNT NO. 1110

DATE		ITEM	POST. REF.	DEBIT	CREDIT	BALANCE	
						DEBIT	CREDIT
Dec.	31	Balance	✔			5 1 2 4 12	

ACCOUNT Petty Cash   ACCOUNT NO. 1120

DATE		ITEM	POST. REF.	DEBIT	CREDIT	BALANCE	
						DEBIT	CREDIT
Dec.	31	Balance	✔			2 5 0 00	

ACCOUNT Accounts Receivable   ACCOUNT NO. 1130

DATE		ITEM	POST. REF.	DEBIT	CREDIT	BALANCE	
						DEBIT	CREDIT
Dec.	31	Balance	✔			14 8 4 3 30	

ACCOUNT Allow. for Uncoll. Accts.   ACCOUNT NO. 1135

DATE		ITEM	POST. REF.	DEBIT	CREDIT	BALANCE	
						DEBIT	CREDIT
Dec.	31	Balance	✔				1 2 4 55

ACCOUNT Merchandise Inventory   ACCOUNT NO. 1140

DATE		ITEM	POST. REF.	DEBIT	CREDIT	BALANCE	
						DEBIT	CREDIT
Dec.	31	Balance	✔			154 3 1 8 22	

16-5 MASTERY PROBLEM (continued)

ACCOUNT Supplies—Office   ACCOUNT NO. 1145

DATE	ITEM	POST. REF.	DEBIT	CREDIT	BALANCE DEBIT	BALANCE CREDIT
20-- Dec. 31	Balance	✔			3 4 1 5 58	

ACCOUNT Supplies—Store   ACCOUNT NO. 1150

DATE	ITEM	POST. REF.	DEBIT	CREDIT	BALANCE DEBIT	BALANCE CREDIT
20-- Dec. 31	Balance	✔			6 1 8 4 56	

ACCOUNT Prepaid Insurance   ACCOUNT NO. 1160

DATE	ITEM	POST. REF.	DEBIT	CREDIT	BALANCE DEBIT	BALANCE CREDIT
20-- Dec. 31	Balance	✔			7 0 0 0 00	

ACCOUNT Office Equipment   ACCOUNT NO. 1205

DATE	ITEM	POST. REF.	DEBIT	CREDIT	BALANCE DEBIT	BALANCE CREDIT
20-- Dec. 31	Balance	✔			21 4 8 2 66	

ACCOUNT Acc. Depr. —Office Equipment   ACCOUNT NO. 1210

DATE	ITEM	POST. REF.	DEBIT	CREDIT	BALANCE DEBIT	BALANCE CREDIT
20-- Dec. 31	Balance	✔				6 4 8 0 00

ACCOUNT Store Equipment   ACCOUNT NO. 1215

DATE	ITEM	POST. REF.	DEBIT	CREDIT	BALANCE DEBIT	BALANCE CREDIT
20-- Dec. 31	Balance	✔			40 4 8 1 66	

ACCOUNT Acc. Depr. —Store Equipment   ACCOUNT NO. 1220

DATE		ITEM	POST. REF.	DEBIT	CREDIT	BALANCE	
						DEBIT	CREDIT
20-- Dec.	31	Balance	✔				18 4 8 0 00

ACCOUNT Accounts Payable   ACCOUNT NO. 2110

DATE		ITEM	POST. REF.	DEBIT	CREDIT	BALANCE	
						DEBIT	CREDIT
20-- Dec.	31	Balance	✔				8 4 1 8 36

ACCOUNT Federal Income Tax Payable   ACCOUNT NO. 2120

DATE		ITEM	POST. REF.	DEBIT	CREDIT	BALANCE	
						DEBIT	CREDIT

ACCOUNT Employee Income Tax Payable   ACCOUNT NO. 2130

DATE		ITEM	POST. REF.	DEBIT	CREDIT	BALANCE	
						DEBIT	CREDIT
20-- Dec.	31	Balance	✔				4 5 8 00

ACCOUNT Social Security Tax Payable   ACCOUNT NO. 2135

DATE		ITEM	POST. REF.	DEBIT	CREDIT	BALANCE	
						DEBIT	CREDIT
20-- Dec.	31	Balance	✔				5 2 8 24

ACCOUNT Medicare Tax Payable   ACCOUNT NO. 2140

DATE		ITEM	POST. REF.	DEBIT	CREDIT	BALANCE	
						DEBIT	CREDIT
20-- Dec.	31	Balance	✔				1 2 3 54

ACCOUNT Sales Tax Payable   ACCOUNT NO. 2145

DATE	ITEM	POST. REF.	DEBIT	CREDIT	BALANCE DEBIT	BALANCE CREDIT
20-- Dec. 31	Balance	✔				1 4 1 5 30

ACCOUNT Unemployment Tax Payable—Federal   ACCOUNT NO. 2150

DATE	ITEM	POST. REF.	DEBIT	CREDIT	BALANCE DEBIT	BALANCE CREDIT
20-- Dec. 31	Balance	✔				4 00

ACCOUNT Unemployment Tax Payable—State   ACCOUNT NO. 2155

DATE	ITEM	POST. REF.	DEBIT	CREDIT	BALANCE DEBIT	BALANCE CREDIT
20-- Dec. 31	Balance	✔				2 7 00

ACCOUNT Health Insurance Premiums Payable   ACCOUNT NO. 2160

DATE	ITEM	POST. REF.	DEBIT	CREDIT	BALANCE DEBIT	BALANCE CREDIT
20-- Dec. 31	Balance	✔				2 5 0 00

ACCOUNT U.S. Savings Bonds Payable   ACCOUNT NO. 2165

DATE	ITEM	POST. REF.	DEBIT	CREDIT	BALANCE DEBIT	BALANCE CREDIT
20-- Dec. 31	Balance	✔				4 0 00

ACCOUNT United Way Donations Payable   ACCOUNT NO. 2170

DATE	ITEM	POST. REF.	DEBIT	CREDIT	BALANCE DEBIT	BALANCE CREDIT
20-- Dec. 31	Balance	✔				6 0 00

ACCOUNT Dividends Payable   ACCOUNT NO. 2180

DATE		ITEM	POST. REF.	DEBIT	CREDIT	BALANCE	
						DEBIT	CREDIT
20-- Dec.	31	Balance	✔				4 0 0 0 00

ACCOUNT Capital Stock   ACCOUNT NO. 3110

DATE		ITEM	POST. REF.	DEBIT	CREDIT	BALANCE	
						DEBIT	CREDIT
20-- Dec.	31	Balance	✔				80 0 0 0 00

ACCOUNT Retained Earnings   ACCOUNT NO. 3120

DATE		ITEM	POST. REF.	DEBIT	CREDIT	BALANCE	
						DEBIT	CREDIT
20-- Dec.	31	Balance	✔				89 7 6 1 21

ACCOUNT Dividends   ACCOUNT NO. 3130

DATE		ITEM	POST. REF.	DEBIT	CREDIT	BALANCE	
						DEBIT	CREDIT
20-- Dec.	31	Balance	✔			16 0 0 0 00	

ACCOUNT Income Summary   ACCOUNT NO. 3140

DATE		ITEM	POST. REF.	DEBIT	CREDIT	BALANCE	
						DEBIT	CREDIT

16-5 MASTERY PROBLEM (continued)

ACCOUNT Sales   ACCOUNT NO. 4110

DATE		ITEM	POST. REF.	DEBIT	CREDIT	BALANCE DEBIT	BALANCE CREDIT
20-- Dec.	31	Balance	✔				514 8 1 5 35

ACCOUNT Sales Discount   ACCOUNT NO. 4120

DATE		ITEM	POST. REF.	DEBIT	CREDIT	BALANCE DEBIT	BALANCE CREDIT
20-- Dec.	31	Balance	✔			2 1 5 4 94	

ACCOUNT Sales Returns and Allowances   ACCOUNT NO. 4130

DATE		ITEM	POST. REF.	DEBIT	CREDIT	BALANCE DEBIT	BALANCE CREDIT
20-- Dec.	31	Balance	✔			6 1 8 4 74	

ACCOUNT Purchases   ACCOUNT NO. 5110

DATE		ITEM	POST. REF.	DEBIT	CREDIT	BALANCE DEBIT	BALANCE CREDIT
20-- Dec.	31	Balance	✔			301 5 4 8 60	

ACCOUNT Purchases Discount   ACCOUNT NO. 5120

DATE		ITEM	POST. REF.	DEBIT	CREDIT	BALANCE DEBIT	BALANCE CREDIT
20-- Dec.	31	Balance	✔				2 1 5 4 65

ACCOUNT Purch. Returns and Allowances   ACCOUNT NO. 5130

DATE		ITEM	POST. REF.	DEBIT	CREDIT	BALANCE DEBIT	BALANCE CREDIT
20-- Dec.	31	Balance	✔				2 88 9 41

ACCOUNT Advertising Expense   ACCOUNT NO. 6105

DATE		ITEM	POST. REF.	DEBIT	CREDIT	BALANCE DEBIT	BALANCE CREDIT
20-- Dec.	31	Balance	✔			2 49 1 95	

ACCOUNT Cash Short and Over   ACCOUNT NO. 6110

DATE		ITEM	POST. REF.	DEBIT	CREDIT	BALANCE DEBIT	BALANCE CREDIT
20-- Dec.	31	Balance	✔			5 25	

ACCOUNT Credit Card Fee Expense   ACCOUNT NO. 6115

DATE		ITEM	POST. REF.	DEBIT	CREDIT	BALANCE DEBIT	BALANCE CREDIT
20-- Dec.	31	Balance	✔			8 1 5 4 62	

ACCOUNT Depr. Exp. —Office Equipment   ACCOUNT NO. 6120

DATE		ITEM	POST. REF.	DEBIT	CREDIT	BALANCE DEBIT	BALANCE CREDIT

ACCOUNT Depr. Exp. —Store Equipment   ACCOUNT NO. 6125

DATE		ITEM	POST. REF.	DEBIT	CREDIT	BALANCE DEBIT	BALANCE CREDIT

16-5 MASTERY PROBLEM (continued)

ACCOUNT Insurance Expense   ACCOUNT NO. 6130

DATE	ITEM	POST. REF.	DEBIT	CREDIT	BALANCE DEBIT	BALANCE CREDIT

ACCOUNT Miscellaneous Expense   ACCOUNT NO. 6135

DATE	ITEM	POST. REF.	DEBIT	CREDIT	BALANCE DEBIT	BALANCE CREDIT
Dec. 31	Balance	✔			4 1 0 00	

ACCOUNT Payroll Taxes Expense   ACCOUNT NO. 6140

DATE	ITEM	POST. REF.	DEBIT	CREDIT	BALANCE DEBIT	BALANCE CREDIT
Dec. 31	Balance	✔			14 1 8 4 60	

ACCOUNT Rent Expense   ACCOUNT NO. 6145

DATE	ITEM	POST. REF.	DEBIT	CREDIT	BALANCE DEBIT	BALANCE CREDIT
Dec. 31	Balance	✔			15 4 0 0 00	

ACCOUNT Salary Expense   ACCOUNT NO. 6150

DATE	ITEM	POST. REF.	DEBIT	CREDIT	BALANCE DEBIT	BALANCE CREDIT
Dec. 31	Balance	✔			102 2 4 0 30	

ACCOUNT Supplies Expense—Office   ACCOUNT NO. 6155

DATE	ITEM	POST. REF.	DEBIT	CREDIT	BALANCE DEBIT	BALANCE CREDIT

ACCOUNT Supplies Expense—Store   ACCOUNT NO. 6160

DATE	ITEM	POST. REF.	DEBIT	CREDIT	BALANCE DEBIT	BALANCE CREDIT

ACCOUNT Uncollectible Accounts Expense   ACCOUNT NO. 6165

DATE	ITEM	POST. REF.	DEBIT	CREDIT	BALANCE DEBIT	BALANCE CREDIT

ACCOUNT Utilities Expense   ACCOUNT NO. 6170

DATE	ITEM	POST. REF.	DEBIT	CREDIT	BALANCE DEBIT	BALANCE CREDIT
20-- Dec. 31	Balance	✔			4 1 5 4 51	

ACCOUNT Federal Income Tax Expense   ACCOUNT NO. 7105

DATE	ITEM	POST. REF.	DEBIT	CREDIT	BALANCE DEBIT	BALANCE CREDIT
20-- Dec. 31	Balance	✔			4 0 0 0 00	

16-5 **MASTERY PROBLEM (concluded)**

5.

ACCOUNT TITLE	DEBIT	CREDIT

CHALLENGE PROBLEM, p. 502

Inventory auditing challenges

1. Grain in a grain elevator:

2. Lumber in a lumber yard:

3. Diamond rings in a jewelry store:

4. Nails in a home improvement store:

[This page left blank intentionally]

An accounting cycle for a corporation: end-of-fiscal-period work

12., 13., 14.

ACCOUNT TITLE	TRIAL BALANCE		ADJUSTMENTS		INCOME STATEMENT		BALANCE SHEET	
	1 DEBIT	2 CREDIT	3 DEBIT	4 CREDIT	5 DEBIT	6 CREDIT	7 DEBIT	8 CREDIT
1								
2								
3								
4								
5								
6								
7								
8								
9								
10								
11								
12								
13								
14								
15								
16								
17								
18								
19								
20								
21								
22								
23								
24								
25								
26								
27								

REINFORCEMENT ACTIVITY 2 PART B (continued)

ACCOUNT TITLE	TRIAL BALANCE		ADJUSTMENTS		INCOME STATEMENT		BALANCE SHEET	
	1 DEBIT	2 CREDIT	3 DEBIT	4 CREDIT	5 DEBIT	6 CREDIT	7 DEBIT	8 CREDIT
28								
29								
30								
31								
32								
33								
34								
35								
36								
37								
38								
39								
40								
41								
42								
43								
44								
45								
46								
47								
48								
49								
50								
51								
52								
53								

15.

												*% OF NET SALES

REINFORCEMENT ACTIVITY 2 PART B (continued)

16.

17.

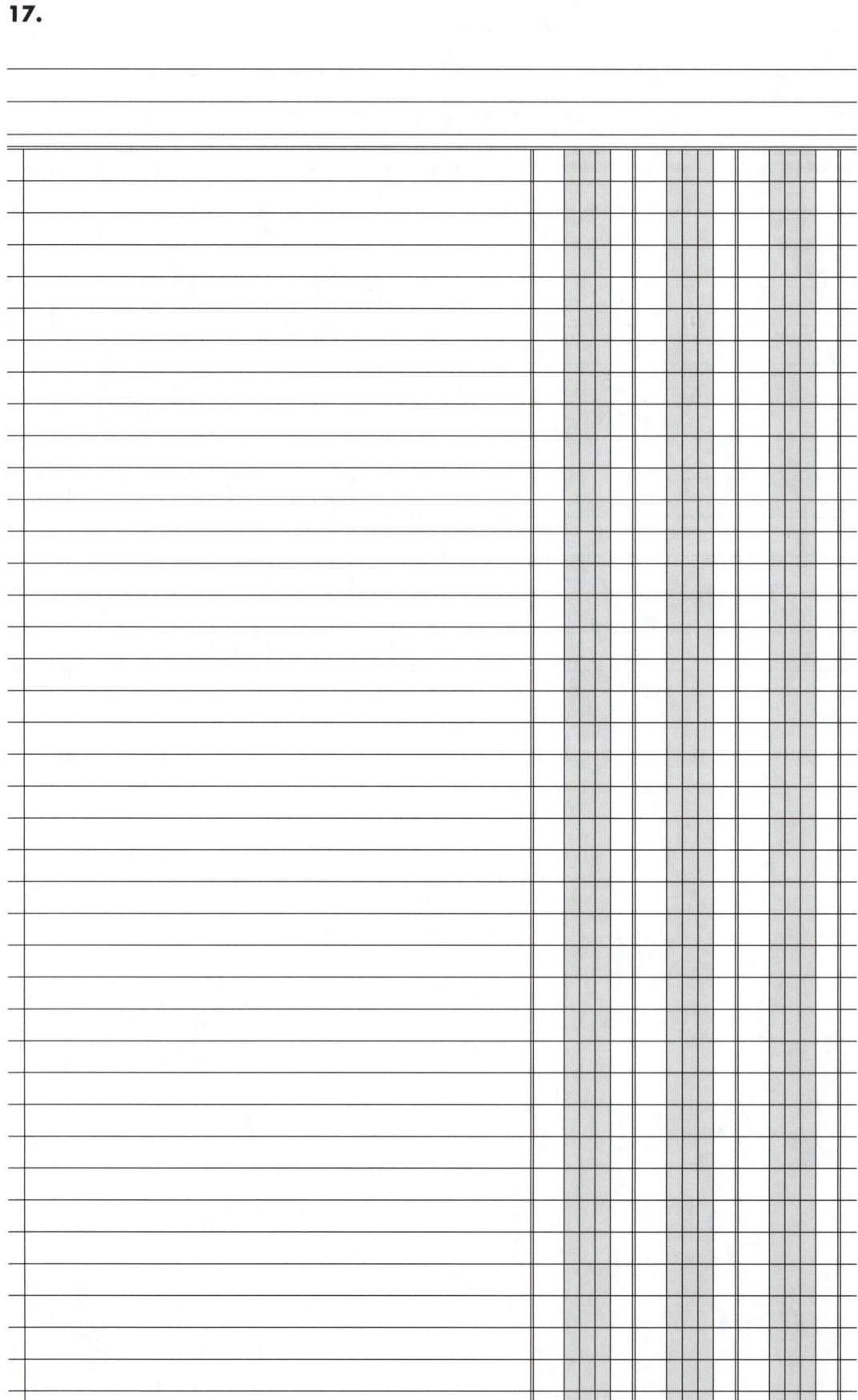

REINFORCEMENT ACTIVITY 2 PART B (continued)

18.

Earnings per share:

Price-earnings ratio:

19.

GENERAL JOURNAL

PAGE 13

	DATE		ACCOUNT TITLE	DOC. NO.	POST. REF.	DEBIT	CREDIT	
1								1
2								2
3								3
4								4
5								5
6								6
7								7
8								8
9								9
10								10
11								11
12								12
13								13
14								14
15								15
16								16
17								17

20.

GENERAL JOURNAL   PAGE 14

	DATE		ACCOUNT TITLE	DOC. NO.	POST. REF.	DEBIT	CREDIT	
1								1
2								2
3								3
4								4
5								5
6								6
7								7
8								8
9								9
10								10
11								11
12								12
13								13
14								14
15								15
16								16
17								17
18								18
19								19
20								20
21								21
22								22
23								23
24								24
25								25
26								26
27								27
28								28
29								29
30								30
31								31
32								32
33								33

REINFORCEMENT ACTIVITY 2 PART B (concluded)

21.

ACCOUNT TITLE	DEBIT	CREDIT

San

San